INDIA'S REFUGEE REGIME AND RESETTLEMENT POLICY

INDIA'S REFUGEE REGIME AND RESETTLEMENT POLICY

(Chakma's and The Politics of Nationality in Arunachal Pradesh)

Chunnu Prasad

KALPAZ

India's Refugee Regime and Resettlement Policy

ISBN: 978-81-7835-952-6

Published in 2013 in India by
Kalpaz Publications
C - 30 Satyawati Nagar
Delhi - 110052
E-mail: kalpaz@hotmail.com
Phone : 9212142040

Leser type setting : Lucky Graphic, Delhi
Printed at : Chawla Offset Printers, Delhi

DEDICATED TO:

Master Buddha

and

ALL THE REFUGEES OF THIS UNIVERSE WHO

ARE FIGHTING FOR THEIR SURVIVAL

"Happy indeed we live, friendly amidst the hostile.

Amidst hostile men we dwell free from hatred"

-Dhamapada. 197

"We may have different religions, different languages, different colored skin, but we all belong to one human race. We all share the same basic values"

- Kofi Annan

Contents

Preface

India's refugee regime and resettlement policy is not simply a book but a reality of life. Refugees are an integral part of the international system in ways that we do not usually realise in India. The current international refugee regime, embodied in core legal documents such as the *Refugee Convention*, the *Refugee Protocol*, institutions such as the United Nations High Commission for Refugees and the International Organization for Migration, and prominent non-governmental organizations, represents only the most recent manifestation of what, in fact, is a fundamental institution of the international system. Refugees matter because of a substantive change in the nature of the state-citizen relationship and one of the most important concerned to any state system, which saw a mutually constitutive relationship created between states and their citizens in which states guaranteed sets of rights in exchange for legitimacy.

The refugee problem continues to be a major international concern. This study is based on the situation of Chakma refugees in Arunachal Pradesh in particular and northeast in general. It provides some general insights in the on-going debate about the notions of home, trans-nationalism, issue of citizenship and return migration. The thesis examines the factors that influence the decision of refugees in concerning their status and various rights for survival and possibilities of return to their origin. Different sources of data and several methods of data collection have been used. These include participant observation as well as interviews with refugees and certain officials. A central question is, what or where is "home". The notions of home and of exile are continuously negotiated, contested and transformed in the context of ever-changing socio-economic and political conditions in the refugees' country of asylum and their country of origin. The study shows that the decision concerning return migration is not only influenced by socio-economic conditions, but also by human rights violations in both countries, the arrival of new asylum-seekers, and the hope for resettlement in countries. One of the most significant findings is that whether refugees return to their country of origin or not has little or nothing to do with the initial factors that prompted them to flee.

As we know India has been the home for a large number and different types of refugees throughout the past. India has dealt with the issues of 'refugees' on a bilateral basis. India's 'refugee regime' generally confirms to the international instruments on the subject without, however, giving a formal shape to all practices adopted by in a form of separate statute. The current position in India is that they are dealt with under the existing Indian laws, both general as well as special, which is, applicable to all the foreigners who came to India over a period of time. This is only because there is no separate law and policies to deal with 'refugees'. India does not have on its statute book a specific and separate law to govern refugees. India is also not a signatory to the 1951 convention on refugees and also the 1967 protocol, but a signatory to a number of United Nation and world Conventions on Human Rights, Refugee Issues and other related matters. Generally refugees are allowed freedom concerning their movement, practice of religion and residence. In case of refugees whose entry into India is either legal or is subsequently legalised, there is limited interference by the administration regarding these basic freedom. Those refugees who enter India illegally or over stay beyond permissible limits, have strict restriction theoretically impose upon them in accordance with the statutes governing refugees in India, i.e. the Foreigners Act of 1946, Foreigners Order, Passport Act and etc.

India is home to over 320,000 refugees and various reports say some of the refugee camps in India were well maintained, but others were neglected. Shelter and sanitation facilities were inadequate. Indian authorities gave camp residents cash grants and provided them some items at subsidised rates. The refugees were allowed to work, but restrictions on their movement made it difficult for them to keep their jobs. It says the Indian government keeps the international community at bay regarding refugees on its soil, discourages discussions of refugee issues and bars access to some regions where refugees live and does not permit the UNHCR access to most refugees. Of the more than 323,000 refugees in India, only some 18,500 receive UNHCR protection and even they experience many difficulties. This examines the question as to whether international refugee law is in conflict in any way with Indian legislations or, in the absence of such legislations, with Indian attitude and policy on refugees. India never had a clear policy as to whom to grant refugee status. There is a need for a change in the law. The model law has not been sufficiently considered by the Union government. For the last so many decades, the NHRC has been requesting the government to provide refugee protection. The argument of terrorism and numbers having been met, there is no reason why the minimal protection against non-refoulement should not be enacted. This can probably be done even through rules.

India's refugee regime is yet to evolve a transparent framework linking rights, laws and policies. It results in great prevarication between policies and practices. Treatment of refugees widely differs in India from state to state and is subject to much pressure from civil society groups. Largely research would be focused on the India's refugee regime, its re-settlement policies, laws, working of civil society and etc.

Largely, research focused on the India's refugee regime, its settlement policies as well as the socio-economic and political conditions of the Chakmas in the region. The genesis of this refugee groups and their treatment has to be looked out. Also, review the shifting ad-hoc and confusing stands of the state machineries through the various laws and policies over time to time. The inadequacies of the national as well as international regime for the protection of the Chakma refugees particularly in Arunachal Pradesh and Northeast India in general would have been examined. The study would like to address a wide range of research questions relating to the refugees of the Indian state of Arunachal Pradesh like; Who is a refugee and what are his or her rights under international law? What are the rights of those asylum seekers who fail to qualify as refugees under the 1951 Convention and the 1967 Protocol? What are the determinants of India's refugee regime in general and Arunachal Pradesh in Particular? How state government and civil society groups dealing with the refugee situations in Arunachal Pradesh? How can refugees be distinguished from economic and other migrants? Can the International community deny protection to those who claim not to receive protection from their country of origin? Are the refugees in India treated well and fair? Moreover, what exactly is the link between India's refugee regime and resettlement policies? In what ways can the rights of refugees be violated in the process of asylum-seeking in host countries? Can repatriation be truly voluntary when the country of origin is unable, or unwilling, to guarantee respect for the civil, political, economic, social and cultural rights of its citizens? India needs to review its ambivalent refugee laws and policies, evolve a regional approach and enact rules or legislation to protect persecuted refugees.

This is one step towards supporting a humanitarian law for those who need it. As a refugee-prone area, South Asia requires India to take the lead to devise a regional policy consistent with the region's needs and the capacity to absorb refugees under conditions of global equity.

Research is largely based on two broad hypotheses firstly; India's refugee regime is yet to evolve a transparent framework linking rights, laws and policies. It results in great prevarication between policies and practices and secondly, the treatment of refugees widely differs in India from state to state and is subject to much pressure from civil society groups.

Every research needs help and support not only from various institutions but also from people who support as a supervisor and contribute directly or indirectly to bring a concrete research based on new findings and interpretations. Considering all this I urged many institutions and individuals to support my research and successfully I got positive response and all type of support in all areas except some difficulties which every researcher generally faces particularly at the time of field work. First of all I take an opportunity to thank *Professor Rakesh Gupta,* Centre far Political Studies Jawaharlal Nehru University, New Delhi, who deserves special thanks for his guidance and help from the very inception to the production of the work. He has taken all the pain with me to suggest many things timely and guided not just like a teacher but as my guardian and rendered his full cooperation to enable me to produce before scholars.

Secondly, I would like to thanks all the people who really helped me particularly at the time of my field work and took all the pain to bring the truth of the real problems. First and foremost I would like to thank Susanta Chakma, Director, SNEHA, New Delhi, arindam Dewan, Head Master SNEHA School deserves special thanks for providing me accommodation and very much needed social contacts during my stay in Changlang and Lohit, is due for their companionship and encouragements. Further I would like to extend my heartfelt gratitude to all the teachers who are working in SNEHA schools Students and friends of Rajiv Gandhi University, North Eastern Regional Institute of Science and Technology, Doimuk, Indira Gandhi College, Tezu, Jawaharlal Nehru College, Pasighat, Arunachal Pradesh, Jawaharlal Nehru University, University of Delhi, Jamia Milia Islamia, New Delhi, North East Hill University, Meghalaya, Assam University, and Tezpur University, Assam, Manipur University, Manipur, Babasaheb Bhimrao Ambedkar University, Lucknow, Uttar Pradesh, Oxford University, London, Amida Trust, Narborough, United Kingdom, Indiana

University and Sussex University, United States of America and all Grade- A officers (APPSC) with whom I had an opportunity to discuss the problem of Chakmas related issues in detail. I should also not forget to thank National Human Rights Commission for providing official documents and courts judgments, United Nation and World Bank, South Asian Human Rights Commission and SNEHA for producing relevant materials time to time related to the Chakmas and their problems. I personally, thanks to Council for the Development of Social Science Research in Africa (CODESRA) and The South-South Exchange Programme for Research on the History of Development (SEPHIS) for giving me an opportunity to visit African countries like Ethiopia and Senegal to participate in a workshop on social history where I received lots of suggestions to improve my work.

Thirdly, my special thanks to the list of a few well known scholars from whom I got lots of literature directly or indirectly on the issues related to Chakma problems. This list includes B.S. Chimni, S.P. Talukdar, Mahendra P. Lama, S. Dutta, Pradeep Kumar Bose, Tapan Kumar Bose, Deepak K. Singh, Suhas Chakma, Miranal Kanti Chakma, Subanil Chakma, Bhumitra Chakma and others who are regularly writing on the issues related to the Chakmas in particular and other refugees in general.

Apart from this I personally remain indebted to my family members and very close friends for their consistent encouragement and support who have been a great source of inspiration and assistance.

CHUNNU PRASAD

CESCR	:	Committee on Economics, Social and Cultural Rights
CHR	:	Commission on Human Rights
CHT	:	Chittagong Hill Tract
CHTSP	:	Chittagong Hill Tracts Solidarity Party
CI	:	Circle Inspector
CM	:	Chief Minister
CO	:	Circle Officer
CRF	:	Central Relief Fund
CRRF	:	Central Relief and Rehabilitation Fund
CSPE	:	Civil, Social and Political Education
DC	:	Deputy Commissioner
DHC	:	Deputy High Commissioner
EA	:	Excluded Area
EAC	:	Extra Assistant Commissioner
EC	:	Election Commissioner
ECI	:	Election Commission of India
EGS	:	Employment Grantee Scheme
EL	:	Electoral Law
EO	:	European Office
EPG	:	Eminent Persons Group
ERO	:	Electoral Registration Officers
ESCAP	:	Economic and Social Commission for Asia and the Pacific
ESCR	:	Economic, Social and Cultural Rights
FRRO	:	Foreigners Regional Registration Office
FSP	:	Federal State Party
GIA	:	Government of Indian Act
GOI	:	Government of India

Abbreviation

AAPSU	:	All Arunachal Pradesh Student Union
AASU	:	All Assam Student Union
AC	:	Arunachal Congress
ADC	:	Additional Deputy Commissioner
ADC	:	Autonomous District Council
ADSU	:	All Adi Student Union
AERO	:	Assistant Electoral Registration Officers
AL	:	Awami League
AMSU	:	Arunachal Mismi Student Union
ANSU	:	All Nishi Student Union
AP	:	Arunachal Pradesh
APCC	:	Arunachal Pradesh Congress Committee
APCSU	:	Arunachal Pradesh Chakma Students Union
APSCW	:	Arunachal Pradesh State Commission for Women
BJP	:	Baharatiya Janata Party
BLW	:	Bangladesh Liberation War
BPL	:	Below Poverty Line
CBSE	:	Central Board of Secondary Education
CCRCAP	:	Committee for Citizenship Rights of the Chakmas of Arunachal Pradesh

CESCR : Covenant on Economics, Social and Cultural Rights
CHR : Commission on Human Rights
CHT : Chittagong Hill Tract
CHTSP : Chittagong Hill Tracts Solidarity Party
CI : Circle Inspector
CM : Chief Minister
CO : Circle Officer
CRF : Central Relief Fund
CRRF : Central Relief and Rehabilitation Fund
CSPE : Civil, Social and Political Education
DC : Deputy Commissioner
DHC : Deputy High Commissioner
EA : Excluded Area
EAC : Extra Assistant Commissioner
EC : Election Commissioner
ECI : Election Commission of India
EGS : Employment Grantee Scheme
EL : Electoral Law
EO : European Office
EPG : Eminent Persons Group
ERO : Electoral Registration Officers
ESCAP : Economic and Social Commission for Asia and the Pacific
ESCR : Economic, Social and Cultural Rights
FRRO : Foreigners Regional Registration Office
FSP : Federal State Party
GIA : Government of Indian Act
GoI : Government of India

HRD	:	Human Resource Development
HRL	:	Human Rights Law
HSZ	:	High Security Zone
IAS	:	Indian Administrative Services
IC	:	Identity Card
ICA	:	Indian Citizenship Act
ICJ	:	International Court of Justice
ICRC	:	International Committee of Red Cross
IDP	:	Internally Displaced People
IHL	:	International Humanitarian Law
IHRL	:	International Human Rights Law
ILO	:	International Labour Organization
ILP	:	Inner Line Permit
ILRA	:	Inner Line Regulation Act
IMC	:	International Magna Carta
INR	:	Indian Rupee
IRL	:	India Rule of Law
IRO	:	International Refugee Organization
JUMNAPA	:	Jumma People's Network of Asia Pacific Australia
LoC	:	Line of Control
LTTE	:	Liberation of Tamil Tiger Eelam
MFA	:	Ministry of Foreign Affairs
MHA	:	Ministry of Home Affairs
MLA	:	Member of Legislative Assemblies
MoU	:	Memorandum of Understanding
MP	:	Member of Parliament
MSU	:	Mizo Student Union
NCCHT	:	National Committee on Chittagong Hill Tract

NEFA	:	North East Frontier Agency
NGO's	:	Non Government Organizations
NHPCL	:	National Hydroelectric Power Corporation Limited
NHRC	:	National Human Right Commission
NRRP	:	National Relief and Rehabilitation Policy
OAUC	:	Organization for African Unity Convention
OHC	:	Office of the High Commissioner
PBD	:	Pravasi Bhartiya Diwas
PCJSS	:	Parbattya Chattagram Jana Sanghati Samity
PDS	:	Public Distribution System
PHC	:	Primary Health Centre
PIL	:	Public Interest Litigation
PIO	:	Persons of Indian Origin
PO	:	Political Officer
PRC	:	Permanent Residence Certificate
PTA	:	Parent Teacher Association
PUCL	:	Peoples Union for Civil Liberties
RIL	:	Relevant Indian Legislation
RP	:	Residential Permit
SAARC	:	South Asian Association for Regional Cooperation
SAHRC	:	South Asian Human Right Commission
SAHRDC	:	South Asia Human Rights Documentation Centre
SC	:	Supreme Court
SDO	:	Sub Divisional Officer
SLIC	:	Socio-Legal Information Centre
SSA	:	Sarva Siksha Abhiyan
ST's	:	Scheduled Tribes
TAWS	:	Tapun Area Welfare Society

UDHR : Universal Declaration of Human Rights

UHM : Union Home Ministry

UK : United Kingdom

UN : United Nation

UNDP : United Nation Development Programme

UNHRC : United Nation Human Rights Commission for Refugees

UNR : United Nations Relief

UNRC : United Nation Refugees Convention

UNRRA : United Nations Relief and Rehabilitation Administration

UNRWA : United Nations Relief and Works Agency

UPA : United Progressive Alliance

USA : United States of America

WGIP : Working Groups on Indigenous Populations

WRD : World Refugee Day

ZPM : Zila Parishad Member

1

Introduction

The problem of refugees is among the most complicated issues before the world community. Much discussion is taking place at the United Nations (UN) as it continues to search for more effective ways to protect and assist these particularly vulnerable groups. While some call for increased levels of cooperation and coordination among relief agencies, others point to gaps in international legislation and appeal for further standard setting in this area. Everyone, however, agrees that the problem is both multidimensional and global. Any approach or solution would therefore have to be comprehensive and to address all aspects of the issue, from the causes of mass exodus to the elaboration of responses necessary to cover the range of refugee situations from emergencies to repatriation. In this debate, some facts remain beyond dispute.

The first is that while some mass displacements may be preventable, none is voluntary. No one likes or chooses to be a refugee. Being a refugee means more than being an alien. It means living in exile and depending on others for such basic needs as food, clothing and shelter. Information on the number of the world's refugees, their geographical distribution, and the causes of their exodus is generally available. The refugee problem has undergone drastic quantitative and qualitative changes in the past five decades. Since its creation, the UN has worked to protect refugees around the world[1]. It is surprisingly true that the international refugee regime has not been given greater prominence in international relations[2].

There is a fundamental contradiction between the principles of sovereignty and human rights, but argued that this conspiracy is mitigated by the practice of granting rights of asylum to foreign political refugees? Refugees actually buttressed a territoriality based conception of sovereignty because states could allow unwanted populations to flee without taking more extreme actions, and the international community could assist refugees without direct intervention. Refugees were, in essence, a necessary relief regulator for the system of sovereign states. Refugee regime represents a salient case for exploring the role of interconnections between issue-areas as an independent variable in cooperation. The absence of a binding normative framework on burden-sharing, and the fact that states have few interests in contributing to burden-sharing for its own sake, mean that the prospects for international cooperation have been determined largely by the ability of United Nations High Commissioner for Refugees (UNHCR) to use linkages to connect refugee protection to states' interests in issue-areas outside the immediate scope of the regime.

In 1951, the year in which the office of the UNHCR was established, there were estimated one million refugees within UNHCR's mandate. In 2005 the total number of persons of concerned office of the UNHCR rose by 8 per cent to 20.8 million from 19.2 million in 2004, an additional 2.5 million refugees cared for by the United Nations Relief (UNR) and Works Agency for Palestine refugees in the Near East and more than 25 million Internally Displaced Persons (IDP). In 1951, most of the refugees were European[3]. The majority of today's refugees are from Africa and Asia. Current refugee movements, unlike those of the past, increasingly take the form of mass exoduses rather than individual flights. Eighty percent of today's refugees are women and children. The causes of exodus have also multiplied and now include natural or ecological disasters and extreme poverty. As a result, many of today's refugees do not fit into the definition contained in the Convention relating to the Status of Refugees. This refers to victims of persecution for reasons of race, religion, nationality, membership of a particular social group or political opinion. The UN system has also been very concerned by the rise in the number of mass internal displacements in recent years. The *'internally displaced'* are persons who are forced to flee their homes but remain within the territory of their own country. Since they remain inside their own countries, these persons are excluded from the present system of refugee protection[4]. In India the total IDP is about 600,000[5] looking for a durable solution.

Millions of people crossed over from one country to another when India got partitioned into two viz., India and Pakistan. These have been recorded as the largest mass migration in history. Roughly seven million people each; Hindus, Sikhs and Muslims in Punjab and Bengal. The burning towns and villages, blood-soaked trains, the dead and dying in huge foot convoys, 40,000-50,000 strong, with desperation and fear as constant companions[6]. On the issue of their rehabilitation and development India's first prime minister Pt. Jawaharlal Nehru stated in the parliament that, *"You will notice that we call it the 'Rehabilitation and Development board', meaning thereby that we are combining the two functions or rather, looking at the two problems-rehabilitation and development together"*[7].

On the other hand the Minister for Relief and Rehabilitation, A.P. Jain put it like these, *"I consider rehabilitation to be a psychological question, and a person who feels that he is living well, that he can educate his children that he is a citizen of India like any other person, well, I treat him as rehabilitated. Unfortunately, no psychologist has yet been able to measure psychological rehabilitation"*[8].

Further, K.C. Neogy, another minister for relief and rehabilitation, of the Government of India drew the attention towards the problem of planning and development by saying that, *"we may have to be grateful to the refugees for having drawn our attention to the urgency of the problem of planning and development of this country, and perhaps future generations will acknowledge their gratitude to the so-called refugees for having punished the man power which is necessary for the purpose of developing the resources of the country as a whole"*[9].

Whatever the case may be, the relief and rehabilitation were the first major administrative challenges of independent India. It would test its capacity to cope with disaster, formulate policy with regard to migrants and refugees, provide itself as a humane, welfare oriented government organised relief on a massive scale, and at the same time engaged in rebuilding the nation's economic, social and political life[10].

Nationally, a number of bills were introduced in the parliament to cover practically every aspect of refugee rehabilitation and resettlement. The evacuee property act in 1947; the finance administration bill dealing with loans to small business and urban refugees, was introduced in February 1948; the displacement persons (institution of Suits bill) in August 1948; the resettlement of displaced persons (land acquisition) bill in September 1948; the influx from Pakistan (control) bill April 1949; the administration of evacuee property bill and displaced persons (claim) act in August 1950; the interim compensation scheme in 1953; and finally, the displaced persons (compensation and rehabilitation act) in 1954. These acts were largely made to resettle the refugees who migrated to India just after partition or before the commencement of the Indian constitution in 1950. No doubt many refugees other then Muslims who came to India before 1950 got the Indian citizenship status but the second influx of those refugees who come to India after 1950 but before 1971 are still fighting for their status and basic human rights[11].

India has played the role of big brother with its neighbouring open border South Asian countries which is a refugee-prone region. India discovered this while absorbing the Tibetan Refugees in 1959, the Bangladeshi refugees in 1971, the Chakma influx in 1963, the Tamil influx from Sri Lanka in 1983, 1989 and again in 1995, the Afghan refugees 1980s, the Myanmar refugees for a similar period migration and refugee movements from Bangladesh over the years. India's ambivalence towards the UNHCR is characterised by its act of indirectly seeking its assistance through the Red Cross in the 1960s, and later allowing the UNHCR to determine the refugee status of those from beyond South Asia, asking the UNHCR to assist in verifying the volunteers for repatriation of the Tamils to Sri Lanka, and permitting an office in Delhi through the United Nation Development Programme (UNDP).

In 1995, India, following Pakistan's example, joined the Executive of the UNHCR. Though welcome, this halfway house seems odd since India refuses to sign the 1951 Convention. Meanwhile, a series of judgments by the Supreme Court and the Gujarat, Punjab, Gauhati and Tamil Nadu High Courts has reinforced the need for a humane due process for the Chakmas, Sri Lankan and other refugees. Some of the judgments expressly recognise the value and worth of the UNHCR and invite it to involve itself more in the refugee questions in India. Unfortunately, this pro-refugee jurisprudence sits uneasily with the normal law relating to foreigners, which grants the government near-arbitrary powers of deportation. Following the Law Commission's 175th Report of 2000, the law was made stricter to treat *'illegal entrants'* harshly, irrespective of the cruel circumstances that may occasion their migration. India blows hot and cold when dealing with the UNHCR, making policy statements at its UNHCR meetings in Geneva and negating either joining the Convention or changing its law to provide reliable legal entitlements to refugees in India[12].

By contrast, Article 17 of the Additional Terrorism Protocol of the South Asian Association for Regional Cooperation (SAARC) of January 2004 permits SAARC nations not to extradite and, perforce, to protect those being prosecuted or punished on account of their race, religion, nationality, ethnic origin or political opinion. This stand is mystifying. Thus, in South Asia, India agreed to the SAARC protocol in 2004. Globally, India steadfastly refuses to join the Convention of

1951 even though it is on the Executive Committee of the UNHCR without being a signatory to the Convention under which the Committee is constituted. Indeed, from 1997, its envoys to the UNHCR have been pleading for a more equitable global regime to participate in a discourse that India does not carry any further.

One needs to examine what India's doubts about protecting refugees are all about. The *Cold War* reasons for not having a global refugee policy have gone cold. Refugees are a global problem. The latest UNHCR statistics show that in 2003, there were 20.55 million displaced persons of international concern, including 10.34 million refugees. Refugees are being created all the time no less due to America's Afghanistan and Iraq wars. But even otherwise, this is a problem that permanently haunts Africa and South Asia. Europe and Australia want to tighten their immigration walls with all kinds of sophisticated arguments to deal with refugees on a regional, rather than a global, basis. India, instead of leading the debate, is being evasive.

So far humanitarian definition is concerned on refugees it is said that, a refugee is someone who has fled his country because he has a well-founded fear of persecution if he remains. The major obligation of refugee protection is the principle of non-refoulement, which ensures that a person is not returned to a life-threatening situation. For India to evade such a principle appears subversive of its constitutional principles unless there are weighty reasons for doing so. New Delhi's reasons for resisting refugee protection are paradoxical. On the one hand, its track record in dealing with the Tibetan, the Sri Lankan and the Chakma crises has been exemplary. Its hesitation to provide an intelligible and comprehensive protection to refugees seems to stem from two major considerations, which are artificial ghosts in the machine.

If India wants to play a role in global affairs and make SAARC a success, it must act as a global player entitled to its just seat in the Security Council of the UN. But it cannot do so as long it pursues narrow policies. The South Asia Region deserves better treatment. For strategic reasons, India was surprisingly quiet when virtually one-sixth of Bhutan's population was forced to leave the country for camps in Nepal. In 2003, Nepal and Bhutan entered into a kind of agreement whereby Bhutan agreed to take back about three to five percent of its citizens of Nepali origin whilst offering illusory promises to some of the rest.

India's refugee regime needs a strong change in its law. The model law has not been sufficiently considered by the Union Government. For the last five years, the National Human Rights Commission (NHRC) has been requesting the Government to provide refugee protection. The argument of terrorism and numbers having been met, there is no reason why the minimal protection against non-refoulement should not be enacted. This can probably be done even through rules. But the argument is not just over the Sri Lankan refugees, the Bangladeshis, the Afghans, the Bhutanese or the Myanmarese. It is whether India wants its voice on the world's most persecuted to be heard so as to mould future policy. If India is waiting for a cue from its neighbour, China has joined the convention and enacted refugee protection legislation. African countries have got together to devise both national and regional solutions. India needs to review its ambivalent refugee law policy, evolve a regional approach and enact rules or legislation to protect persecuted refugees. This is one step towards supporting a humanitarian law for those who need it. As a refugee-prone area, South Asia requires India to take the lead to devise a regional policy consistent with the region's needs and the capacity to absorb refugees under conditions of global equity.

The various reports say that some of the refugee camps in India were well maintained, but others were neglected. Shelter and sanitation facilities were inadequate. Indian authorities gave camp residents cash grants and provided them some items at subsidized rates. The refugees were allowed to work, but restrictions on their movement made it difficult for them to keep their jobs. It says the Indian government keeps the international community at bay regarding refugees on its soil, discourages discussions of refugee issues and bars access to some regions where refugees live. It does not permit the UNHCR access to most refugees.

The Indian Government deals refugees with at both political and administrative level which is largely applicable to the aliens. In the case of refugees' protection, the constitution of India guarantees certain fundamental rights, which are applicable to non-citizen, namely the right to equality (Article 14), the right to life and personal liberty (Article 21) and the freedom to practice and propagate their own religion (Article 25). Any violation of these rights can be remedied through recourse to the judiciary as the Indian Supreme Court has held that refugees or asylum seeker can not be discriminated against because of their non- citizen status.

India refugee's policy is further governed by certain administrative regulations. The standard of humane treatment set by these administrative regulations flowed from the ethos that persons displaced from their home need both protection and economic sustenance. The administrative experience of the ministry/department of rehabilitation and the laws adjudicated at the time of Partition contributed towards a refugee policy for India. India's refugees are registered under the 1939 Registration act, which is applicable to all foreigners entering in India. Under the 1946 Foreigners Acts, the Government is empowered to regulate the entry, presence and departure of aliens in India, though the word 'alien' itself is nowhere defined. Entry is also governed by the Passport Act 1967. Entry can be restricted if a person does not have a valid passport or visa, though the government can exempt person when it so desires. These procedures are linked at this stage to individuals who enter India without a valid visa or any other document. Though it is related to illegal migrants, the exemption provision is applicable to refugees. Under these circumstances, refugees become an administrative to oversee the relief and rehabilitation process rather than to supervise who stays or does not stay.

As mentioned, the government of India alone determine refugee status and has no specific legislation to deal with refugees. Despite this lacuna India does apply in practice certain articles of the 1951 Convention. This includes:

Article 7. India provides refugees the same treatment as all aliens,

Article 3. India fully applies a policy of non–discrimination,

Article 3A. No penalty is imposed on illegal entry,

Article 4. Religious freedom is guaranteed,

Article 16. Free access to courts is provided,

Articles 17 and 18. It provide wage-earning rights and as work permits have no meaning and refugees do work, this article is complied with,

Article 21. Freedom of housing allowed and refugees need stay in camps. Freedom of movement as guaranteed to aliens except in certain areas where special permits are required not only for aliens but also all Indians.

Article 27 and 28. the issuing of identity and travel cards.

India is not a party to the 1951 United Nation Refugees Convention (UNRC) or it's Protocol and domestic laws have not been found to be in conflict with international laws. It followed a program of humane treatment of different refugees, with respect to refugee's rights; there is still an absence of assistance and opportunities. To protect the refugees by means of the activists' approach has its own limitations.

Brief History of Arunachal Pradesh

When the Constitution of India came into force in 1950, another change was effected in the administrative set up. The Government of Assam was relieved of its responsibility of looking after administration of the *'Excluded Areas'*. However, the discretionary power was vested in the Governor of Assam, who served as the agent of the President of the Republic of India. In 1954, all these tracts formed into the North East Frontier Agency (NEFA). On the enactment of North Eastern Area (Reorganization) Act 1971, NEFA was made Union Territory of Arunachal Pradesh on 21st January 1972. On 20th February 1987, Arunachal Pradesh was made a full fledged state within the Indian Union.

The Scheduled District Act 1874

This area was declared as *'Scheduled District'* under the provisions of the Scheduled Districts Act, 1874. The Governor-General In-Council had power to make laws for these territories.

The North-Eastern Areas (Re-organisation) Act and Central Act 81 of 1971

The Governor of Assam who until then administered the area as the agent of the president under Para 18 of the Sixth Scheduled ceased to function as such with effect from 21st January, 1972, the date when this Act came into force. The 'Tribal Areas' which formed this Territory was granted the status of a Union Territory from 21st August, 1972.

On 15th August, 1975 the provisions of the Government of Union Territories Act 1973 made applicable and the existing 'Pradesh Council' was constituted as the Union Territories Legislature. The first general election was held on February 1978 and the Chief Commissioner of the territory came to be known as *'Lt Governor'* in 20th February, 1987 this area become a full fledged state under the provisions of the state of Arunachal Pradesh Act, 1986 compassing the territories which immediately before that day were comprised in the existing Union Territory of Arunachal Pradesh. Keeping in view the sensitivity of the area, the ILP was introduced to restrict the entry of outsiders in the area and it continues to be in force even now. The employees of the State Government, Central Government, Public Enterprises, Business

Communities and Working Labourers who are all Indian citizens, by virtue of their service within the state have been given the ILP and have to leave the area when the contractual work is over, in view of the fact that they cannot reside or settle as per the laws applicable to the area, principles for Administering Tribal Areas[13].

Arunachal Pradesh, the youngest (21st) State of the Union of India which has been the most peaceful state in the northeastern region of India. Much credit for it goes to Jawaharlal Nehru, the first Prime Minister of India who spelt out '*Panchasheela*'- five fundamental principles for administration of tribal areas.

1. People should develop along the line of their genius and we should avoid imposing anything on them.
2. Tribal rights on land and forest should be respected.
3. We should try to train and build up a team of their own people to do the work of administration and developments.
4. We should not over-administer these areas or overwhelm them with multiplicity of schemes; we should rather work through and not as rivals to their own social and cultural institutions.
5. We should judge not by statistics or the amount of money spent but by the quality of human character that is evolved.

The above principles have been underlined as the policy of the Government in the various developmental activities in the tribal areas[14].

References

1. *Ibid*, pp. 1300-1320.
2. *Ibid.*
3. See Global Internally Displaced Persons Projects, August, 2005.
4. Year book of United Nation (2005), Towards Development, Security and Human Rights for all, Vol. 59, United Nation Publication, New York, pp. 711-908.
5. B.S. Chimni (2005), Outside the Bounds of Citizenship: The Status of Aliens, Illegal Migrants and Refugees in India in edited book by Rajiv Bhargava and Helmut Reifeld, Civil Society, Public Sphere and Citizenship, Dialogues and Perceptions, Sage Publication, New Delhi, pp. 277-313.

6. Rita Menon (2003), Birth of Social Security Commitments: What Happen in the West, in Ranabir Samaddar (ed.) Refugees and the State; Practices of Asylum and Care in India, 1947-2000, Sage Publication, New Delhi, p. 153.
7. Constituent Assembly of India (Legislative) Debates, Vol. 1 February, 1948, p.187.
8. Constitute Assembly Debates, *op. cit.*, Vol. VI. 5 February, 31, March 1951, Part-1, p. 1315.
9. *Ibid.*, pp.187.
10. Rita Menon (2003), Birth of Social Security Commitments: What Happened in the West, in Ranabir Samaddar (ed.) Refugees and the State; Practices of Asylum and Care in India, 1947-2000, Sage Publication, New Delhi, p. 155.
11. Protection of Human Rights Act, 1993 [As amended by the Protection of Human Rights (Amendment) Act, 2006–No. 43 of 2006] National Human Rights Commission, Faridkot House, Copernicus Marg, New Delhi - 110 001 Website: www.nhrc.nic.in, pp. 1-19.
12. See Law Commission's 175th Report of 2000.
13. White paper on Chakma-Hajong, issued by the Government of Arunachal Pradesh, Itanagar, 12 March 1996.
14. *Ibid.*

2

Refugee Laws and Policies

A refugee is a person who *"owing to a well-founded fear of being persecuted for reasons of race, religion, nationality, membership of a particular social group, or political opinion, is outside the country of their nationality, and is unable to or, owing to such fear, is unwilling to avail him/herself of the protection of that country or who, not having a nationality and being outside the country of his former habitual residence as a result of such events, is unable or, owing to such fear, is unwilling to return to it"*[1]. Every person has the right to live free from persecution, or the fear of persecution, based on their race, caste, sex, religion, nationality, membership in a particular social group, or political opinion[2]. The concept of a refugee was expanded by the Conventions' 1967 Protocol and by regional conventions in Africa and Latin America to include persons who had fled war or other violence in their home country. A person who is seeking to be recognised as a refugee is an asylum seeker. In the United States a recognized asylum seeker is known as an asylee[3].

Refugee was defined as a legal group in response to the large number of people fleeing Eastern Europe following World War Second[4]. The leading international agency coordinating refugee protection is the UNHCR, which counted 8.4 million refugees worldwide at the beginning of 2006[5]. This was the lowest number since 1980. The major exception is the 4.3 million Palestinian refugees under the authority of the United Nations Relief and Works Agency for Palestine Refugees in the Near East (UNRWA). The United States Committee for Refugees and Immigrants gives the world total as 12,019,700 refugees and estimates there are over 34,000,000 displaced by war, including IDP, who remains within the same national borders. The majority of refugees who leave their country seek asylum in countries neighbouring their country of nationality[6]. The *'durable solutions'* to refugee populations, as defined by UNHCR and governments, are: voluntary repatriation to the country of origin; local integration into the country of asylum; and resettlement to a third country[7].

UNHCR was established on December 14, 1950, and succeeded the earlier United Nations Relief and Rehabilitation Administration (UNRRA). The agency is mandated to lead and co-ordinate international action to protect refugees and resolve refugee problems worldwide. Its primary purpose is to safeguard the rights and wellbeing of refugees. It strives to ensure that everyone can exercise the right to seek asylum and find safe refuge in another state, with the option to return home voluntarily, integrate locally or to resettle in a third country. UNHCR's mandate has gradually been expanded to include protecting and providing humanitarian assistance to what it describes as other *persons of concern,* including IDP's who would fit in the legal definition of a refugee under the 1951 United Nations Convention Relating to the Status of Refugees and 1967 Protocol, the 1969 Organization for African Unity Convention (OAUC) or some other treaty if they left their country, but who presently remain in their country of origin[8]. It is having headquartered office in Geneva, Switzerland to protect and support refugees at the request of a government or the UN itself and assists in their voluntary repatriation, local integration or resettlement to a third country[9].

Convention relating to the Status of Refugees Adopted on 28 July 1951 by the United Nations Conference of Plenipotentiaries on the Status of Refugees and Stateless Persons convened under General Assembly resolution 429 (V) of 14 December 1950. In more than six decades, the agency has helped an estimated fifty million people restart their lives. Today, staffs of around 5,000 people in more than 20 countries continue to help some more than 17 million persons[10].

Table: 3 (A)

Estimated Asylum Seekers, Refugees Concern to UNHCR (1st January, 2007)

Continent	*Total No's*
Asia	14,910,900
Africa	9,752,600
Europe	3,426,700
Latin America and Caribbean	1,143,100

Northern America	3,542,500
Oceania	85,700
Total	32,861,500

Report on Migration (UNHCR), 2007.

To deal with some of the important questions like what is protection, who protects, is the convention still relevant for the new millennium, and how refugees protected. As we know governments are responsible for enforcing a country's laws. When they are unable or unwilling to do so, often during a conflict or civil unrest, people whose basic human rights are threatened flee their homes, often to another country, where they may be classed as refugees and be guaranteed basic rights. The host government particularly responsible for protecting refugees and the 143 parties to the convention and the Protocol are obliged to carry out its provisions. The UNHCR maintains a *watching brief,* intervening if necessary to ensure bona fide refugees are granted asylum and are not forcibly returned to countries where their lives may be in danger. The agency seeks ways to help refugees restart their lives, either through local integration, voluntary return to their homeland or, if that is not possible, through resettlement in third countries[11].

Government normally guarantees the basic human rights and physical security of their citizens but when civilians become refugees this safety net disappears. The UNHCR's main role in pursuing international protection is to ensure that states are aware of and act on, their obligations to protect refugees and persons seeking asylum[12]. However, it is not a supranational organisation and cannot be considered as a substitute for government responsibility. Countries may not forcibly return refugees to a territory where they face danger or discriminate between groups of refugees. Convention was originally adopted to deal with the aftermath of World War-II in Europe and growing East-West political tensions. But though the nature of conflict and migration patterns have changed in the intervening decades, the convention has proved remarkably resilient in helping to protect an estimated fifty million people in all types of situations. As long as persecution of individuals and groups persists, there will be a need for the convention. In 2007, world refugee day focused the search for, and implementation of, durable solutions for refugee and declared World Refugee Day (WRD) theme as *a new home, a new life.*

Refugees

Definitions of Populations

Refugee. Persons who flee persecution for protection in another country. These persons are so designated by international law and their entry into a host country is determined by internationally cooperating governmental and private agents.

Displaced Person

Persons who flee persecution in their locality but remain in their own country.

Evacuee

Persons who flee their locality due to natural or man-made disasters.

Asylee

Persons fleeing persecution who enter another country by means other than the established refugee process and who later seek legal protection status in the country to which they fled. These persons must establish conditions similar to those required by refugees, and they may not be eligible for some services until their legal status is regularised.

Unaccompanied Minor

Persons under the legal majority age in any country who arrive as refugees but not as members of families or related to persons who are of majority age. While these persons may have been considered adults in their country, they are deemed to be in need of child welfare protection services here.

Victims of Torture

Persons who establish that they, personally, suffered torture as part of the persecution they fled, and, as such, were at such risk that they could not await the normal refugee process to escape, resulting in their seeking asylum as a torture victim.

Victims of Human Trafficking

Persons who come to any country understanding that they are

arriving legally for employment purpose, but are in reality brought illegally through traffickers and are held captive in their places of work. These persons often are required to turn their passports over to their 'handlers' and then have no proof of citizenry in any country[13].

UNHCR Provisions Related to the Refugees

Preamble

The High Contracting Parties,

(a) Considering that the Charter of the UN and the Universal Declaration of Human Rights (UDHR) approved on 10 December 1948 by the General Assembly have affirmed the principle that human beings shall enjoy fundamental rights and freedoms without discrimination.

(b) Considering that the UN has, on various occasions, manifested its profound concern for refugees and endeavoured to assure refugees the widest possible exercise of these fundamental rights and freedoms.

(c) Considering that it is desirable to revise and consolidate previous international agreements relating to the status of refugees and to extend the scope of and the protection accorded by such instruments by means of a new agreement.

(d) Considering that the grant of asylum may place unduly heavy burdens on certain countries, and that a satisfactory solution of a problem of which the UN has recognised the international-scope and nature cannot therefore be achieved without international co-operation.

(e) Expressing the wish that all States, recognising the social and humanitarian nature of the problem of refugees, will do everything within their power to prevent this problem from becoming a cause of tension between States.

(f) Noting that the UNHCR is charged with the task of supervising international conventions providing for the protection of refugees, and recognising that the effective co-ordination of measures taken to deal with this problem will depend upon the co-operation of States with the High Commissioner[14].

Have agreed as follows:

Chapter -1 (General Provisions)

Article 1- Definition of the term 'Refugee'

(A) For the purposes of the present Convention, the term refugee, shall apply to any person who:

(1) Has been considered a refugee under the Arrangements of 12 May 1926 and 30 June 1928 or under the Conventions of 28 October 1933 and 10 February 1938, the Protocol of 14 September 1939 or the Constitution of the International Refugee Organisation (IRO);

(2) Decisions of non-eligibility taken by the IRO during the period of its activities shall not prevent the status of refugee being accorded to persons who fulfil the conditions of paragraph 2 of this section;

(3) As a result of events occurring before 1st January 1951 and owing to well-founded fear of being persecuted for reasons of race, religion, nationality, membership of a particular social group or political opinion, is outside the country of his nationality and is unable, or owing to such fear, is unwilling to avail himself of the protection of that country; or who, not having a nationality and being outside the country of his former habitual residence as a result of such events, is unable or, owing to such fear, is unwilling to return to it.

In the case of a person who has more than one nationality, the term *the country of his nationality* shall mean each of the countries of which he is a national, and a person shall not be deemed to be lacking the protection of the country of his nationality if, without any valid reason based on well-founded fear, he has not availed himself of the protection of one of the countries of which he is a national[15].

(B) For the purposes of this Convention;

(1) For the purposes of this convention, the words *'events occurring before 1st January 1951'* in article 1, section A, shall be understood to mean either (a) *'events occurring in Europe before I January* 1951'; or (b) *'events occurring in Europe or elsewhere before I January 1951'*; and each Contracting State shall make a declaration at the time of signature, ratification or accession, specifying which of these meanings it applies for the purpose of its obligations under this Convention.

(2) Any contracting state which has adopted alternative (a) may at any time extend its obligations by adopting alternative (b) by means of a notification addressed to the Secretary-General of the UN.

(C) This convention shall cease to apply to any person falling under the terms of section A if:

(a) He has voluntarily re-availed himself of the protection of the country of his nationality.

(b) Having lost his nationality, he has voluntarily reacquired it.

(c) He has acquired a new nationality, and enjoys the protection of the country of his new nationality.

(d) He has voluntarily re-established himself in the country which he left or outside which he remained owing to fear of persecution.

(e) He can no longer, because the circumstances in connection with which he has been recognised as a refugee have ceased to exist, continue to refuse to avail himself of the protection of the country of his nationality; Provided that this paragraph shall not apply to a refugee falling under section A (I) of this article who is able to invoke compelling reasons arising out of previous persecution for refusing to avail himself of the protection of the country of nationality.

(f) Being a person who has no nationality he is, because the circumstances in connection with which he has been recognised as a refugee have ceased to exist, able to return to the country of his former habitual residence; Provided that this paragraph shall not apply to a refugee falling under section A (I) of this article who is able to invoke compelling reasons arising out of previous persecution for refusing to return to the country of his former habitual residence.

(D) This convention shall not apply to persons who are at present receiving from organs or agencies of the UN other than the UNHCR protection or assistance. When such protection or assistance has ceased for any reason, without the position of such persons being definitively settled in accordance with the relevant resolutions adopted by the

General Assembly of the UN, these persons shall ipso facto be entitled to the benefits of this Convention.

(E) This convention shall not apply to a person who is recognised by the competent authorities of the country in which he has taken residence as having the rights and obligations which are attached to the possession of the nationality of that country.

(F) The provisions of this convention shall not apply to any person with respect to whom there are serious reasons for considering that[16].

(a) He has committed a crime against peace, a war crime, or a crime against humanity, as defined in the international instruments drawn up to make provision in respect of such crimes;

(b) He has committed a serious non-political crime outside the country of refuge prior to his admission to that country as a refugee;

(c) He has been guilty of acts contrary to the purposes and principles of the UN.

Article 2-General Obligations

Every refugee has duties to the country in which he finds himself, which require in particular that he conforms to its laws and regulations as well as to measures taken for the maintenance of public order.

Article 3-Non-discrimination

The Contracting States shall apply the provisions of this Convention to refugees without discrimination as to race, religion or country of origin.

Article 4-Religion

The contracting states shall accord to refugees within their territories treatment at least as favourable as that accord to their nationals with respect to freedom to practise their religion and freedom as regards the religious education of their children.

Article 5-Rights Granted Apart from this Convention

Nothing in this Convention shall be deemed to impair any rights and benefits granted by a Contracting State to refugees apart from this Convention.

Article 6-The Term in the same Circumstances

For the purposes of this convention, the term in the same circumstances, implies that any requirements (including requirements as to length and conditions of sojourn or residence) which the particular individual would have to fulfil for the enjoyment of the right in question, if he were not a refugee, must be fulfilled by him, with the exception of requirement which by their nature a refugee is incapable of fulfilling.

Article 7-Exemption from Reciprocity

Except where this convention contains more favourable provisions, a contracting state shall accord to refugees the same treatment as is accorded to aliens generally. After a period of three year's residence, all refugees shall enjoy exemption from legislative reciprocity in the territory of the contracting states. Each Contracting State shall continue to accord to refugees the rights and benefits to which they were already entitled, in the absence of reciprocity, at the date of entry into force of this convention for that State. The Contracting States shall consider favourably the possibility of according to refugees, in the absence of reciprocity, rights and benefits beyond those to which they are entitled according to paragraphs 2 and 3, and to extending exemption from reciprocity to refugees who do not fulfil the conditions provided for in paragraphs 2 and 3. The provisions of paragraphs 2 and 3 apply both to the rights and benefits referred to in articles 13, 18, 19, 21 and 22 of this convention and to rights and benefits for which this Convention does not provide.

Article 8-Exemption from Exceptional Measures

With regard to exceptional measures which may be taken against the person, property or interests of nationals of a foreign state, the Contracting States shall not apply such measures to a refugee who is formally a national of the said State solely on account of such nationality. Contracting States which, under their legislation, are prevented from applying the general principle expressed in this article, shall, in appropriate cases, grant exemptions in favour of such refugees[17].

Article 9-Provisional Measures

Nothing in this convention shall prevent a contracting state, in time of war or other grave and exceptional circumstances, from taking provisional measures which it considers to be essential to the national security in the case of a particular person, pending a determination by the contracting state that that person is in fact a refugee and that the continuance of such measures is necessary in his case in the interests of national security.

Article 10-Continuity of Residence

Where a refugee has been forcibly displaced during the Second World War from the territory of a contracting state and has, prior to the date of entry into force of this convention, returned there for the purpose of taking up residence, the period of residence before and after such enforced displacement shall be regarded as one uninterrupted period for any purposes for which uninterrupted residence is required.

Article 11- Refugee Seamen

In the case of refugees regularly serving as crew members on board a ship flying the flag of a contracting state, that State shall give sympathetic consideration to their establishment on its territory and the issue of travel documents to them or their temporary admission to its territory particularly with a view to facilitating their establishment in another country[18].

***Chapter – 2* (Juridical Status)**

Article 12- Personal Status

The personal status of a refugee shall be governed by the law of the country of his domicile or, if he has no domicile, by the law of the country of his residence. Rights previously acquired by a refugee and dependent on personal status, more particularly rights attaching to marriage, shall be respected by a contracting state, subject to compliance, if this be necessary, with the formalities required by the law of that State, provided that the right in question is one which would have been recognized by the law of that State had he/she not become a refugee.

Article 13-Movable and immovable property

The contracting states shall accord to a refugee treatment as favourable as possible and, in any event, not less favourable than that accorded to aliens generally in the same circumstances, as regards the acquisition of movable and immovable property and other rights pertaining thereto, and to leases and other contracts relating to movable and immovable property.

Article 14-Artistic Rights and Industrial Property

In respect of the protection of industrial property, such as inventions, designs or models, trade marks, trade names, and of rights in literary, artistic and scientific works, a refugee shall be accorded in the country in which he has his habitual residence the same protection as is accorded to nationals of that country. In the territory of any other contracting states, he shall be accorded the same protection as is accorded in that territory to nationals of the country in which he has his habitual residence.

Article 15-Right of Association

As regards non-political and non-profit-making associations and trade unions the Contracting States shall accord to refugees lawfully staying in their territory the most favourable treatment accorded to nationals of a foreign country, in the same circumstances[19].

Article 16-Access to courts

A refugee shall have free access to the courts of law on the territory of all contracting states. A refugee shall enjoy in the Contracting State in which he has his habitual residence the same treatment as a national in matters pertaining to access to the courts, including legal assistance. A refugee shall be accorded in the matters referred to in paragraph- 2 in countries other than that in which he has his habitual residence the treatment granted to a national of the country of his habitual residence.

***Chapter – 3* (Gainful Employment)**

Article 17- Wage-earning Employment

The contracting states shall accord to refugees lawfully staying in their territory the most favourable treatment accorded to nationals of a foreign country in the same circumstances, as regards the right to engage in wage-earning employment. In any case, restrictive measures imposed on aliens or the employment of aliens for the protection of the national labour market shall not be applied to a refugee who was already exempted from them at the date of entry into force of this convention for the contracting state concerned, or who fulfils one of the following conditions:

(a) He has completed three years' residence in the country;

(b) He has a spouse possessing the nationality of the country of residence. A refugee may not invoke the benefit of this provision if he has abandoned his spouse;

(c) He has one or more children possessing the nationality of the country of residence.

The contracting states shall give sympathetic consideration to assimilating the rights of all refugees with regard to wage-earning employment to those of nationals, and in particular of those refugees who have entered their territory pursuant to programmes of labour recruitment or under immigration schemes.

Article 18-Self-employment

The contracting states shall accord to a refugee lawfully in their territory treatment as favourable as possible and, in any event, not less favourable than that accorded to aliens generally in the same circumstances, as regards the right to engage on his own account in agriculture, industry, handicrafts and commerce and to establish commercial and industrial companies.

Article 19- Liberal Professions

Each contracting state shall accord to refugees lawfully staying in their territory, who hold diplomas recognised by the competent authorities of that State, and who are desirous of practising a liberal profession, treatment as favourable as possible and, in any event, not less favourable than that accorded to aliens generally in the same circumstances. The Contracting States shall use their best endeavours consistently with their laws and constitutions to secure the settlement of such refugees in the territories, other than the metropolitan territory, for whose international relations they are responsible.

Chapter – 4 (Welfare)

Article 20- Rationing

Where a rationing system exists, which applies to the population at large and regulates the general distribution of products in short supply, refugees shall be accorded the same treatment as nationals.

Article 21- Housing

As regards housing, the contracting states, in so far as the matter is regulated by laws or regulations or is subject to the control of public authorities, shall accord to refugees lawfully staying in their territory treatment as favourable as possible and, in any event, not less favourable than that accorded to aliens generally in the same circumstances.

Article 22- Public Education

The Contracting States shall accord to refugees the same treatment as is accorded to nationals with respect to elementary education. The contracting states shall accord to refugees treatment as favourable as possible, and, in any event, not less favourable than that accorded to aliens generally in the same circumstances, with respect to education other than elementary education and, in particular, as regards access to studies, the recognition of foreign school certificates, diplomas and degrees, the remission of fees and charges and the award of scholarships.

Article 23- Public relief

The contracting states shall accord to refugees lawfully staying in their territory the same treatment with respect to public relief and assistance as is accorded to their nationals.

Article 24- Labour Legislation and Social Security

The contracting states shall accord to refugees lawfully staying in their territory the same treatment as is accorded to nationals in respect of the following matters;

(a) In so far as such matters are governed by laws or regulations or are subject to the control of administrative authorities: remuneration, including family allowances where these form part of remuneration, hours of work, overtime arrangements, holidays with pay, restrictions on home work, minimum age of employment, apprenticeship and training, women's work and the work of young persons, and the enjoyment of the benefits of collective bargaining;

(b) Social security (legal provisions in respect of employment injury, occupational diseases, maternity, sickness, disability, old age, death, unemployment, family responsibilities and any other contingency which, according to national laws or regulations, is covered by a social security scheme), subject to the following limitations;

(c) There may be appropriate arrangements for the maintenance of acquired rights and rights in course of acquisition.

National laws or regulations of the country of residence may prescribe special arrangements concerning benefits or portions of benefits which are payable wholly out of public funds, and concerning allowances paid to persons who do not fulfil the contribution conditions prescribed for the award of a normal pension. The right to compensation for the death of a refugee resulting from employment injury or from occupational disease shall not be affected by the fact that the residence of the beneficiary is outside the territory of the contracting state. The contracting states shall extend to refugees the benefits of agreements concluded between them, or which may be concluded between them in the future, concerning the maintenance of acquired rights and rights in the process of acquisition in regard to social security, subject only to the conditions which apply to nationals of the states signatory to the agreements in question. The contracting states will give sympathetic consideration by extending to refugees so far as possible the benefits of similar agreements which may at any time be in force between such Contracting States and non- contracting States[20].

***Chapter* – *5* (Administrative Measures)**

Article 25- Administrative Assistance

When the exercise of a right by a refugee would normally require the assistance of authorities of a foreign country to whom he cannot have recourse, the contracting states in whose territory he is residing shall arrange that such assistance be afforded to him by their own authorities or by an international authority. The authority or authorities mentioned in paragraph-1 shall deliver or cause to be delivered under their supervision to refugees such documents or certifications as would normally be delivered to aliens by or through their national authorities. Documents or certifications so delivered shall stand in the stead of the official instruments delivered to aliens by or through their national authorities, and shall be given credence in the absence of proof to the contrary. Subject to such exceptional treatment as may be granted to indigent persons, fees may be charged for the services mentioned herein, but such fees shall be moderate and commensurate with those charged to nationals for similar services. The provisions of this article shall be without prejudice to articles 27 and 28.

Article 26- Freedom of Movement

Each contracting state shall accord to refugees lawfully in its territory the right to choose their place of residence and to move freely within its territory subject to any regulations applicable to aliens generally in the same circumstances.

Article 27- Identity Papers

The contracting states shall issue identity papers to any refugee in their territory who does not possess a valid travel document.

Article 28- Travel Documents

The contracting states shall issue to refugees lawfully staying in their territory travel documents for the purpose of travel outside their territory, unless compelling reasons of national security or public order otherwise require, and the provisions of the schedule to this convention shall apply with respect to such documents. The contracting states may issue such a travel document to any other refugee in their territory; they shall in particular give sympathetic consideration to the issue of such a travel document to refugees in their territory who are unable to obtain a travel document from the country of their lawful residence. Travel documents issued to refugees under previous international agreements by Parties thereto shall be recognized and treated by the Contracting States in the same way as if they had been issued pursuant to this article.

Article 29- Fiscal charges

The contracting states shall not impose upon refugee's duties, charges or taxes, of any description whatsoever, other or higher than those which are or may be levied on their nationals in similar situations. Nothing in the above paragraph shall prevent the application to refugees of the laws and regulations concerning charges in respect of the issue to aliens of administrative documents including identity papers.

Article 30- Transfer of assets

A contracting state shall, in conformity with its laws and regulations, permit refugees to transfer assets which they have brought into its territory, to another country where they have been admitted for the purposes of resettlement. A contracting state shall give sympathetic consideration to the application of refugees for permission to transfer assets wherever they may be and which are necessary for their resettlement in another country to which they have been admitted.

Article 31- Refugees Unlawfully in the Country of Refuge

The contracting states shall not impose penalties, on account of their illegal entry or presence, on refugees who, coming directly from a territory where their life or freedom was threatened in the sense of article 1, enter or are present in their territory without authorisation, provided they present themselves without delay to the authorities and show good cause for their illegal entry or presence. The contracting states shall not apply to the movements of such refugees restrictions other than those which are necessary and such restrictions shall only be applied until their status in the country is regularized or they obtain admission into another country. The contracting states shall allow such refugees a reasonable period and all the necessary facilities to obtain admission into another country.

Article 32- Expulsion

The contracting states shall not expel a refugee lawfully in their territory saves on grounds of national security or public order. The expulsion of such a refugee shall be only in pursuance of a decision reached in accordance with due process of law. Except where compelling reasons of national security otherwise require, the refugee shall be allowed to submit evidence to clear himself, and to appeal to and be represented for the purpose before competent authority or a person or persons specially designated by the competent authority. The contracting states shall allow such a refugee a reasonable period within which to seek legal admission into another country. The contracting states reserve the right to apply during that period such internal measures as they may deem necessary.

Article 33- Prohibition of Expulsion or Return (Refoulement)

No contracting state shall expel or return (refouler) a refugee in any manner whatsoever to the frontiers of territories where his life or freedom would be threatened on account of his race, religion, nationality, membership of a particular social group or political opinion. The benefit of the present provision may not, however, be claimed by a refugee whom there are reasonable grounds for regarding as a danger to the security of the country in which he is, or who, having been convicted by a final judgement of a particularly serious crime, constitutes a danger to the community of that country[21].

Article 34- Naturalisation

The Contracting States shall as far as possible facilitate the assimilation and naturalisation of refugees. They shall in particular make every effort to expedite naturalisation proceedings and to reduce as far as possible the charges and costs of such proceedings.

***Chapter – 6* (Executory and Transitory Provisions)**

Article 35- Co-operation of the National Authorities with the United Nations

The contracting states undertake to co-operate with the office of the UNHCR, or any other agency of the UN which may succeed it, in the exercise of its functions, and shall in particular facilitate its duty of supervising the application of the provisions of this Convention. In order to enable the Office of the High Commissioner or any other agency of the UN which may succeed it, to make reports to the competent organs of the UN, the contracting states undertake to provide them in the appropriate form with information and statistical data requested concerning:

(a) The condition of refugees;

(b) The implementation of this Convention, and

(c) Laws, regulations and decrees which are, or may hereafter be, in force relating to refugees.

Article 36 - Information on National Legislation

The contracting states shall communicate to the Secretary-General of the UN the laws and regulations which they may adopt to ensure the application of this Convention.

Article 37 - Relation to Previous Conventions

Without prejudice to article 28, paragraph 2, of this Convention, this Convention replaces, as between parties to it, the Arrangements of 5 July 1922, 31 May 1924, 12 May 1926, 30 June 1928 and 30 July 1935, the Conventions of 28 October 1933 and 10 February 1938, the Protocol of 14 September 1939 and the Agreement of 15 October 1946..

***Chapter* – 7 (Final Clauses)**

Article 38- Settlement of disputes

Any dispute between parties to this Convention relating to its interpretation or application, which cannot be settled by other means, shall be referred to the International Court of Justice (ICJ) at the request of any one of the parties to the dispute.

Article 39- Signature, Ratification and Accession

This Convention shall be opened for signature at Geneva on 28 July 1951 and shall thereafter be deposited with the Secretary-General of the UN. It shall be open for signature at the European Office (EO) of the UN from 28 July to 31 August 1951 and shall be re-opened for signature at the headquarters of the UN from 17 September 1951 to 31 December 1952. This convention shall be open for signature on behalf of all states members of the UN, and also on behalf of any other state invited to attend the Conference of Plenipotentiaries on the Status of Refugees and Stateless Persons or to which an invitation to sign will have been addressed by the general assembly. It shall be ratified and the instruments of ratification shall be deposited with the Secretary-General of the UN. This Convention shall be open from 28 July 1951 for accession by the States referred to in paragraph-2 of this article. Accession shall be effected by the deposit of an instrument of accession with the secretary-general of the UN[22].

Article 40- Territorial Application Clause

Any State may, at the time of signature, ratification or accession, declare that this convention shall extend to all or any of the territories for the international relations of which it is responsible. Such a declaration shall take effect when the convention enters into force for the State concerned. At any time thereafter any such extension shall be made by notification addressed to the Secretary-General of the UN and shall take effect as from the ninetieth day after the day of receipt by the secretary- general of the UN of this notification, or as from the date of entry into force of the convention for the State concerned, whichever is the later. With respect to those territories to which this convention is not extended at the time of signature, ratification or accession, each state concerned shall consider the possibility of taking the necessary steps in order to extend the application of this convention to such territories, subject, where necessary for constitutional reasons, to the consent of the governments of such territories.

Article 41- Federal Clause

In the case of a federal or non-unitary state, the following provisions shall apply:

(a) With respect to those articles of this convention that come within the legislative jurisdiction of the federal legislative authority, the obligations of the federal government shall to this extent be the same as those of parties which are not Federal States;

(b) With respect to those articles of this Convention that come within the legislative jurisdiction of constituent states, provinces or cantons which are not, under the constitutional system of the federation, bound to take legislative action, the Federal Government shall bring such articles with a favourable recommendation to the notice of the appropriate authorities of States, provinces or cantons at the earliest possible moment;

(c) A Federal State Party to this Convention shall, at the request of any other Contracting State transmitted through the Secretary-General of the UN, supply a statement of the law and practice of the federation and its constituent units in regard to any particular provision of the Convention showing the extent to which effect has been given to that provision by legislative or other action[23].

Article 42- Reservations

At the time of signature, ratification or accession, any state may make reservations to articles of the convention other than to articles 1, 3, 4, 16 (1), 33, 36-46 inclusive. Any State making a reservation in accordance with paragraph- 1 of this article may at any time withdraw the reservation by a communication to that effect addressed to the secretary-general of the UN.

Article 43- Entry into Force

This convention shall come into force on the ninetieth day following the day of deposit of the sixth instrument of ratification or accession. For each State ratifying or acceding to the convention after the deposit of the sixth instrument of ratification or accession, the convention shall enter into force on the ninetieth day following the date of deposit by such state of its instrument of ratification or accession.

Article 44- Denunciation

Any contracting State may denounce this convention at any time by a notification addressed to the Secretary-General of the UN. Such denunciation shall take effect for the contracting state concerned one year from the date upon which it is received by the secretary-general of the UN. Any state which has made a declaration or notification under article 40 may, at any time thereafter, by a notification to the secretary-general of the UN, declare that the convention shall cease to extend to such territory one year after the date of receipt of the notification by the secretary-general.

Any Contracting State may denounce this convention at any time by a notification addressed to the secretary-general of the UN. Such denunciation shall take effect for the contracting state concerned one year from the date upon which it is received by the Secretary-General of the UN. Any State which has made a declaration or notification under article 40 may, at any time thereafter, by a notification to the secretary-general of the UN, declare that the convention shall cease to extend to such territory one year after the date of receipt of the notification by the Secretary-General.

Article 45 - Revision

Any Contracting State may request revision of this convention at any time by a notification addressed to the Secretary-General of the UN. The General Assembly of the UN shall recommend the steps, if any, to be taken in respect of such request.

Article 46- Notifications by the Secretary-General of the UN

The Secretary-General of the UN shall inform all members of the UN and non-member states referred to in article 39;

(a) Of declarations and notifications in accordance with section B of article 1;

(b) Of signatures, ratifications and accessions in accordance with article 39;

(c) Of declarations and notifications in accordance with article 40;

(d) Of reservations and withdrawals in accordance with article 42;

(e) Of the date on which this Convention will come into force in accordance with article 43;

(f) Of denunciations and notifications in accordance with article 44;

(g) Of requests for revision in accordance with article 45.

In faith where of the undersigned, duly authorised, have signed this convention on behalf of their respective governments, done at Geneva, this 28.07.1951, in a single copy, of which the English and French texts are equally authentic and which shall remain deposited in the archives of the UN, and certified true copies of which shall be delivered to all members of the UN and to the non-member states referred to in article 39[24].

Refugee Laws

Refugee law is the branch of international law which deals with the rights and protection of related to, but distinct from, international human rights law and international humanitarian law, which deal respectively with human rights in general, and the conduct of war in particular[25]. On 12 May 1993 Ministry of Foreign Affairs (MFA), SG No 88/1993 (Protocol, considering the convention relating to the status of refugees done at Geneva on 28 July 1951)[26] mainly covers only those persons who have become refugees as a result of events occurring before 1 January, 1951, considering that new refugee situations have arisen since the convention was adopted[27]. The refugees concerned may therefore not fall within the scope of the convention, considering is desirable equal status should be enjoyed by all refugees covered by the definition in the convention irrespective of the dateline 1 January 1951, have agreed as follows[28]:

Article 1- (General Provision)

(1) The States that are Parties to the present Protocol undertake to apply Articles 2 to 34 inclusive of the convention to refugees as hereinafter defined.

(2) For the purpose of the present Protocol, the term 'refugee' shall, except as regards the application of paragraph- 3 of this Article, mean any person within the definition of Article 1 of the convention as if the words '*As a result of events occurring before 1 January 1951 and a result of such events*' in Article 1 A (2) were omitted.

(3) The present Protocol shall be applied by the states parties hereto without any geographic limitation, save that existing declarations made by states already parties to the convention in accordance with Article 1 B (1)(a) of the convention shall, unless extended under Article 1 B (2) thereof, apply also under the present protocol.

Article 2 – (Co-operation of the National Authorities with the United Nations)

(1) The states parties to the present protocol undertake to co-operate with the office of the UNHCR, or any other agency of the UN which may succeed it, in the exercise of its functions, and shall in particular facilitate its duty of supervising the application of the provisions of the present Protocol.

(2) In order to enable the office of the high commissioner, or any other agency of the UN which may succeed it, to make reports to the competent organs of the UN, the states parties to the present Protocol undertake to provide them with the information and statistical data requested, in the appropriate form, concerning:

(a) The condition of refugees;

(b) The implementation of the present Protocol;

(c) Laws, regulations and decrees which are, or may hereafter be, in force relating to refugees.

Article 3 – (Information on National Legislation)

The states parties to the present protocol shall communicate to the secretary-general of the UN the laws and regulations which they may adopt to ensure the application of the present Protocol.

Article 4 – (Settlement of disputes)

Any dispute between states parties to the present Protocol which relates to its interpretation or application and which cannot be settled by other means shall be referred to the ICJ at the request of any one of the parties to the dispute.

Article 5 – (Accession)

The present protocol shall be open for accession on behalf of all states parties to the convention and of any other state member of the UN or member of any of the specialized agencies or to which an invitation to accede may have been addressed by the General Assembly of the UN. Accession shall be effected by the deposit of an instrument of accession with the secretary-general of the UN.

Article 6

Federal clause in the case of a federal or non-unitary state, the following provisions shall apply:

(a) With respect to those articles of the convention to be applied in accordance with Article I, paragraph- 1, of the present Protocol that come within the legislative jurisdiction of the federal legislative authority, the obligations of the Federal Government shall to this extent be the same as those of States Parties which are not Federal States;

(b) With respect to those articles of the convention to be applied in accordance with Article I, paragraph- 1, of the present Protocol that come within the legislative jurisdiction of constituent states, provinces or cantons which are not, under the constitutional system of the federation, bound to take legislative action, the Federal Government shall bring such articles with a favourable recommendation to the notice of the appropriate authorities of States, provinces or cantons at the earliest possible moment;

(c) A federal state party (FSP) to the present Protocol shall, at the request of any other state party hereto transmitted through the secretary-general of the UN, supply a statement of the law and practice of the federation and its constituent units in regard to any particular provision of the convention to be applied in accordance with Article I, paragraph- 1, of the present Protocol, showing the extent to which effect has been given to that provision by legislative or other action.

Article 7 - (Reservations and Declarations)

(1) At the time of accession, any state may make reservations in respect of Article IV of the present protocol and in respect of the application in accordance with Article I of the present Protocol of any provisions of the convention other than those contained in Articles 1, 3, 4, 16 (1) and 33 thereof, provided that in the case of a state party to the convention reservations made under this Article shall not extend to refugees in respect of whom the convention applies.

(2) Reservations made by states parties to the convention in accordance with article 42 thereof shall, unless withdrawn, be applicable in relation to their obligations under the present Protocol[29].

(3) Any State making a reservation in accordance with paragraph 1 of this Article may at any time withdraw such reservation by a communication to that effect addressed to the Secretary-General of the UN.

(4) Declarations made under Article 40, paragraphs - 1 and 2, of the convention by a State Party thereto which accedes to the present Protocol shall be deemed to apply in respect of the present Protocol, unless upon accession a notification to the contrary is addressed by the State Party concerned to the secretary-general of the UN. The provisions of Article 40, paragraphs 2 and 3, and of Article 44, paragraph 3, of the convention shall be deemed to apply mutatis mutandis to the present Protocol.

Article 8 – (Entry into Force)

(1) The present protocol shall come into force on the day of deposit of the sixth instrument of accession.

(2) For each State acceding to the protocol after the deposit of the sixth instrument of accession, the protocol shall come into force on the date of deposit by such state of its instrument of accession.

Article 9- (Denunciation)

(1) Any State Party hereto may denounce this Protocol at any time by a notification addressed to the Secretary-General of the UN.

(2) Such denunciation shall take effect for the State Party concerned one year from the date on which it is received by the Secretary-General of the UN.

Article 10 – (Notifications by the Secretary-General of the UN)

The Secretary-General of the UN shall inform the states referred to in Article V above of the date of entry into force, accessions, reservations and withdrawals of reservations to and denunciations of the present Protocol, and of declarations and notifications relating hereto.

Article 11 – (Deposit in the Archives of the Secretariat of the United Nations)

A copy of the present Protocol, of which the Chinese, English, French, Russian and Spanish texts are equally authentic, signed by the President of the general Assembly and by the Secretary-General of the UN, shall be deposited in the archives of the Secretariat of the UN. The secretary-general will transmit certified copies thereof to all states members of the UN and to the other states referred to in Article V above[30].

Refugees in India

The 1991 final census count gave India a total population of 846,302,688. However, estimates of India's population vary widely. According to the Population Division of the UN Department of International Economic and Social Affairs, the population had already reached 866 million in 1991. The population division of the UN Economic and Social Commission for Asia and the Pacific (ESCAP) projected 896.5 million by mid-1993 with a 1.9 per cent annual growth rate. The United States Bureau of the census, assuming an annual population growth rate of 1.8 per cent, put India's population in July 1995 at 936,545,814[31].

India accounts for some 2.4 per cent of the world's landmass but is home to about 16 per cent of the global population. The magnitude of the annual increase in population can be seen in the fact that India adds almost the total population of Australia or Sri Lanka every year. A 1992 study of India's population notes that India has more people than all of Africa and also more than North America and South America together. Between 1947 and 2001, India's population more than doubled[32].

The upward population spiral began in the 1920s and is reflected in inter censual growth increments. South Asia's population increased roughly 5 percent between 1901 and 1911 and actually declined slightly in the next decade. Population increased some 10 per cent in the period from 1921 to 1931 and 13 to 14 per cent in the 1930s and 1940s. Between 1951 and 1961, the population rose 21.5 per cent. Between 1961 and 1971, the country's population increased by 24.8 per cent. Thereafter a slight slowing of the increase was experienced: from 1971 to 1981, the population increased by 24.7 per cent, and from 1981 to 1991, by 23.9 per cent. The 1991 census, which was carried out under the direction of the Registrar General and Census Commissioner of India (part of the MHA), in keeping with the previous two censuses, used the term *urban agglomerations*. In India urban agglomerations with a population of 1 million or more, there were 24 in 1991 are referred to as metropolitan areas. Places with a population of 100,000 or more are termed '*cities*' as compared with '*towns*,' which have a population of less than 100,000. Including the metropolitan areas, there were 299 urban agglomerations with more than 100,000 populations in 1991. These large urban agglomerations are designated as Class I urban units. There were five other classes of urban agglomerations, towns, and villages based on the size of their populations: Class II (50,000 to 99,999), Class III (20,000 to 49,999), Class IV (10,000 to 19,999), Class V (5,000 to 9,999), and Class VI. In 1991 the 24 metropolitan cities accounted for 51 per cent of India's total population living in Class I urban centres, with Bombay and Calcutta the largest at 12.6 million and 10.9 million, respectively. In the early 1990s, growth was the most dramatic in the cities of central and southern India[33]. About 20 cities in those two regions experienced a growth rate of more than 100 per cent between 1981 and 1991. Areas subject to an influx of refugees also experienced noticeable demographic changes. Refugees from Bangladesh, Burma, and Sri Lanka contributed substantially to population growth in the regions in which they settled. Less dramatic population increases occurred in areas where Tibetan refugee settlements were founded after the Chinese annexation of Tibet in the 1950s[34].

The partition of the Indian subcontinent into India and Pakistan in 1947 resulted in the largest human movement in history resulted an exchange of 18 millions Hindus and Sikhs (from Bangladesh-65 per cent and Pakistan-35 percent) for Muslims (from India)[35]. During the Bangladesh Liberation War (BLW) in 1971, owing to the West Pakistani army's operation searchlight, more than 10 million Bengalis fled to neighbouring India. As a result of the BLW, on 27 March 1971, Prime

Minister of India, Indira Gandhi, expressed full support of her Government to the Bangladeshi struggle for freedom. The Bangladesh-India border was opened to allow panic-stricken Bengalis safe shelter in India. The governments of West Bengal, Bihar, Assam, Meghalaya and Tripura established refugee camps along the border. Exiled Bangladeshi army officers and the Indian military immediately started using these camps for recruitment and training members of Mukti Bahini[36]. During the Bangladesh War of Independence around 10 million Bengalis fled the country to escape the killings and atrocities committed by the Pakistan army. Following the war, the Bangladesh government actively supported by the Indian military indiscriminately tortured and killed thousands of Biharies who were mostly against the independence of Bangladesh. Those who survived the massacre were forced into squalid camps where they live to this day. There are between 126,000 and 159,000 Biharis who have been living in camp-like situations in Bangladesh ever since the war. As mentioned before India is the home of largest number of refugees particularly from the South Asian Countries. Some of the major refugee groups are Chakmas, Srilankan, Afghan, Tibetan, Myanmar (Burma), Kashmir, Chin and etc[37].

Chakma Refugees

Chakmas originally are the people from the CHT of Bangladesh. CHT was the part of India before Independence, when India was the colony of British. British had followed a policy of exclusion in the CHT in order to exploit the natural resources of the region, thereby isolating the Chakmas from national politics. After Independence, the CHT were awarded to East Pakistan, much against the wishes of the Chakmas, who wanted to integrate into India[38]. In 1964, the Pakistan president, Ayub Khan, abolished earlier regulation preventing settlement of plains people (Bengalis) in the hills. Consequently, Bengali Muslims were encouraged to settle in the area to counter the Chakmas who were thought to be pro-Indian. After the creation of Bangladesh, the Chakmas continued to struggle under an oppressive regime. The Awami League government, led by Sheikh Mujibur Rahman, advocated a Bangladesh for Bengalis only. This alienated the Chakmas further and pushed them on to the path of violence.

In 1976, the Shanti Bahini, the armed wing of the Parbattya Chattagram Jana Samhati Samiti (PCJSS), attacked the Bangladeshi army[39]. The ensuing violence forced over 56,000 Chakmas to seek refuge in the Indian state of Tripura. Not wanted however, this was not the first time that Chakmas had been forced to fee to India. In the early sixties, a dam[40] built in the hill districts in East Pakistan displaced nearly 18,000 Chakma families[41]. They were the first batch of Chakmas who migrated to India in search of a new life[42].

Eventually, they ended up in refugee camps in the Lohit, Tirap, Changlang, and Papumpare districts of Arunachal Pradesh[43], where they remained largely forgotten by the administration. Despite a Supreme Court order in 1996, the Chakmas were denied the right to vote[44]. The Arunachalees feared that if the Chakmas were given voting rights, they would end up controlling politics in the state in the future. In neighbouring Mizoram, the Chakmas, some of whom were regarded as Congress-backers, were granted an autonomous district council in 1972. The Mizos resented the move and lent their support to a militant campaign that sought to intimidate the Chakmas. As a result, members of the community were assaulted, their houses torched and their names struck off the electoral lists. They were also pushed to the Myanmar-Bangla border. A hostile indigenous population is not the only problem that the Chakmas face. The hilly terrain makes it impossible to provide adequate healthcare facilities in the region. The absence of infrastructure, education and a common language are some of the other problems that have stalled the uplift of this community. The conflict in the CHT was largely a struggle for militarisation and Islamisation of this particular region. Ironically, a decision taken nearly sixty five years ago continues to torment a small community on either side of the Indo-Bangladesh border. Unfortunately, for the Chakmas, military oppression in their home country has forced the community to flee and seek refuge in an alien land[45]. Even today after many decades they continue their struggle for a homeland and an identity.

Srilankan Refugees

Tamil refugees from Sri Lanka began fleeing to India in 1983 when violence broke out in their country between the majority Sinhalese and the minority Tamil militant group, the Liberation Tigers of Tamil Eelam (LTTE). Although many of the refugees have been repatriated to Sri Lanka over the years, at present 61,000 Sri Lankan Tamils are living in 103 government-run camps in the South Indian state of Tamil Nadu and an additional 20,000 refugees live outside the camps[46].

The camp-based refugees were aided by the Indian Government and permitted to stay in India and ensured that educational and health facilities be made available to their children[47]. In particular, the Sri Lankan refugees were pleased with the opportunities they have for the education of their children in India, although a quota is imposed on Sri Lankan refugees attending universities. They receive a small stipend each month and a few basic supplies from the Indian Government, which are inadequate for survival. In one camp more than a thousand people have been living for a decade in crowded warehouses where each family lives in a 10 feet by 10 feet partitioned area. In other camps, refugees are living in '*temporary*' shelters, which were built prior to the refugee influx as short-term housing and are now falling apart. Basic facilities in the camps, such as toilets and water pumps, constructed by Indian authorities in the early 1990s, broke down long ago and have not been repaired. Sanitary problems in the camps were cited by many as a serious problem. They have had very few options to living in the camps, especially as returning to their homes in Sri Lanka was not feasible in the past due to the ongoing war between the LTTE and the Government[48].

With the cease-fire agreement between the Sri Lankan Government and the LTTE in early 2002, the security situation has improved significantly in Sri Lanka. Several thousand refugees have returned perhaps 10 per cent of those in India to Sri Lanka. Some of the returning refugees have been assisted by the UNHCR, which is facilitating their return via air, while others have paid fishermen thousands of rupees to smuggle them back by boat. The UNHCR's policy is not to encourage returns to Sri Lanka because of concerns about security, but the agency assists voluntary returnees. That policy seems correct and prudent at the present time. None of the refugees alleged to the government of India pressuring them to go home, although they fear that pressure may come in the future[49].

Other refugees are hesitant to return to Sri Lanka at this point because their homes lie in High Security Zones (HSZ), occupied by the Sri Lankan army, from where all residents have been displaced. These refugees only want to return when they will be able to go back to their original homes. A reason also mentioned by the refugees for not returning is the fear that their children will be recruited by the LTTE, which continues to fill its ranks with child soldiers. An additional cause affecting return is the standard of educational facilities in parts of Sri Lanka, which is not as high as the standard in India. As Sri Lankan Tamils place a high value on education, they do not want to return before the education of their children is completed in India[50]. The number of Sri Lankan refugees in India has risen to 12,062, resulting in Indian authorities opening a new camp in South India's Coimbatore to accommodate the number of overflowing refugees[51].

Afghan Refugees

From the Soviet invasion of Afghanistan in 1979 through the early 1990s, the Afghan War (1978–92) caused more than six million refugees to flee to the neighbouring countries of Pakistan and Iran, making Afghanistan the greatest refugee-producing country[52]. Since the early 1980s, approximately 3 million Afghan refugees were settled in Pakistan and about two million in Iran. Many of them also made their way into the European Union, North America, Australia, India[53], Turkey, and other parts of the world. The United States invasion of Afghanistan in 2001 and continued ethnic cleansing and reprisals also caused additional displacement. Though there has been some repatriation sponsored by the UN from Iran and Pakistan[54]. India is a home to 8,400 Afghan refugees of whom 7,560 are Hindus and Sikhs refugees and according to the UNHCR about 4,000 applying for Indian citizenship and as on date more then 510 now Indian nationals[55].

Since the beginning of 1999, the Indian Government's Foreigners Regional Registration Office (FRRO) has refused to renew their residence visas. As a result, the residence visas of most of these refugees have expired and they are now living in the country illegally. This situation has had predictable consequences. For example, most of these refugees are now wary about travelling outside their own neighbourhoods for fear of extortion, or, even worse, deportation, at the hands of the Indian police[56]. The situation for Afghan refugees is rapidly deteriorating[57]. The Indian Government's new policy of non-renewal is in significant part of the product of tensions between India and Pakistan, which reached a fever pitch during the Kargil crisis[58] and because of this Afghans were victimised by both private individuals and the state[59].

Tibetan Refugees

There are an estimated 110,000[60] Tibetan refugees in India, who fled their homeland in 1959 after Chinese troops crushed their uprising. The total of 68,639 Tibetan refugees has resettled with government assistance and self-employment under agriculture and handicraft schemes. The rehabilitation of these refugees is being achieved through the scheme of Government of India as well as relief agencies under the Tibetan Administration in India[61]. They mainly settled in Delhi, Bangalore and several places, but their main centre is in the Himalayan resort of Dharamsala, the home of the Tibetan government-in-exile[62]. In India the overwhelming majority of Tibetans born are still stateless and carry a document called an Identity Card issued by the Indian

Government in lieu of a passport. This document states the nationality of the holder as Tibetan. It is a document that is frequently rejected as a valid travel document by many customs and immigrations departments. Tibetan leaders in India consistently state that the government of India has treated them extremely well, but these understandably sincere statements of gratitude fail to testify to a changing reality both practical and political under which Tibetan refugees in India must live[63]. Tibetans, as one of the only refugee groups to be officially recognized by the Indian government and thus legally permitted to stay in India, are often considered to be in a more advantageous position than other refugees in India[64].

It is, however, necessary to recognise that the proximity and strategic importance of their country of origin, China, makes their situation politically delicate. As political pressure continues to mount on India from China, human rights observers fear that the practice of tolerance and permissive freedom will give way to subtle and even overt forms of repression, which are technically supported under Indian law[65]. As the Tibetan refugee community in India has existed for over 50 years and many Tibetans have been born in India. However, conflicting information exists about whether or not Tibetan refugees living in India are able to acquire Indian citizenship. Further, a number of sources indicate that only 1-3 percent of Tibetans are eligible to apply for Indian citizenship[66]. Few of them apply because there is a general belief that their exile in India is temporary and a return to Tibet will eventually follow[67]. Many do not see India as their country and look forward to returning to a free Tibet[68]. As a result, they see no need for the acquisition of Indian citizenship. Other sources, however, reveal that the acquisition of Indian citizenship is not so straightforward for Tibetans[69]. In an interview with the Unites States Bureau of Citizenship and Immigration Services, a Liaison Officer from the Office of Tibet in New York stated that in general, Tibetans have trouble obtaining Indian citizenship and are subsequently denied the concomitant rights it bestows[70].

Kashmiri Refugees

Kashmiri Hindus are living in Kashmir only due to the ongoing anti-Indian insurgency. Some 300,000 Hindus have been internally displaced from Kashmir due to the violence[71]. Azad Kashmir is a territory of Kashmir under Pakistan's jurisdiction twelve miles (19 km) outside of Muzaffarabad, capital of Azad Kashmir. More than 100 refugees have just moved into a new camp there above the Jhelum

River. The refugees, Kashmiri Muslims, are trying to rebuild lives ravaged by the decades-old Pakistan-Indian Kashmir conflict. The newcomers join the 17,000 other refugees who have made Azad Kashmir their home some since 1989. More than 350,000 refugees have flooded other parts of Kashmir. In 1999, the latest group of refugees began a slow mass migration to Azad Kashmir from villages near the Neelum Valley, which straddles the Line of Control (LoC) between Indian and Pakistan Kashmir. The refugees claim that Indian soldiers forced them out of their homes[72]. At first the refugees migrated only five miles from their villages, hoping they might soon return to their homes in India. But constant shelling near the LoC forced them to start new lives elsewhere. For Kashmiri Muslims, Pakistan appeared safer than main Kashmir. With the Kashmir conflict in its more than sixth decade of deadlock, the outlook for resolution is bleak[73].

Chin Refugees

A majority of Chin forced to flee Burma cross into neighbouring India and settle in the Mizoram hills, which are adjacent to the Chin Hills. Although it is impossible to accurately determine their true number, it is estimated to be nearly 80,000. Out of this 1,800 Chin living in Delhi, 1,000 have been granted refugee status by UNHCR. Another 300 Chin cases have been registered by UNHCR and are awaiting refugee status determination[74]. In mid 2006, UNHCR also began resettling the Chin to third countries. Obtaining refugee status through UNHCR, however, has become increasingly difficult for the Chin community in India. Most Chin live in Mizoram, where UNHCR is not operational. As a result, Chin living in Mizoram seeking UNHCR recognition must make an arduous and expensive journey to Delhi. Once registered, they are required to remain in Delhi, where it is difficult to make a living and assimilate culturally. Further limiting the accessibility of refugee status for the Chin, UNHCR announced the closure of general registration in September 2007. Only *'priority'* cases or those considered especially vulnerable, such as pregnant women, the elderly and the infirm, are now eligible for registration. *'Non-priority'* cases will have to wait until the general registration process re-opens, which is unlikely to happen as per rules[75].

Although India is not a signatory to the 1951 UN Refugee Convention, New Delhi has always taken an active role in refugee-related problems. A report by the United States Committee for Refugees says there are more than 2,00,000 refugees living in India, including people from Sri Lanka, Tibet, Bhutan, Myanmar and Afghanistan[76]. Gradually, both state and citizens began to ignore the refugees. At one point, when a short-lived peace reigned in Sri Lanka, many refugees were coaxed (some say forced) to leave India in an organised repatriation process. Accusations that Tamil militants were responsible for the assassination of India's former Prime Minister, Rajiv Gandhi, took away any remaining sympathy local people had for refugees. Sri Lankans suspected to be militants were thrown into what were *special camps,* where their movement was restricted and treatment was harsher. Some innocents were also detained here. Suspects could not seek judicial or political support. There have been many reports of ill treatment and torture, and human rights groups have recorded forced repatriation of ordinary refugees. In most cases, relief is not provided. It is clear, although nothing has been said officially, that India no longer wants the refugees. Article 33 of the 1951 UN convention on the status of refugees says that no contracting state shall expel or return (refouler in French) a refugee in any manner whatsoever to the frontiers of territories where his life or freedom would be threatened. It means a nation cannot send back a refugee unless his or her claim to refugee status has been properly determined. But India is not a signatory to the Convention, and it treats rights of refugees differently. In India, there is no mechanism for redress for refugees when a right is refused. Like most countries, India's stance on refugees depends on many things, most of them political or economic. Refugees who might have been acceptable last year are unacceptable this year, perhaps. Much depends on where they come from and when. Accepting large numbers of refugees is not always popular with the electorate. So, governments sometimes adopt a policy of pre-emptive deterrence to ensure that the flow is stopped at the point of origin itself. Here in India, it has been said that Bangladesh refugees in 1971, Tibetan refugees since the 50s and Tamil refugees since 1983 were all greeted with open arms because of political exigencies of that time. But that was not the case when Chakmas came into Arunachal Pradesh and Tripura. Now the UNHCR has been given the mandate to provide *"protection and assistance"* to refugees as legally defined by the UN. India, however, has taken the stand that it will deal with refugees itself, and that the UNHCR need not come into the picture. In many ways, then, the UN body does not have a very active role to play in matters concerning refugees in India[77]. It played a big role in the repatriation of 10 million Bangladeshi refugees, and it has been called in occasionally to play a limited role in other cases, but even that has sometimes ended on a sour note. And inevitably, if large number of refugees do come into the country as with the Sri Lankan Tamils they will face all manner of human rights and other problems unless they are given a clear legal status[78].

It has been mainly seen that the laws are affecting the rights of refugees in India. Here is one; the Foreigners Act of 1946 gives the executive wide powers of discretion to control foreigners in India. They can be prohibited, arrested, detained or confined and even asked to leave the country. The rights set out in the Refugees Convention are duplicated and complemented in the international human rights treatises and declarations, covering the Universal Declaration of Human Rights (UDHR) and the Covenant on Economics, Social and Cultural Rights (ESCR). In India, whether a person seeking asylum is termed an illegal alien or a refugee, the State is obligated to respect their fundamental rights. This was confirmed by the Supreme Court in the case of NHRC vs. State of Arunachal Pradesh[79], in which an attempt to drive out the Chakma refugees was brought before the court. It has been noticed on many occasions that India does not grant permission to media, non-governmental organisations (NGOs) and international bodies to visit the refugee camps, thus stifling investigations into the affairs there. The question of repatriation of refugees and India's stand on this has come into focus and discussion during the repatriation process involving the Sri Lankan Tamil refugees. There is no clarity on this issue either, leading to interpretations governed apparently, which leads to abuse. So India's policy on refugees presents a paradox[80]. While it has joined the UNHCR's Executive Committee, it does not concur with the Executive's policies on treatment of refugees and has declined to sign either the 1951 Refugee Convention or the 1967 Protocol. India's policy works more on a bilateral country-to-country basis, as with the Tamils of Sri Lanka[81].

UN body stresses need for law in India on refugee issues. The UNHCR has made out a strong case for enactment of a national law by India that would lay down the policy guidelines for recognising and assisting refugees who seek shelter in the country. The NHRC has turned little attention to such issues. Perusal of its annual reports shows that little or nothing has been done on the rights of refugees in India, the judiciary has played a very important role in protecting refugees. Court orders have filled legislative gaps and in many cases have provided a humanitarian solution to the problems of refugees. Moreover, Indian courts have allowed refugees and intervening NGOs to file cases before them. Furthermore, the courts have interpreted provisions of the Indian Constitution, existing laws and, in the absence of municipal law, provisions of international law to offer protection to refugees and asylum seekers.

References

1. Article 1 of the Convention as amended by the 1967 Protocol provides the definition of a refugee as well as the 1951 United Nations Convention, relating to the status of refugees.

2. Year book of United Nation (2005), Towards Development, Security and Human Rights for all, Vol. 59, United Nation Publication, New York, pp. 711-908.

3. *Ibid.*

4. UNHCR (2000), The State's of the World Refugees, Oxford University Press, Oxford.

5. Year book of United Nation (2005), Towards Development, Security and Human Rights for all, Vol. 59, United Nation Publication, New York, pp. 711-908.

6. UNHCR (2006), Statistical Yearbook.

7. Year book of United Nation (2005), Towards Development, Security and Human Rights for all, Vol. 59, United Nation Publication, New York, pp. 711-908.

8. Handbook for the Protection of Internally Displaced Persons (provisional release), p.6, Global Protection Cluster Working Group, December 2007, www.humanitarianreform.org.

9. Year book of United Nation (2005), Towards Development, Security and Human Rights for all, Vol.59, United Nation Publication, New York, pp. 1300-1320.

10. *Ibid.*

11. *Ibid.*

12. *Ibid.*

13. *Ibid.*

14. Prakesh, Talwar (ed.) (2006), *Human Rights*, Isha Books Publication, Delhi, pp. 32-41, also See the preamble of the UNHCR for detail information.

15. UNHCR (2001), Ministerial Declaration of States Parties, Geneva, Switzerland, 12-13 December, Declaration of States Parties to the 1951 Convention and/or its 1964 Protocol Relating to the Status of the Refugees.

16 *Ibid.*

17. *Ibid.*

18. Prakesh, Talwar (ed.) (2006), "Human Rights", Isha Books Publication, Delhi, pp. 32-41.

19. *Ibid.*

20. UNHCR (2001), Ministerial Declaration of States Parties, Geneva, Switzerland, 12-13 December, Declaration of States Parties to the 1951 Convention and/or its 1964 Protocol Relating to the Status of the Refugees.

21. *Ibid.*

22. *Ibid.*

24. *Ibid.*, pp. 33-41, also See the Preamble of the UNHCR for detail information.

25. *Ibid,* pp. 711-908.

26. Protocol relating to the status of refugees of 31 January 1967 ratified by a Law of the National Assembly (LNA), 22.05.1992, SG No 36/1992, supplemented by the LNA, 1. 04. 1993, SG No 30/1993.

27. P. Oberoi (2006), Exile and Belonging: Refugees and State Policy in South Asia, Oxford University Press, New Delhi, pp. 77 – 103.

28. *Ibid.*

29. Prakesh, Talwar (ed.) (2006), Human Rights, Isha Books Publication, Delhi, pp. 32-41.

30. Year book of United Nation (2005), Towards Development, Security and Human Rights for all, Vol. 59, United Nation Publication, New York, pp. 711-908.

31. These higher projections merit attention in light of the fact that the Planning Commission had estimated a figure of 844 million for 1991 while preparing the Eighth Five-Year Plan (FY 1992-96; see Population Projections, this chapter).

32. *Ibid.*

33. P. Oberoi (2006), Exile and Belonging: Refugees and State Policy in South Asia, Oxford University Press, New Delhi, pp. 77 –103.

34. See U.S. Library of Congress Report for detail information.
35. B.R.Ambedkar (1992), Pakistan or Partition of India, Writing and Speeches, Vol. 8, Mumbai, pp. 29-39.
36. Mukti Bahini was the Liberation Army and also termed as the "Freedom Fighters" collectively refers to the armed organizations fought against the Pakistan Army during the Bangladesh Liberation War.
37. P. Oberoi (2006), Exile and Belonging: Refugees and State Policy in South Asia, Oxford University Press, New Delhi, pp. 77–103.
38. Deepak K. Singh (2001), Refugee question in Arunachal Pradesh: Some conflicting currents' Journal of Anthropological Survey of India, 50(4), December, pp. 95-102.
39. The Shanti Bahini is the Peace Force was the name of the military wing of the Parbatya Chattagram Jana Sanghati Samti, the United People's Party of the CHT in Bangladesh. It was formed in 1972 to preserve the rights of the tribal people in south-eastern Bangladesh, and fought for many years against the central government. It abandoned militancy following the peace treaty signed by the government and the Shamiti on December 2, 1997.
40. Kaptai Dam (Kaptai Hydel Power Project) was built in CHT by the Pakistan Government in which Chakmas lost more than 60 percent of their cultivated land and largely displaced.
41. S. Dutta (1996), Chakma-Hajong Refugee Problem in Arunachal Pradesh: Historical Background, Journal Title IASSI Quarterly, Vol. 15, No.1, July-September, pp.111-26.
42. Deepak K. Singh (2001), Stateless Chakmas in Arunachal Pradesh: From Rejected Peoples to Unwanted Migrants, Social Science Research Journal, 9(1), pp. 47-82.
43. Arunachal Pradesh was known as North East Frontier Agency (NEFA) before 1982.
44. See Judgment of Supreme Court of India (1996), Original Civil Jurisdiction, Writ Petition (Civil) No. 720 of 1995 (Between NHRC versus State of Arunachal Pradesh), 9th January, New Delhi.
45. The Telegraph, 19, July, 2007.

46. See website, http://www.fmreview.org, article by K.C. Saha, Learning from Empowerment of Sri Lankan Refugees in India.
47. Annual Report (2007), Ministry of Home Affairs, Government of India, Chapter XIV, Rehabilitation of Displaced Persons, pp. 1-3.
48. P. Oberoi (2006), Exile and Belonging: Refugees and State Policy in South Asia, Oxford University Press, New Delhi, pp. 77–103.
49. Rohini, Hensman (2008), Democracy as Solution to Sri Lanka's Ethnic Crisis, Economic and Political Weekly, 9 August, pp. 46-49.
50. See website, http://www.refugeesinternational.org, Srilankan Refugees in India: Hesitant to Return, Refugee International.
51. Asian Tribune, 26 September, 2006.
52. The Hindu, 6 July, 2002.
53. UNHCR (2005), The UN Refugee Agency, Afghan refugees in search of Indian identity, New Delhi, India, 18 May, http://www.unhcr.org.
54. UNHCR (2007) Census identified over two million Afghan refugees still living in Pakistan alone.
55. The Hindu, 19 June, 2009.
56. Margesson, Rhoda (ed.) (2007), Afghan Refugees: Current Status and Future Prospects, Foreign Affairs, Defence and Trade Division, 26 January, New Delhi, p. 2.
57. SAHRD (1999), No Place to Turn: Afghan Refugees in New Delhi, Human Rights Features, 26 July, http://www.hrdc.net.
58. *Times of India*, 9 July 1999.
59. *Hindustan Times*, 5 July 1999.
60. United States Department of State (2007), Country Reports on Human Rights Practices - India, Bureau of Democracy, Human Rights and Labour, 11 March 2008, available at http://www.state.gov.
61. Annual Report (2007), Ministry of Home Affairs, Government of India, Chapter XIV, Rehabilitation of Displaced Persons, pp. 1-3.

62. Indo Asian News Service, August 30, 2008.
63. R. Kharat (2003), Tibetan Refugees in India, Kaveri Books, New Delhi, pp. 46 –94.
64. United States Committee for Refugees and Immigrants, World Refugee Survey 2007, India, available at http://www.refugees.org. This report indicates that unlike other refugees with the exception of Sri Lankan Tamils, Tibetans are provided with documents that legalize their stay in India; permission to work though there is no legal basis for doing so, certification to practice profession that was not available to other refugee groups, and have been successful in acquiring land, something that other refugees are unable to do.
65. R. Kharat (2003), Tibetan Refugees in India, Kaveri Books, New Delhi, pp. 46–94.
66. The Hindu, 26 May 2005.
67. See Immigration and Refugee Board of Canada, Responses to Information Requests (100699.E), *op. cit.*
68. The Hindu, 26 May 2005.
69. See Immigration and Refugee Board of Canada, Responses to Information Requests (IND42508.E), 26 March 2004, available at http://www.cisr-irb.gc.ca.
70. United States Bureau of Citizenship and Immigration Services, India: Information on Tibetan Refugees and Settlements, op. cit.
71. See website, http://www.britishcouncil.org.in.
72. Annual Report (2007), Ministry of Home Affairs, Government of India, Chapter VIII, Human Rights, p. 4.
73. See website, http://news.nationalgeographic.com, Zoltan Istvan (2003), Refugee Crisis Worsening in Western Kashmir.
74. P. Oberoi (2006), Exile and Belonging: Refugees and State Policy in South Asia, Oxford University Press, New Delhi, pp. 77–103.
75. Hindustan Times, 23 February, 2007.
76. The Hindu, 10 May, 2000.

77. P. Oberoi (2006), Exile and Belonging: Refugees and State Policy in South Asia, Oxford University Press, New Delhi, pp. 77–103.

78. *Ibid.*

79. See Judgment of Supreme Court of India (1996), Original Civil Jurisdiction, Writ Petition (Civil) No. 720 of 1995, Between NHRC versus State of Arunachal Pradesh, 9 January, New Delhi.

80. The Hindu, May 10, 2000.

81. *Ibid.*

3

India's Refugee Regime and Resettlement Policy

Humanitarian Law, Human Rights and Refugee Law are the three Pillars of International Humanitarian Law (IHL). Refugee Law and Human Rights Law (HRL) are complementary bodies of law that share a common goal and the protection of the lives, health and dignity of persons. They form a complex network of complementary protections and it is essential that we understand how they interact. International law is the term commonly used for referring to the system of implicit and explicit agreements that bind together nation-states in adherence to recognized values and standards, differing from other legal systems in that it concerns nations rather than private citizens[1]. IHL is a set of rules which seek, for humanitarian reasons, to limit the effects of armed conflict. It protects persons who are not or are no longer participating in the hostilities and restricts the means and methods of warfare. It does not regulate whether a State may actually use force; this is governed by an important, but distinct, part of international law set out in the United Nations Charter[2].

IHL is rooted in the rules of ancient civilizations and religions warfare has always been subject to certain principles and customs. Universal codification of IHL began in the nineteenth century. Since then, States have agreed to a series of practical rules, based on the bitter experience of modern warfare. These rules strike a careful balance between humanitarian concerns and the military requirements of States. As the international community has grown, an increasing number of States have contributed to the development of those rules. IHL today forms a universal body of law[3]. A major part of IHL is contained in the fourth *Geneva Convention of 1949*. Nearly every State in the world has agreed to be bound by them. The

Conventions have been developed and supplemented by two further agreements: the *Additional Protocols of 1977 relating to the protection of victims of armed conflicts.* Other agreements prohibit the use of certain weapons and military tactics and protect certain categories of people and goods. These agreements include:

(a) The 1954 convention for the protection of cultural property in the event of armed conflict, plus its two protocols;

(b) The 1972 biological weapons convention;

(c) The 1980 conventional weapons convention and its five protocols;

(d) The 1993 chemical weapons convention;

(e) The 1997 Ottawa convention on anti-personnel mines;

(f) The 2000 optional protocol to the convention on the rights of the child on the involvement of children in armed conflict. Many provisions of international humanitarian law are now accepted as customary law – that is, as general rules by which all States are bound.

IHL applies only to armed conflict; it does not cover internal tensions or disturbances such as isolated acts of violence. The law applies only once a conflict has begun, and then equally to all sides regardless of who started the fighting. IHL distinguishes between international and non-international armed conflict[4]. International armed conflicts are those in which at least two States are involved. They are subject to a wide range of rules, including those set out in the fourth Geneva Convention and Additional Protocol- I (one).

Non-international armed conflicts are those restricted to the territory of a single State, involving either regular armed forces fighting groups of armed dissidents, or armed groups fighting each other. A more limited range other. A more limited range of rules apply to internal armed conflicts and are laid down in Article 3 common to the fourth Geneva Convention as well as in Additional Protocol-II (two). It is important to differentiate between IHL and HRL. While some of their rules are similar, these two bodies of law have developed separately and are contained in different treaties. In particular, human rights law unlike IHL applies in peacetime, and many of its provisions may be suspended during an armed conflict[5].

International humanitarian law largely covers two areas:

(i) The protection of those who are not, or no longer, taking part in fighting;

(ii) Restrictions on the means of warfare in particular weapons and the methods of warfare, such as military tactics.

IHL protects those who do not take part in the fighting, such as civilians and medical and religious military personnel. It also protects those who have ceased to take part, such as wounded, shipwrecked and sick combatants, and prisoners of war. These categories of person are entitled to respect for their lives and for their physical and mental integrity. They also enjoy legal guarantees. They must be protected and treated humanely in all circumstances, with no adverse distinction. More specifically it is forbidden to kill or wound an enemy who surrenders or is unable to fight; the sick and wounded must be collected and cared for by the party in whose power they find themselves. Medical personnel, supplies, hospitals and ambulances must all be protected. There are also detailed rules governing the conditions of detention for prisoners of war and the way in which civilians are to be treated when under the authority of an enemy power. This includes the provision of food, shelter and medical care, and the right to exchange messages with their families. The law sets out a number of clearly recognizable symbols which can be used to identify protected people, places and objects. The main emblems are the Red Cross, the Red Crescent and the symbols identifying cultural property and civil defense facilities[6].

International humanitarian law prohibits all means and methods of warfare which:

(a) Fail to discriminate between those taking part in the fighting and those, such as civilians, who are not, the purpose being to protect the civilian population, individual civilians and civilian property;

(b) Cause superfluous injury or unnecessary suffering;

(c) Cause severe or long-term damage to the environment. Humanitarian law has therefore banned the use of many weapons, including exploding bullets, chemical and biological weapons, blinding laser weapons and anti-personnel mines.

Sadly, there are countless examples of violation of IHL and there is increasingly, the victims of war are civilians. However, there are important cases where the IHL has made a difference in protecting civilians, prisoners, the sick and the wounded, and in restricting the use of barbaric weapons. Given that this body of law applies during times of extreme violence, implementing the law will always be a matter of great difficulty. That said striving for effective compliance remains as urgent as ever. Measures must be taken to ensure respect for IHL. States have an obligation to teach its rules to their armed forces and the general public. They must prevent violations or punish them if these nevertheless occur. In particular, they must enact laws to punish the most serious violations of the Geneva Convention and Additional Protocols, which are regarded as war crimes. The states must also pass laws protecting the Red Cross and Red Crescent Emblems. Measures have also been taken at an international level and tribunals have been created to punish acts committed in two recent conflicts (the former Yugoslavia and Rwanda). An international criminal court, with the responsibility of repressing *inter alia* war crimes, was created by the 1998 Rome Statute. Whether as individuals or through governments and various organisations, we can all make an important contribution to compliance with IHL[7].

1. International Humanitarian Law in Refugee Law and Protection

Armed conflict and IHL are of relevance to refugee law and refugee protection in a number of ways, first to determine who is a refugee. Many asylum seekers are persons fleeing armed conflict and this made them refugees? Not every person fleeing an armed conflict automatically falls within the definition of the 1951 Refugee Convention, which lays down a limited list of grounds for persecution. While there may be situations, notably in conflicts with an ethnic dimension, where persons are fleeing because of a fear of persecution based on their "race, religion, nationality or membership of a particular social group", this is not always the case[8].

The majority of persons, forced to leave their state of nationality today are fleeing the indiscriminate effect of hostilities and the accompanying disorder, including the destruction of homes, food stocks and means of subsistence. All violations of the IHL but with no specific element of persecution, subsequent regional refugee instruments, such as the 1969 OAU Refugee Convention and the 1984 Cartagena Declaration on Refugees have expanded their definitions to include persons fleeing armed conflict. Moreover, states that are not party to these regional instruments have developed a variety of legislative and administrative measures, such as the notion of *'temporary protection'* for example, to extend protection to persons fleeing armed conflict. A second point of interface between the IHL and refugee law is in relation to issues of exclusion. Violations of certain provisions of IHL are war crimes and their commission may exclude a particular individual from entitlement to protection as a refugee[9].

2. Protection of Refugees under International Humanitarian Law

IHL offers refugees who find themselves in a state experiencing armed conflict a two tiered protection. First, provided that they are not taking a direct part in hostilities, as civilians, refugees are entitled to protection from the effects of hostilities. Secondly, in addition to this general protection, the IHL grants refugees additional rights and protections in view of their situation as aliens in the territory of a party to a conflict and their consequent specific vulnerabilities.

(a) General Protection

If respected, the IHL operates so as to prevent displacement of civilians and to ensure their protection during displacement, should they nevertheless have moved.

(i) The Express Prohibition of Displacement

Parties to a conflict are expressly prohibited from displacing civilians. This is a manifestation of the principle that the civilian population must be spared as much as possible from the effects of hostilities. During occupation, the fourth Geneva Convention prohibits individual or mass forcible transfers, both within the occupied territory and beyond its borders, either into the territory of the occupying power or, as is more often the case in practice, into third states.

There is a limited exception to this rule, which permits an occupying power to *'evacuate'* the inhabitants of a particular area if this is necessary for the security of the civilian population or for imperative military reasons. Even in such cases the evacuations should not involve the displacement of civilians *'outside the occupied territory'* unless this is impossible for material reasons. Moreover, displaced persons must be transferred back to their homes as soon as the hostilities in the area in question have ceased. The prohibition on displacing the civilian population for reasons related to the conflict unless the security of the civilians or imperative military reasons so demand also applies in non-international armed conflicts.

(ii.) Protection from the Effects of Hostilities in order to Prevent displacement

In addition to these express prohibitions, the rules of IHL which shield civilians from the effects of hostilities also play on important role in the prevention of displacement, as it is often violations of these rules which are at the root of displacements in situations of armed conflict of particular relevance are:

(a) The prohibition to attack civilians and civilian property and of indiscriminate attacks;

(b) The duty to take precautions in attack to spare the civilian population;

(c) The prohibition of starvation of the civilian population as a method of warfare and of the destruction of objects indispensable to its survival; and

(d) The prohibition on reprisals against the civilian population and its property.

Also of relevance are the prohibitions on collective punishments which, in practice have often taken form of destruction of homes, leading to displacement; and the rules requiring parties to a conflict, as well as all other states, to allow the unhindered passage of relief supplies and assistance necessary for the survival of the civilian population.

(iii) Protection during Displacement

Although prohibited by IHL, displacement of civilians frequently occurs in practice and once displaced or evacuated civilians are entitled to various protections and rights. Thus we find rules regulating the manner in which evacuations must be effected and transfers must be carried out are in satisfactory conditions of hygiene, health, safety and nutrition. During displacement persons must be provided with appropriate accommodation and members of the same family must not be separated. Although these provisions relate to conditions to be ensured on situations of evacuation i.e. 'lawful' displacements for the safety of the persons involved, security or for imperative military necessity these conditions should be applicable *a fortiori* in situations of unlawful displacement[11]. In addition to these special provisions relating specifically to persons who have been displaced, such persons are civilians and, as such, entitled, even during displacement, to the whole range of protection appertaining to civilians[12].

(b) Specific Protection of Refugees

In addition to this general protection, the IHL affords refugees further specific protection. In international armed conflicts refugees are covered by the rules applicable to aliens in the territory of a party to a conflict generally as well as by the safeguards relating specifically to refugees.

(i) Protection as Aliens in the Territory of a Party to a Conflict

Refugees benefit from the protections afforded by the fourth Geneva Convention to aliens in the territory of a party to a conflict, including:

(a) The entitlement to leave the territory in which they find themselves unless their departure would be contrary to the national interests of the state of asylum;

(b) The continued entitlement to basic protections and rights to which aliens had been entitled before the outbreak of hostilities;

(c) Guarantees with regards to mean of existence, if the measures of control applied to the aliens by the party to the conflict means that they are unable to support themselves.

While recognising that the party to the conflict in whose control the aliens find themselves if its security makes this absolutely necessary, intern the aliens or place them in assigned residence, the convention provides that these are the strictest measures of control to which aliens may be subjected.

Finally, the fourth convention also lays down limitations on the power of a belligerent to transfer aliens. The particular relevance is the rule providing that a protected person may in no circumstances be transferred to a country where he or she may have reason to fear persecution for his or her political opinions or religious beliefs; a very early expression of the principle of *non refoulement*[13].

(ii) Additional Protections for Refugees

In addition to the aforementioned rules for the benefit of all aliens in the territory of a party to a conflict, the fourth Geneva Convention contains two further provisions expressly for the benefit of refugees. The first provides that refugees should not be treated as enemy aliens and thus susceptible to the measures of control-solely on the basis of their nationality. This recognises the fact that refugees no longer have a link of allegiance with that state and are thus not automatically a potential threat to their host state.

The second specific provision deals with the precarious position in which refugees may find themselves if the state which they have fled occupies their state of asylum. In such circumstances, the refugees may only be arrested, prosecuted, convicted or deported from the occupied territory by the occupying power for offences committed after the outbreak of hostilities, or for offences unrelated to the conflict committed before the outbreak of hostilities which, according to the law of the now occupied state of asylum, would have justified extradition in time of peace. The objective of this provision is to ensure that refugees are not punished for acts- such as political offences, which may have been the cause of their departure from their state of nationality, or for the mere fact of having sought asylum[14].

All of this being said, who is a refugee for the purposes of IHL? Although the fourth Geneva Convention expressly refers to refugees, it does not define this term. Instead, it focuses on their *de facto* lack of protection from any government. The matter was developed in Additional Protocol-I. This provides that persons who, before the beginning of hostilities, were considered refugees under the relevant international instruments accepted by the parties concerned or under the national legislation of the state of refuge or of residence are to be considered *'protected persons'* within the meaning of the fourth convention in all circumstances and without any adverse distinction[15].

The Office of the High Commissioner (OHC), monitoring bodies and the Commission on Human Rights (CHR), where the ICRC has observer status, is increasingly addressing the IHL in both country and thematic work and, where appropriate, the ICRC provides informal expert advice on IHL. To give but one example, earlier this week the CHR adopted the basic principles and guidelines on the right to a remedy and reparation for victims of gross violations of International Human Rights Law (IHRL) and serious violations of IHL. The ICRC participated in the expert meetings leading to the adoption of this instrument and provided legal input on the IHL dimension[16].

B. Non-refoulement

The practical challenge that the ICRC has faced in recent years is to find very difficult that how to ensure the respect of principle of *non-refoulement*. *Non-refoulement* is the keystone of refugee law and also forms part of IHL and HRL, notably as part of the prohibition of torture; no one must be transferred to a place where she/he risks torture or other forms of ill-treatment. While the precise contours of the principle may differ slightly in the different bodies of law, the essence of the principle is uncontroversial[17].

The Geneva Conventions came into being between 1864 and 1949 as a result of efforts by Henry Duant, the founder of the International Committee of Red Cross (ICRC). The conventions safeguard the human rights of individuals involved in armed conflict, and build on the 1899 and 1907 Hague Conventions, the international community's first attempt to formalise the laws of war and war crimes in the nascent body of secular international law. The conventions were revised as a result of World War-II and readopted by the international community in 1949. The Geneva Conventions define what is today referred to as humanitarian law. The ICRC is the controlling body of the Geneva conventions[18].

Human Rights

The idea of rights provides an essential tool of analysis of the relations between individual and the state. Hobbes and Bentham suggest that the rights are generally a claim of the citizens which are recognized by the state and enforced by the society. As Bosanquet opines that we have a right to the means that are necessary to the development of our lives in the direction of the highest good of the community of which we are a part. In other sense the human rights is one the most important natural rights of human kind in this universe. Human rights are those rights to which an individual is entitled by virtue of his or her status as a human being. While the civil, political and socio-economic rights are dependent on an individual's status as a citizen of a particular state, his/her human rights are not determined by this condition. As we know the scope of human rights is very wide. Human rights constitute the very source of all rights of human beings[19].

Human Rights Law is a system of laws, both domestic and international, designed to promote human rights. HRL is made up of various international human rights instruments which are binding to its parties (nation-states that have ratified the treaty). An important concept within human rights law is that of universal jurisdiction. This concept, which is not widely accepted, is that any nation is authorised to prosecute and punish violations of human rights wherever and whenever they may have occurred. Some customary peremptory norms of human rights are also recognised, and these are considered binding on all nations, even those that have not ratified the relevant treaty. In principle the HRL is enforced on a domestic level and nation-states that ratify human rights treaties commit themselves to enact domestic human rights legislations[20].

Human rights refer to the 'basic rights and freedoms to which all humans are entitled'. Examples of rights and freedoms which are often thought of as human rights include civil and political rights, such as the right to life and liberty, freedom of expression, and equality before law; and social, cultural and economic rights, including the right to participate in culture, the right to food, the right to work, and the right to education[21].

The history of human rights covers thousands of years and draws upon religious, cultural, philosophical and legal developments throughout recorded history. Several ancient documents and later religions and philosophies included a variety of concepts that may be considered to be human rights. Notable among such documents are the Cyrus calendar of 539 BC, a declaration of intentions by the Persian emperor Cyrus, the great after his conquest of the Neo-Babylonia empire; the Edits of Ashoka issued by Ashoka the Great of India between 272-231 BC; and the Constitution of Medina of 622 AD, drafted by Muhammad to mark a formal agreement between all of the significant tribes and families of Yathrib (later known as Medina), including Muslims, Jews and Pagans. The English Magna Carta of 1215 is particularly significant in the history of English law, and is hence significant in international law and constitutional law today and the declaration of the rights of man and of the citizen approved by the National Assembly of France, August 26, 1789. Much of modern HRL and the basis of most modern interpretations of human rights can be traced back to relatively recent history. The British Bill of Rights (An Act Declaring the Rights and Liberties of the Subject and Settling the Succession of the Crown) of 1689 made illegal a range of oppressive governmental actions in the United Kingdom.

Two major revolutions occurred during the 18th century, in the United Kingdom (1776) and in France (1789), leading to the adoption of the United States Declaration of Independence and the French Declaration of the Rights of Man and of the Citizen respectively, both of which established certain rights. Additionally, the Virginia Declaration of Rights of 1776 set up a number of fundamental rights and freedoms. These were followed by developments in philosophy of human rights by philosophers such as Thomas Paine, John Stuart Mill and Hegel during the 18th and 19th centuries. The term *'human rights'* probably came into use sometime between Paine's *'The Rights of*

Man' and William Lloyd Garrison's 1831 writings in The Liberator saying he was trying to enlist his readers in 'the great cause of human rights'[22]. The Magna Carta or 'Great Charter' was one of England's first documents containing commitments by a sovereign to his people to respect certain legal rights. All human beings are born free and equal in dignity and rights. They are endowed with reason and conscience and should act towards one another in a spirit of brotherhood[23].

Universal Declaration of Human Rights

The Universal Declaration of Human Rights (UDHR) is a non-binding declaration adopted by the UN's General Assembly in 1948, partly in response to the atrocities of World War-II. Although the UDHR is a non-binding resolution, it is now considered to be a central component of international customary law which may be invoked under appropriate circumstances by national and other judiciaries. The UDHR urges member nations to promote a number of human, civil, economic and social rights, asserting these rights as a part of the *'foundation of freedom, justice and peace in the world.'* The declaration was the first international legal effort to limit the behavior of states and press upon them duties to their citizens following the model of the rights-duty duality.

The UDHR was framed by members of the HRC, with former First Lady Eleanor Roosevelt as Chair, who began to discuss an *'International Bill of Rights'* in 1947. The members of the commission did not immediately agree on the form of such a bill of rights, and whether, or how, it should be enforced. The commission proceeded to frame the UDHR and accompanying treaties, but the UDHR quickly became the priority. Canadian law professor John Humprey and French lawyer Rene Cassin were responsible for much of the cross-national research of the structure of the document respectively, where the articles of the declaration were interpretative of the general principle of the preamble. The document was structured by Cassin to include the basic principles of *'dignity, liberty, equality and brotherhood'* in the first two articles, followed successively by rights pertaining to individuals; rights of individuals in relation to each other and to groups; spiritual, public and political rights; and economic, social and cultural rights. The final three articles place, according to Cassin, rights in the context of limits, duties and the social and political order in which they are to be realised. Humphrey and Cassin intended the rights in the UDHR to be legally enforceable through some means, as is reflected in the third clause of the preamble:

"Whereas it is essential, if man is not to be compelled to have recourse, as a last resort, to rebellion against tyranny and oppression, that human rights should be protected by the rule of law"[24]

Some of the UDHR was researched and written by a committee of international experts on human rights, including representatives from all continents and all major religions, and drawing on consultation with leaders such as Mohan Das Karamchand Gandhi. The inclusion of both civil and political rights and economic, social and cultural rights was predicated on the assumption that basic human rights are indivisible and that the different types of rights listed are inextricably linked[25]. This principle was not then opposed by any of the member states (the declaration was adopted unanimously, with the abstention of the Eastern Bloc, Apartheid South Africa and Saudi Arabia), however this principle was later subject to significant challenges.

The universal declaration was bifurcated into two distinct and different covenants, a covenant on civil and political rights and another covenant on economic, social and cultural rights. Over the objection of the more developed states (capitalist), which questioned the relevance and propriety of such provisions in covenants on human rights, both begin with the right of people to self-determination and to sovereignty over their natural resources. Then the two covenants go different ways[26].

The drafters of the covenants initially intended only one instrument. The original drafts included only political and civil rights, but economic and social rights were added early. Western states then fought for, and obtained, a division into two covenants. They insisted that economic and social rights were essential aspirations or plans, not rights, since their realisation depended on availability of resources and on controversial economic theory and ideology. There was wide agreement and clear recognition that the means required to enforce or induce compliance with socio-economic undertakings were different from the means required for civil-political rights[27].

Because of the divisions over which rights to include, and because some states declined to ratify any treaties including certain specific interpretations of human rights, and despite the Soviet bloc and a number of developing countries arguing strongly for the inclusion of all rights in a so-called Unity Resolution, the rights enshrined in the UDHR were split into two separate covenants, allowing states to adopt some rights and derogate others. Though this allowed the covenants to be created, one commentator has written that it denied the proposed principle that all rights are linked which was central to some interpretations of the UDHR[28]. The Refugee Act of 1980 created a new system for refugee admissions, dropping the seventh preference and reducing the world-wide ceiling to 270,000. The total number of immigrant visa to be distributed is currently made up of three components[29].

National Human Rights Commission

India is a country of 28 states and 7 union territory of different form of culture, tradition, history and so on so forth, but only few states have a proper human rights commission body to see the basic human dignity in the states as well as to extend thehuman rights features to its citizens, particularly to the states like Andhra Pradesh, Jammu and Kashmir, Madhya Pradesh, Odisha, Tamil Nadu, Chhattisgarh, Assam, Kerala, Maharashtra, Punjab, Uttar Pradesh, Gujarat, Himachal Pradesh, Karnataka, Manipur, Rajasthan, West Bengal[30].

Nationality

Nationality is a relationship between a person and their state of origin, culture, association, affiliation or loyalty. Nationality affords the state jurisdiction over the person and affords of the person, the protection of the state. Traditionally under international law and conflict of laws principles, it is the right of each state to determine who its nationals are. Today the law of nationality is increasingly coming under more international regulation by various conventions on statelessness, as well as some multilateral treaties such as the European Convention on nationality.

Generally, nationality is established at birth by a child's place of birth (jus soil) or bloodline (jus sanguinis). Nationality may also be acquired later in life through naturalisation. Corporations, ships, and other legal persons also have a nationality, generally in the state under whose laws the legal person was formed. The legal sense of nationality, particularly in the English speaking world, may often mean citizenship, although they do not mean the same thing everywhere in the world; for instance, in the United Kingdom (UK), citizenship is a branch of nationality which in turn ramifies to include other subcategories[31]. Citizens have rights to participate in the political life of the state of which they are a citizen, such as by voting or standing for election. Nationals need not immediately have these rights; they may often acquire them in due time. Nationality can also mean membership in a cultural/historical group related to political or national identity, even if it currently lacks a formal state. This meaning is said by some authorities to cover many groups, including Kurds, Basques, Catalans, English, Welsh, Scots, Palestinians, Tamils, Quebecers and many others[32].

Citizenship

The very common understanding of citizenship denotes the status of an individual as a full and most responsible member of a political community. Citizenship is a central concept through which the duties of a state are determined. It is therefore 'a powerful instrument of social closer[33]. So far the subaltern concept of citizenship is concerned, largely they believed that the 'Dalits' in India are, so to speak, exiled citizens. They do not enjoy the sort of citizenship that can give them a sense of inclusion on a more permanent basis[34]. Citizen is a person who owes allegiance to a state and in turn receives protection from the state. He or she must fulfill his or her duties and obligations toward the state as state grants him civil, political, and social rights. Thus, citizenship implies the two way relationship between the state and the individuals. There is a distinction between the 'subject' and 'citizen'. A subject is usually subversive to the state where the right to rule is reserved for privileged classes but citizen themselves constitutes the state[35]. Citizenship is the product of a community where the right to rule is decided by a prescribed producer which expresses the will of the general body of its members while ascertaining their will, no body is discriminated on the ground of race, religion, gender, caste, place of birth, etc[36]. Anoski and Bottmore rightly points that the citizenship may be defined as a passive and active membership of individuals in a nation-state with universalistic rights and obligations at a specified level of equality[37].

There are four main definitions, first citizenship determining membership in a nation-state, which means establishing *'personhood'* or who out of the totality of denizens, natives, and subjects of a territory are recognised as being citizens with specific rights. Secondly, citizenship involves active capacities to influence politics and passive rights of existence under a legal system[38]. Thirdly, citizenship rights are universalistic rights enacted into laws and implemented for all citizens, and not informal, un-enacted or special rights. Fourthly and lastly citizenship is a statement of equality; with rights and obligations being balanced within certain limits[39]. In ancient citizenship, the citizenry is its own political master. Modern historians have made much of Aristotle's famous phrase that in democracies the citizen is both ruler and ruled in turn[40].

Citizenship is something that one talks about the legal rights. There is a difference between legal and political rights. Legal right on one hand is largely related to the access to justice, and freedom of conscience. Kriegel rightly points that the rights to personal security include freedoms from government torture, the imposition of the death penalty and freedom to control your own body through contraception. The right to personal security *'consist'* in a person's legal and uninterrupted enjoyment of his life, his/her limbs, body, health and his/her reputation[41]. Legal rights allow individuals to conduct their lives without interference from the state, other groups, and individuals. It obligates the state to protect the individual's rights to personal security. The right to control one's body is the ability to decide how one takes care of one's body and mind and one's health. Legal rights largely support or facilitate access to justice and rights that provide access to gain justice[42].

On the other hand the political rights focus on the four types of rights: personal political rights, organisational political rights, membership rights and the group self-determination rights. Firstly, personal political rights consist of voting in election for a multiplicity of competing candidates chosen through a democratic political process. Secondly, organisational political rights refer to the rights to the political parties, interest groups, and social movements to forms and take action in legislative forums, the courts and in the media. Thirdly, countries differ according to their propensity to grant membership to citizens within and outside of their borders. Naturalisation refers to the procedures that an immigrant must go through in order to become a citizen. And fourthly, the right of a group to self-determination is not an individual right since one person cannot form a government. This is a group's right afforded to regional, ethnic, or racial groups who claim that they are a nation and should stand independently with some form of sovereignty. On the whole the liberal democracies score high on measures of legal and political rights but across categories differences exist with social democracies scoring highest and liberal democracies tending to score lowest. Norton argued that the citizenship varies most across different levels of government in federal system but much less so is more centralised countries[43].

Citizenship is membership in a society, community, (originally that of a city or town but now usually for a country) and carries with it rights to political participation; a person having such membership is a citizen. Citizenship status often implies some responsibilities and duties under social contract theory. It is largely co-terminus with nationality, although it is possible to have a nationality without being a citizen (i.e., be legally subject to a state and entitled to its protection without having rights of political participation in it); it is also possible to have political rights without being a national of a state[44]. In most nations, a non-citizen is a non-national and called either a '*foreigner* or an *alien*'. Citizenship, which is explained above, is the political right of an individual within a society. Thus, you can have a citizenship from one country and be a national of another country[45]. One example might be as follows: A Cuban-American might be considered a national of Cuba due to his being born there, but he could also become an American citizen through naturalization. Nationality often derives either from place of birth (Currently used in few countries other than the United States) (i.e. jus soli) or parentage (i.e. jus sanguinis common in European Union member states such as the United Kingdom, Republic of Ireland, Germany, Italy etc.), or ethnicity (as in Israel). Citizenship derives from a legal relationship with a state. Citizenship can be lost, as in denaturalisation, and gained, as in naturalization, or by marriage. The term active citizenship implies working towards the betterment of one's community through economic participation, public service, volunteer work, and other such efforts to improve life for all citizens. In this vein, schools in England provide lessons in citizenship. In Wales the model used is personal and social. In the Republic of Ireland it is known as civil, social and political education (CSPE).

Discrimination and exclusion of certain groups due to their identity based on social origin, ethnic and religious background, race, colour, gender and nationality is common to several societies. It is well illustrated that the nature and forms of discrimination and social exclusion have undergone changes over time and space. While it has changed to fluid forms, practices of discrimination overwhelmingly exist in the social, economic, political and cultural spheres of every society, irrespective of the existence of legal safeguards and equal opportunity policies. This seeks to extend discussions to the changing nature and forms of discrimination and social exclusion, both in specific and comparative contexts.

Discrimination has multiple ramifications related to exclusion from economic entitlements, basic services and opportunities on one hand and humiliation, subordination, exploitation and denial of citizenship rights on the other. It is well entrenched that discrimination and social exclusion leads to widening of income inequalities, degree of poverty and deprivation by denying equal opportunities and access to resources and services.

Citizenship in India

Legal provisions relating to acquisition and termination of citizenship of India are contained in the Citizenship Act, 1955. Citizenship of India can be acquired by Birth, Decent, Registration, Naturalisation, and Incorporation of territory, Termination, Renunciation, Acquisition of another country and by Deprivation[46].

Citizenship by Birth

Every person born in India on or after the 26th January, 1950, is a citizen of India by birth except if at the time of his birth:

(a) His father possesses such immunity from suits and legal process as is accorded to an envoy of a foreign sovereign power accredited to the President of India and is not a citizen of India; or

(b) His father is an enemy alien and the birth occurs in a place other than under occupation by the enemy.

Citizenship by Descent

A person born outside India on or after 26th January, 1950, but before the commencement of the Citizenship (Amendment) act, 1992, shall be a citizen of India by descent if his father is a citizen of India at the time of his birth; or (b) On or after such commencement, shall be a citizen of India by descent if either of his parents is a citizen of India at the time of his birth; Provided further if either of the parents of such a person referred to in clause (b) was a citizen of India by descent only, that person is not be a citizen of India by virtue of this section unless his birth is registered at an Indian consulate within one year of its occurrence or the commencement of the Citizenship (amendment) act, 1992, whichever is later, or, with the permission of the Central Government, after the expiry of the said period; or Either of his parents is at the time of his birth, in service under a Government of India[47].

Citizenship by Registration

Subject to certain conditions and restrictions, the central government, in the ministry of home affairs may, on application made in this behalf, register as a citizen of India any person who is not already such citizen and belongs to any of the following categories:

(a) Persons of Indian origin who are ordinarily resident in India and have been so resident for five years immediately before making an application for registration. Prior to the coming into force of the Citizenship (amendment) Act, 1986 i.e. 1st July 1987, this period was six months. New Delhi, pp. 209-235.

(b) Persons of Indian origin who are ordinarily resident in any country or place outside undivided India;

(c) Persons who are or have been married to citizens of India and are ordinarily resident in India and have been so resident for five years immediately before making an application for registration. Prior to the citizenship (amendment) act, 1986 the clause read 'women who are or have been married to citizens of India'.

(d) Minor children of persons who are citizens of India and persons of full age and capacity who are citizens of a country specified in the first schedule of the citizenship Act, 1955.

Citizenship by Naturalisation

Where an application is made in the prescribed manner by any person of full age and capacity who is not a citizen of a country specified in the First Schedule-I for the grant of a certificate of a naturalization to him, the Central Government may, if satisfied that the applicant is qualified for naturalisation under the provisions of the third schedule, grant to him a certificate of naturalization. Provided that, if in the opinion of the Central Government, the applicant is a person who has rendered distinguished services to the cause of science, philosophy, art, literature, world peace or human progress generally, it may waive all or any of the conditions specified in the third schedule of citizenship Act 1955. The person to whom a certificate of naturalisation is granted shall, on taking oath of allegiance in the form specified in the second schedule, be a citizen of India by naturalisation as from the date on which that certificate is granted[48].

Citizenship by Incorporation of Territory

If any territory becomes a part of India, the central government, may by order notified in the official gazette, specify the persons who shall be citizens of India by reasons of their connection with that territory, and those persons shall be citizens of India as from the date to be specified in the order.

Termination

Citizenship is terminated either by renunciation or acquisition of citizenship of another country. For the purpose a person, who is also a citizen or national of another country of full age and capacity, can make a declaration renouncing his/her Indian citizenship before the prescribed authority in the prescribed manner. Once such a declaration is registered, a person ceases to be a citizen. If such a declaration was made during wartime, a war in which India is engaged, the registration of such a declaration can be withheld until the central government directs otherwise[49].

Renunciation of Citizenship

If any citizen of India of full age and capacity, who is also a citizen or national of another country, makes in the prescribed manner a declaration renouncing his Indian citizenship; the declaration shall be registered by the prescribed authority, and upon such registration, that person shall cease to be a citizen of Indian. Provided that if any such declaration is made during any war in which India may be engaged, registration thereof shall be withheld until the central government otherwise directs. Where a person ceases to be a citizen of India every minor child of that person shall thereupon cease to be a citizen of India, provided that any such child may, within one year after attaining full age, make a declaration that he wishes to resume Indian citizenship and shall thereupon again become a citizen of India. For the purpose of this section any woman who is, or has been, married shall be deemed to be of full age acquisition of citizenship of another country. However, this does not apply to a citizen of India, during any war in which India may be engaged, voluntarily acquires the citizenship of another country, until the central government otherwise directs. If any question arises as to whether, when or how any person has acquired the citizenship of another country, it shall be determined by such authority, in such manner, and having regard to such rules of evidence, as may be prescribed in this behalf [50].

Deprivation

The Central Government under section 10 of the Indian Citizenship Act, 1955 deprives any citizen of Indian citizenship if it is satisfied that:

(a) The registration or certificate of naturalisation was obtained by means of fraud, false representation or concealment of any material fact; or

(b) That citizen has shown himself by act or speech to be disloyal or disaffected towards the Constitution of India as by law established;

(c) That citizen has, during the war in which India may be engaged, unlawfully traded or communicated with an enemy or been engaged in or associated with, any business that was to his knowledge carried on in such manner as to assist any enemy in that war;

(d) That citizen has, within five years after registration or naturalization, been sentenced in any country to imprisonment for a term of not less than two years;

(e) That citizen has been ordinarily resident out of India for a continuous period of seven years, and during that period, has neither been at any time a student of any educational institution in a country outside India or in the service of a Government of India or of an International Organisation of which India is a member, nor registered annually in the prescribed manner at an Indian consulate his intention to retain his citizenship of India.

The central government shall not deprive a person of citizenship unless it is satisfied that it is not conducive to the public good that person should continue to be a citizen of India[51].

Constitutional Rights for Indian Citizens

Fundamental rights are given only to the Indian citizens like Article 15, 16, 19. Some important posts are only for Indian citizens like President, Vice-President, Chief Justice and Judges of Supreme Court and High Court, Attorney General, Governor etc. and right for constituency and assembly elections. In that the Indian citizens areonly allowed to be parliamentarian or member of legislative assemblies.[52] When it comes to the part of law, it is said that the law is a set of understanding rules and practices controlling the function and power of the government and its subsidiary machineries. Law can be distinguished from other social rules on four grounds. Firstly, as law is made by the government and thus reflects the will of the states, it takes precedence over all other norms and social rules. Secondly, law is compulsory, citizens are not allowed to choose which laws to obey and which to ignore because law is backed up by a system of coercion and punishment. Thirdly, law consists in published and recognised rules that have been enacted through a formal and usually public legislative process. Fourthly, law is generally recognised as binding upon those to whom it applies, law thus embodies moral claims, implying that legal rules should be obeyed[53].

However, it must be acknowledged that in the absence of laws, the court of India has played a commendable role in protecting the rights of the migrants. One of the most predominant court precedents is the 1995 Supreme Court ruling in the Chakmas vs. the State of Arunachal Pradesh. The Supreme Court ruled that Article 21 of the constitution-Right to life and liberty is available to all the persons living in India and that definition to refugees as well as several refugee lawyers in the country land laud the role of the courts that have interpreted Article 14 and 19[54].

Citizenship after Amendments

The Constitution of India provides for a single citizenship for the entire country. The provisions relating to citizenship at the commencement of the Constitution are contained in Articles 5 to 11 in Part II of the Constitution of India. Relevant India Legislation (RIL) is the Citizenship Act 1955, which has been amended by the Citizenship (amendment) Act 1986, the Citizenship (amendment) Act 1992, the Citizenship (amendment) Act 2003, and the Citizenship (amendment) Ordinance 2005. The Citizenship (amendment) Act 2003 received the assent of the President of India on 7 January 2004 and came into force on 3 December 2004. The Citizenship (amendment) Ordinance 2005 was promulgated by the President of India and came into force on 28 June 2005. Any person born in India on or after 26 January 1950 but prior to the commencement of the 1986 Act on 1 July 1987 was a citizen of India by birth. A person born in India on or after 1 July 1987 was a citizen of India if either parent was a citizen of India at the time of the birth. Those born in India on or after 3 December 2004 are considered citizens of India only if both of their parents are citizens of India or if one parent is a citizen of India and the other is not an illegal migrant at the time of their birth. Persons born outside India on or after 26 January but before 10 December 1992 are citizens of India by descent if their father was a citizen of India at the time of their birth. Person born outside India on or after 10 December 1992 are considered as citizens of India if either of their parents is a citizen of India at the time of their birth.

From 3 December 2004 onwards, persons born outside of India shall not be considered citizens of India unless their birth is registered at an Indian consulate within one year of the date of birth. In certain circumstances it is possible to register after one year with the permission of the central government. The application for registration of the birth of a minor child must be made to an Indian consulate and must be accompanied by an undertaking in writing from the parents of such minor child that he or she does not hold the passport of another country[55].

Citizenship (Amendment) Act 1955

The position which has to be focused on the provisions of the Constitution on citizenship follows like this[56]:

Article- 5(1) Suggest that those who migrated to India before the commencement of the Constitution (1950) are liable to get citizenship rights.

Article- 5(a) A person born as well as domicile in the territory of India-irrespective of the nationality of his parents.

Article- 5(b) A person domicile in the *'territory of India'*, either of whose parents was born in the territory of India-irrespective of the nationality of his parents or the place of birth of such person.

Article- 5(c) A person who or whose father or mother was not born in India, but who migrated before the commencement of Indian constitution.

Article- 6 Migrants from Pakistan: Provides for citizenship rights of migrants from Pakistan before the commencement of the constitution.

Article- 7 Makes special provisions regarding the citizenship rights of persons who migrated to Pakistan after March, 1, 1947 but return to India subsequently[57].

Article- 8 Provides that any person who or either whose parents or grand parents were born in India as defined in the Government of India Act 1955 and who is ordinarily residing in any country outside India shall be deemed to be a citizen of India if he has been registered as an Indian citizen by diplomatic or consular representative of India in that country on an application made by him in the prescribed form to such diplomatic or consular representative, whether before or after the commencement of the constitution (26 January, 1950, Act of 1955).

As already said constitution makers did not give complete code of nationality and left modification and regulation of citizenship rights to the parliament. In accordance with this provision of the constitution that in 1955 Indian Citizenship Act (ICA) was passed which extended citizenship rights to certain categories of persons and the way it could be renounced[58].

(i) Every person who was born in India on or before 26th January 1950 shall be Indian citizen by birth but children born to foreign diplomats posted in India are not entitled to Indian citizenship. By an Act passed in 1986 it has been provided that a person born in India can become its citizen provided if at the time of his birth either of his parents was a citizen of India.

(ii) If a person is born outside undivided India if either of his/her parents is a citizen of India or deemed to be citizen of India on 26th January, 1950 shall be Indian citizen by descent only.

(iii) Following categories of person can become Indian citizen provided they get themselves registered with the competent authority appointed by the government for purpose:

(a) A person of Indian origin but not an Indian citizen and residing out side India.

(b) Women married to an Indian husband.

(c) Minor children of Indian citizen parents.

(d) Persons belonging to common wealth countries.

Citizenship Amendment Act of 1986

Accordingly the provision under amended act is given below:-

(i) Every person in India, if wants to be registered as an Indian citizen that they have to show their domicile certificate of five year. Earlier it was six months duration only.

(ii) No one can acquire citizenship through birth only. Only those people can have citizenship of India either of whose parents was citizen of India at the time of his birth.

(iii) On the basis of naturalization for foreigners they may become an Indian citizen after continuously residing in India for ten years. Earlier it was five years duration.

(iv) After the 1986 citizenship Amendment Act there is a provision for acquisition of citizenship for an Indian man.

Citizenship Amendment Act of 1992

According to the amendment bill the child who is born outside of India and if his mother belongs to Indian citizenship. Before this any child born outside of India could acquire citizenship only if his father was a citizen of India.

Dual Citizenship Amendment Bill of 2005

The parliament has passed a bill on dual citizenship for Persons of Indian Origin (PIO) living abroad. This was promised at the Pravasi Bhartiya Diwas (PBD). The citizenship (amendment) bill 2005 will help India to expand its horizon and approach person of Indian origin to contribute to India's growth and development. The legislation would simplify the procedure for acquiring Indian citizenship by PIO's especially grown-up children of former Indian citizens who where living abroad and had required citizenship of other countries. It would help such persons to contribute to India's development. The bill provides for overseas citizenship of India to PIO's in sixteen countries who have acquired citizenship of those countries. It would also enable Indians who intend to acquire citizenship of other countries to retain the overseas Indian citizenship. This was not possible earlier and has been a long standing demand of PIO's[59] .

Citizenship (Amendment) Ordinance 2005

The Citizenship (Amendment) Act 2003 received the assent of the President of India on 7 January 2004 and came into force on 3 December 2004. The Citizenship (Amendment) Ordinance 2005 was promulgated by the President of India and came into force on 28 June 2005. Apart from this the Indira-Mujib Agreement between India and Bangladesh follows like that, Bangladeshis those who migrated to India before 1971 and got the refugee status are liable to get the citizenship rights according to the agreement. From 1st July, 1987 i.e. the date of enforcement of the Citizenship (amendment) Act, 1986, except as provided at 9a & 9b above, every person born in India on or after 26th January, 1950 but before the commencement of the act and on or after such commencement and either of whose parents a citizen in India at the time of his birth, shall be citizen of India by birth.

References

1. See for detail information on the site, http://en.wikipedia.org/wiki/International_law.

2. *Ibid.*

3. Year book of United Nation (2005), Towards Development, Security and Human Rights for all, Vol.59, United Nation Publication, New York, pp. 711-908.
4. UNHCR (2001), Ministerial Declaration of States Parties, Geneva, Switzerland, 12-13 December, Declaration of States Parties to the 1951 Convention and/or its 1964 Protocol Relating to the Status of the Refugees.
5. Year book of United Nation (2005), Towards Development, Security and Human Rights for all, Vol.59, United Nation Publication, New York, pp. 711-908.
6. *Ibid.*
7. Advisory Service, on International Humanitarian Law, ICRC, 07/2004, the International Association of Refugee Law Judges, Netherlands.
8. Year book of United Nation (2005), Towards Development, Security and Human Rights for all, Vol.59, United Nation Publication, New York, pp. 711-908
9. *Ibid.*, pp. 1300-1320.
10. *Ibid.*
11. Year book of United Nation (2005), Towards Development, Security and Human Rights for all, Vol.59, United Nation Publication, New York, pp. 711-908.
12. *Ibid.*
13. *Ibid.*
14. *Ibid.*
15. *Ibid.*
16. *Ibid.*
17. *Ibid.*
18. Sarbani, Sen (2003), Paradoxes of the International Regime of Care: The Role of the UNHCR in India in edited book by Ranabir Samaddar, Refugees and the State; Practices of Asylum and care in India, 1947-2000, Sage Publication, New Delhi, pp. 396-442.
19. B.S. Chimni (2000), International Refugee law: A Reader, Sage Publication, New Delhi, pp. 146-152.

20. See website, http://en.wikipedia.org/wiki/International_human_rights_law.
21. Sarbani, Sen (2003), Paradoxes of the International Regime of Care: The Role of the UNHCR in India in edited book by Ranabir Samaddar, Refugees and the State; Practices of Asylum and care in India, 1947-2000, Sage Publication, New Delhi, pp. 396-442.
22. *Ibid.*
23. See for detail of *Article 1 of the United Nations Universal Declaration of Human Rights (UDHR)*
24. See for detail on the *Preamble to the Universal Declaration of Human Rights, 1948.*
25. Jurgen, Hebermas (1955), Citizenship and National Identity: Some Reflection on the Future of Europe in Ronald Beiner edited, Theorizing Citizenship, New York, p. 278.
26. Henkin, Louis (1987), The International Bill of Rights: The Universal Declaration and the Covenants, in International Enforcement of Human Rights, pp. 6-9.
27. See Henkin, Louis, Introduction, The International Bill of Rights 9-10 (1981).
28. See for detail information, http://en.wikipedia.org.
29. V.T.Patil and P.R.Tivedi (2000), Migration, Refugees and Security in the 21st Century, Authors Press, Delhi, p. 252.
30. Protection of Human Rights Act, 1993 [As amended by the Protection of Human Rights (Amendment) Act, 2006–No. 43 of 2006] National Human Rights Commission, Faridkot House, Copernicus Marg, New Delhi - 110 001 Website : www.nhrc.nic.in, pp. 1-19.
31. See for detail British Nationality Law.
32. Year book of United Nation (2005), Towards Development, Security and Human Rights for all, Vol. 59, United Nation Publication, New York, pp. 711-908.
33. Brubaker, Rogers (1992), Citizenship and Nationhood in France and Germany also see detailed article by B.S. Chimni, Outside the Bounds of Citizenship: The Status of Aliens, Illegal Migrants and Refugees in India (pp. 277-313), in edited book

by Rajiv Bhargava and Helmut Reifeld, (2005), Civil Society, Public Sphere and Citizenship, Dialogues and Perceptions, Sage Publication, New Delhi.

34. Gopal, Guru (2005), Citizenship in Exile: A Dalit Case in edited book by Rajiv Bhargava and Helmut Reifeld, Civil Society, Public Sphere and Citizenship, Dialogues and Perceptions, Sage Publication, New Delhi, pp. 260-276.
35. O.P. Gauba (2005), An Introduction to Political Theory, Macmillan India Ltd., Delhi, p. 269.
36. *Ibid.*
37. See for detail information by Anoski 1998, pp. 8-11 and Bottomore 1993.
38. See for detail information by Janoski, 1998 and Thompson, 1990.
39. Engin F Isin and Bryan S Turner (ed.) (2002), Handbook of Citizenship Studies, Sage Publication, pp. 13-14.
40. See for detail in Aristotle's Politics, 1283b.
41. See for detail in Kriegel, 1995 P. 40.
42. Pocock, J. (1995), The Ideal of Citizenship since Classical Times, in Theorizing Citizenship, R. Beiner (ed.), State University of New York Press, Albany, pp. 29–53.
43. See writings of Norton, 1994.
44. B.S.Chimni (2005), Outside the Bounds of Citizenship: The Status of Aliens, Illegal Migrants and Refugees in India in edited by Rajiv Bhargava and Helmut Reifeld, Civil Society, Public Sphere and Citizenship, Dialogues and Perceptions, Sage Publication, New Delhi, pp. 277-313.
45. J. Pocock (1995), The Ideal of Citizenship since Classical Times, in Theorizing Citizenship, R. Beiner (ed.), State University of New York Press, Albany, pp. 29–53.
46. D.D, Basu (2004), The Introduction to the Constitution of India, Particularly the articles related to the Citizenship rights, pp. 54-58.
47. Valerian, Rodrigues (2005), Citizenship and the Indian Constitution in edited book by Rajiv Bhargava and Helmut

Reifeld, Civil Society, Public Sphere and Citizenship, Dialogues and Perceptions, Sage Publication.

48. D.D, Basu (2004), The Introduction to the Constitution of India, Particularly the articles related to the Citizenship rights, pp. 54-58.

49. Valerian, Rodrigues (2005), Citizenship and the Indian Constitution in edited book by Rajiv Bhargava and Helmut Reifeld, Civil Society, Public Sphere and Citizenship, Dialogues and Perceptions, Sage Publication, New Delhi, pp. 209-235.

50. D.D, Basu (2004), The Introduction to the Constitution of India, Particularly the articles related to the Citizenship rights, pp. 54-58.

51. Valerian, Rodrigues (2008), Citizenship and the Indian Constitution in edited book by Rajiv Bhargava Politics and Ethics of the Indian Constitution, Oxford University Press, New Delhi, pp. 164-188.

52. D.D, Basu (2004), The Introduction to the Constitution of India, Particularly the articles related to the Citizenship rights, Pp. 54-58.

53. Judgment of Supreme Court of India (1996), Original Civil Jurisdiction, Writ Petition (Civil) No. 720 of 1995, Between NHRC versus State of Arunachal Pradesh, 9th January, New Delhi.

55. Valerian, Rodrigues (2008), Citizenship and the Indian Constitution in edited book by Rajiv Bhargava Politics and Ethics of the Indian Constitution, Oxford University Press, New Delhi, pp. 164-188.

56. D.D, Basu (2004), The Introduction to the Constitution of India, Particularly the articles related to the Citizenship rights, pp. 54-58.

57. B.R.Ambedkar (1992), Pakistan or Partition of India, Writing and Speeches, Vol. 8, Mumbai, pp. 29-39.

58. D.D, Basu (2004), The Introduction to the Constitution of India, Particularly the articles related to the Citizenship rights, pp. 54-58.

59. *Ibid.*

4

Exclusion and The Question of Livelihood

Generally refugee camp or settled areas is a place built by the government or NGOs to receive refugees. People may stay in these camps, receiving emergency food and medical aid, until it is safe to return to their homes or until they get retrieved by other people outside the camps. In some cases, often after several years, other countries decide it will never be safe to return these people, and they are resettled in *'third countries,'* away from the border they crossed[1]. Since refugee camps are generally set up in an impromptu fashion and designed to meet basic human needs for only a short time, when the return of refugees is prevented (often by civil war), a humanitarian crisis can result.

Displacement, relief and rehabilitation should be viewed from a rights based perspective rather than as an administrative/governance issue that focuses on needs of beneficiaries. For instance, the lexicon of welfare/charity i.e. *'gratuitous relief'* and *'beneficiary'* should be jettisoned for language that respects human rights of the displaced or to-be-displaced people. In all instances of displacement, there should be minimum non-negotiable human rights standards that should be adhered to for all and especially for vulnerable and marginalized groups such as women, children and elderly persons. As part of relief and rehabilitation, authorities provide food, potable water, clothing, shelter, basic health care, education etc. It is important to note that access to these basic minimum services is not a matter of welfare or charity but is a human right. Basic minimum standards for such facilities/services should be defined.

There is a need for Central and State Governments to re-examine and amend laws, policies, plans, regulations and practices to mainstream and integrate human rights concerns on issues related to relief and rehabilitation[2].

Authorities concerned with rehabilitation activities should be sensitised about human rights through capacity building. All affected persons have the right to be treated with dignity. In particular, no arbitrary decision, without reasoning should be taken in the matters that affect their source of food, shelter and livelihood. Furthermore, before any such decision is taken, they should have right to be heard/ consulted.

They should also have the right to appeal against such decisions in appropriate forums. All affected persons have the right to be treated without any discrimination in matters relating to rescue, relief and rehabilitation. In respect of vulnerable groups among them such as women, disabled, elderly persons and children, the appropriate authority shall take special measures to protect their rights. Chakmas who have resettled in Arunachal Pradesh country shall not be discriminated against as a result of their having been displaced. They shall have the right to participate fully and equally in public affairs at all levels and have equal access to public services. All affected persons have the right to information regarding all aspects related to immediate humanitarian assistance, relief and rehabilitation.

Adequate measures to guarantee to those to be resettled, full information on the reasons and procedures for their displacement and, where applicable, on compensation and relocation and proper publicity by the State Government so as to enable the affected people to become aware of their entitlements in the form of relief and compensation. All the third generation Chakmas persons, in particular children, have the right to receive education, which shall be free and compulsory at the primary level. Education should respect their cultural identity, language and religion. Education facilities should be made available as soon as conditions permit. Special efforts should be made to ensure the full and equal participation of women and girls in educational programmes and should have the right to an adequate standard of living. At the minimum, regardless of the circumstances, and without discrimination, competent authorities shall provide with and ensure access to:

(a) Sleeping accommodations (tents).

(b) Hygiene facilities (cleaning and toilets).

(c) Medical supplies.

(d) Communication equipment (e.g. radio).

(a) Essential food and potable water.

(b) Basic shelter, clothing and housing.

(c) Essential medical services and sanitation.

(d) Free and compulsory education to their children.

(e) Transportation and other means of communications.

(f) Security to the life and property.

In many cases it has been reported that the refugee camps are dirty and unhygienic. Chakmas on another hand do not have any of the facilities as mentioned above. The refugee regime in India largely ignored in such a way in which one finds very difficult to understand what exactly the problem with this regime is. The very unfortunate thing of the Chakma new settlement is that they even have not been given shelter or any house material. Chakmas of Arunachal Pradesh are given either open areas or big forest or forced to live as they like particularly in the areas of Papumpare, Changlang and Lohit. Chakmas over a period of time made these places to live and find their livelihood through agriculture. They built houses with bamboos, canes and leafs and cleaned the forest areas which allotted to them. As per my survey is concerned, I found that Chakmas are very hard working people who produce every thing accept salt. This is not easy for any one to clean forests in mountains and made a place to live, particularly in the state like Arunachal Pradesh which is one of the most hilly and tough regions of India[3].

Districts-Villages where Chakmas are Concentrated in Arunachal Pradesh

As per the population of Chakmas is concerned, Changlang is having 40,000 and is the highest in number followed by Lohit with 15,000 which stands second and lastly Papumpare has only 5,000 population respectively. Chakmas in Kokila (Papumpare) is on the border of Assam and Arunachal Pradesh. It is largely one of the most conflicting areas, where always there is a conflict between Assam and Arunachal Pradesh and Chakmas are always getting trouble because Chakmas are on this border land. Also it is highly flooded zone. In rainy season particularly April, May, June, July and August it has floods with lots of destruction of life and property. As per Government of India record is concerned their population is approximately 60,000[4].

Chart: 4 (A)

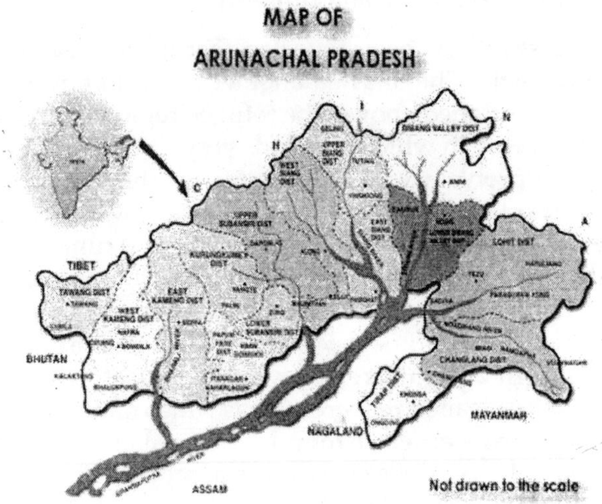

Chart: 4 (B)

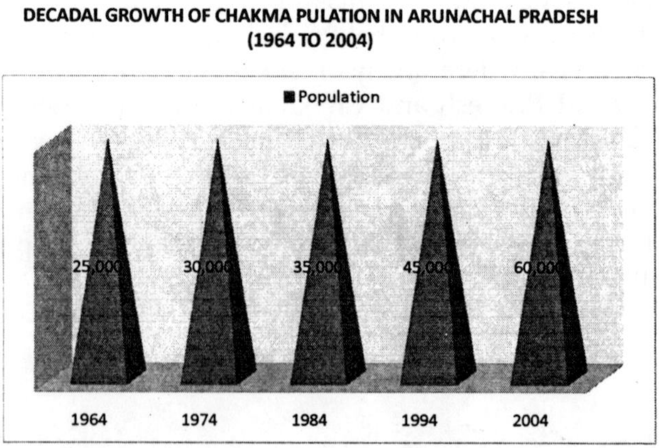

Presently Chakmas are resettled in the three districts/villages respectively which are given as below[5]:

1. Papumpare

   (a) Kokila

2. Changlang

   (a) Gautampur Village

   (b) Santipur Village

   (c) Joytipur Village

   (d) Abhaypur Village

   (e) Dumpani Village

   (f) Rajnagar Village

   (g) Joshnapur Village

   (h) Dumpattar Village

   (i) Udaypur Village

   (j) Modoideep Village –I

   (k) Modoideep Village- II

   (l) Kamakhyapur Village

   (m) Vijoypur Village- I

   (n) Vijoypur Village- II

   (o) Vijoypur Village- III

   (p) Dharmapur Village- I

   (q) Dharmapur Village- II

   (r) Ratnapur Village

   (s) Golakpur Village

(t) Milanpur Village

3. Lohit

(a) Chakma Basti- I

(b) Chakma Basti- II

(c) Chakma Basti- III

Papumpare

It is the most developed city of Arunachal Pradesh because Itanagar is in this district. Largely Nyishi are the majority community in this district. It has a border called Balijan and Kokila which divide Arunachal Pradesh and Assam. It is one of the most conflicting areas as for as state boundary and land is concerned. Earlier Chakmas were largely settled in Balijan but over a period of time they were shifted forcefully and resettled to the new place called Kokila, which is the flooded area. For a period of minimum four to five months, this area remains under flood and heavy rainfall. Being a low-lying area, the Chakma inhabited region is always under a deluge.

Changlang

Changlang the biggest district of Arunachal Pradesh has maximum population, largely of Buddhist origin. Maximum Chakmas are concentrated to Diyun and Mieo. The condition of Chakmas is better of as compared to other two districts where Chakmas are settled and the reason is the activeness of civil society groups particularly the SNEHA[6].

Lohit

Lohit is also having good number of Chakma population. They are living in three bastis (villages). These bastis are always under threat of flood every year. Loss of life and property is very common. My field work found that the oldest people who migrated from CHT and Rangamati are living in these three bastis of Lohit districts.

Chart: 4 (C)

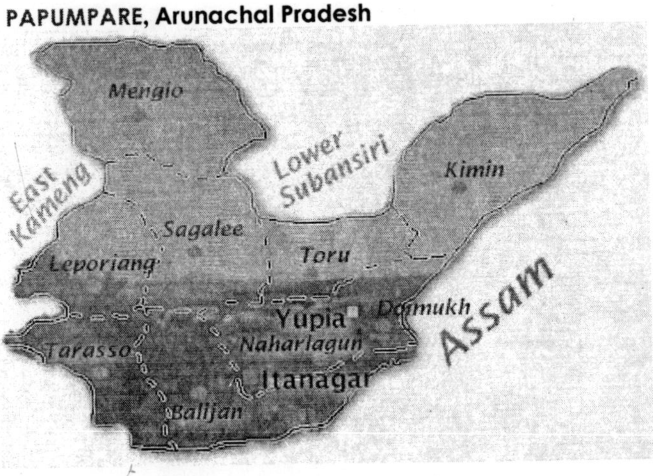

Chart: 4 (D)

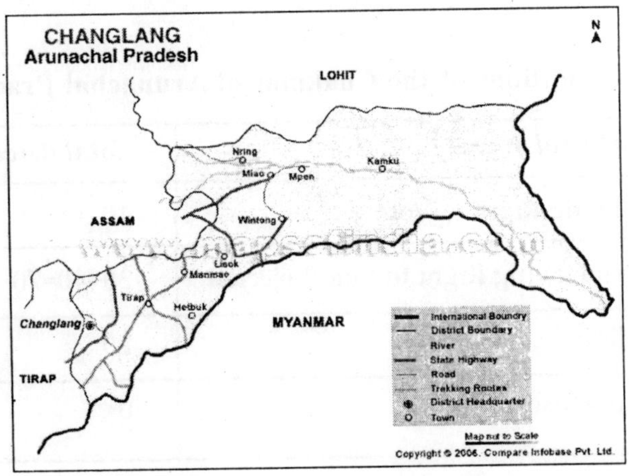

Chart: 4 (E)

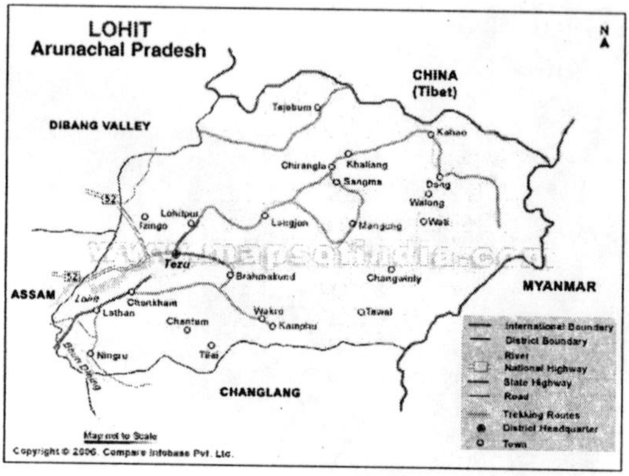

Socio-Economic and Political Conditions of Chakmas in the Settled Areas

Table: 4 (A)

Political Conditions of the Chakmas of Arunachal Pradesh

Political Status	*Total Percentage*
Having Right to Vote	10
Not Having Right to Vote/Rejected	30+40=70
Minor	20
Citizenship Rights	0

The social condition of the Chakmas of Arunachal Pradesh in particular and India in general is very rich. They do not have caste system or any type of division we see in other religions. Socially, they live together, eat and participate in all the occasions without any

Chart: 4 (F)

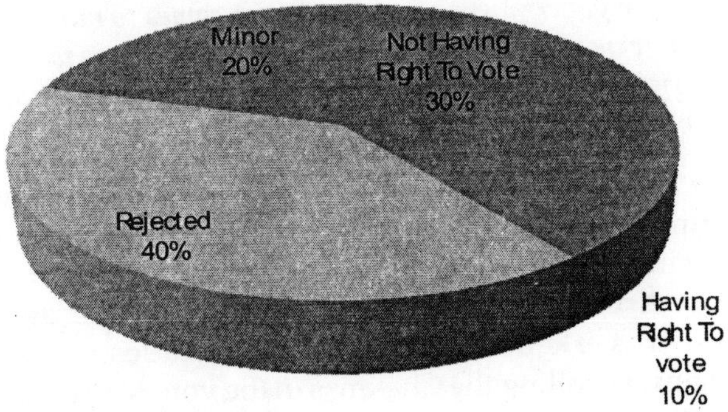

differences. They marry freely without any restriction based on caste, sex, tradition, rich, poor etc. Chakmas are largely Buddhist religiously. During my field work I did not find single Chakma to be other than Buddhist and no report of conversion in any other religion. It is also appreciable that though they are facing huge discrimination from every side of states as well as central government and everyday violence by the AAPSU activists and Arunachalees[7] but even then they have a strong and deep feeling that they are in good religion and one day definitely things will change. Politically very few Chakmas are enrolled in the electoral list and they are voting without choice. Many Chakmas who are born in India are still waiting for their enrolment in the electoral roll and their application is being rejected many times starting from 2004, 2007 and 2008 respectively. There is also a very confusing picture which I could not understand that how many Chakmas are having right to vote but they are not the citizen of India and the dilemma is that the political parties in the state are using these Chakmas as their vote bank. They are interested to include these Chakmas in the electoral process but not interested in the inclusion of citizenship rights. Chakmas are fighting since 1964 and it is almost five decades delay to get their citizenship rights. Their applications for the citizenship rights are still under process. When I asked to one of the Chakma leaders about the issue of citizenship application he told that the Arunachal Government is being run by the AAPSU activists and the politicians as well as State Government is not interested to forward their application to the central authority for the grant of citizenship rights. He gave one funny example also. He said that,

> *"the state government officers throw our application in air, the forms which fall on the mosquito net are being accepted as in process, those fall on the bed are accepted as under process and those fall on the earth being rejected. This is the way of working of state government officials when it comes to our matter, he told Arunachal is more worse than any other state of India and here we see a complete jungle raj. No rights to survive and we have no basic rights which consider us as human being of this universe"*[8].

In 2004 the Election Commission has warned that it would not hold Assembly polls in Arunachal Pradesh unless the State Government includes the Chakmas in the electoral rolls. The Chakmas are living in Arunachal Pradesh for more than five decades. The commission was irked by the Arunachal Pradesh Government's decision against enrolling the Chakmas in the voters' list for not having Inner Line Permit - a permit that is required to visit certain Border States. As a result of this, the commission from January 2 has already stopped its ongoing revision of the electoral rolls in four Assembly segments that also form parts of the Lok Sabha constituencies in both East Arunachal Pradesh and West Arunachal Pradesh constituencies. The conduct of any and all elections in the four assembly constituencies of Doimukh, Chowkham, Bordumsa Diyum, and Miao along with all election related work, including the preparation or revision of the electoral rolls there shall stand suspended until further orders, ruled the commission, and in an order dated January 2, 2004. The commission was compelled to take this drastic measure, as the State Government officials engaged in the electoral roll revision, in an unprecedented step, refused to entertain the commission's repeated instructions to include the Chakmas. Their refusal was based on a State Cabinet decision taken on May 14, 2003, to not include non-Arunachalese people in the electoral roll unless they possessed the Inner Line Permit, issued under the Bengal East Area and Frontier Regulation, 1873. Terming the decision as 'wrong' the commission has pointed out that even the Supreme Court of India and the Delhi High Court, in their respective orders on two different petitions dealing with the question of the settlement of the Chakmas in the state and granting of Indian citizenship to them, have held that the Chakmas, born in India on or after January 26, 1950, but before July 1, 1985, and living in the state, are to be treated as ordinary residents of the state and are entitled to be registered in the electoral roll of the state. The commission had also met the Arunachal Pradesh Chief Minister on August 28, 2003, and on the basis of the Supreme Court order dated January 9, 1996 and the Delhi High Court order dated September 28, 2000, had conveyed to him that so long as the Chakmas were ordinary residents in the state, they could not be denied their Constitutional right of enrolment of their names in the electoral rolls of the state. Subsequently, in September 2003, the commission had also conveyed to him through an official communication that, the preparation and revision of the electoral rolls was a constitutional duty conferred on the commission by Article 324 (1) and the state Cabinet resolution refusing voting rights to the Chakmas was an hindrance to the commission's constitutional obligation to prepare and revise the electoral rolls. This, in turn, will adversely affect the free and fair conduct of the elections, said the commission in its September, 2003 communication to the State Government, requesting it to suitably amend or altogether scrap its Cabinet resolution. The State Government's refusal to comply has resulted in an impasse[9].

Chart: 4 (G)

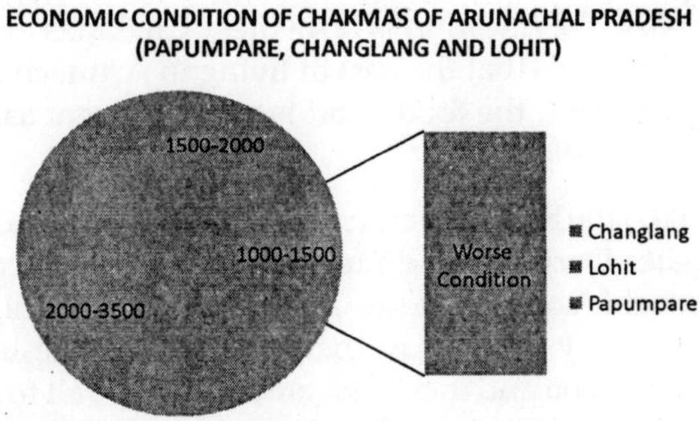

The economic condition of Chakmas is so poor and unfortunate to believe that even after fifty years some sections of the society are living under poverty and just surviving with one time meal in a day. They are living Below Poverty Line (BPL) and government does not have any plan for these marginalized sections of the society. Not a single scheme I found by Government of India, Government of

Arunachal Pradesh as well as any civil society to bring some necessary economic changes to improve the conditions of the poor Chakmas in all the three districts of the Indian state of Arunachal Pradesh. Chakmas are largely concentrated in the three districts of Arunachal Pradesh viz. Papumpare (Kokila), Changlang (Diyun) and Lohit (Chakma Basti's[10]). It is unfortunate to say that the entire settlement of the Chakma is largely on the bank of river which always remains flooded in the rainy seasons. As per my field survey is concerned all the districts where Chakmas are settled are concentrated in the flooded areas. In Kokila (Papumpare) the bank of the river where Chakmas are settled is Hollongi. In Diyun, Changlanng it is called Neo Deheng River and in Lohit it is called Darang River.

Chakmas produce every thing although it is largely a barren and flooded area. They cleaned their settled areas granted by the Government of India in 1964. It is also reported that the land largely captured by the local tribals like Adis, Khamptis, Shingpos and Nyishi. Arunachalees captured the land in Kokila and it is reported that they captured nearly 60 percent of the Chakma land granted by the Government of India. Now the condition is that all the Chakmas are working as labourers[11] in the lands of Arunachalees to get two time meal. It is also reported that some time Chakmas are not given any remuneration as they are working, and beaten up by the local people when ever they ask for their remuneration. The income level of all the Chakmas as per questionnaire is concerned, is not more than INR 2000 to 2500. Now the question is how these Chakmas are surviving. So the simple answer is that the cost of living in Arunachal Pradesh is very low and secondly, the food habit is very different as compare to the other parts of India.

In June 2007, the State government of Arunachal Pradesh headed by Chief Minister Dorjee Khandu formed a high power committee to find out an amicable solution to the Chakma issue[12]. The high powered committee headed by Speaker of the Arunachal Pradesh Legislative Assembly, Setong Sena and included, among others, all four Members of Legislative Assembly of the Chakma inhabited Assembly Constituencies as members. Both the AAPSU and the CCRCAP welcomed the establishment of the Committee[13].

At the same time, over 12,000 Chakmas eligible voters continued to be denied enrollment into electoral rolls. Electoral activities in the four Chakma inhabited Assembly Constituencies of 14-Doimukh, 46-Chowkham, 49-Bordumsa-Diyun and 50-Miao remained suspended as a result of complaints of bias on the part of the local electoral officials.

On 6 September 2007, the Election Commission of India revoked the suspension and ordered the conduct of Special Summary Revision of electoral rolls. The Election Commission issued specific guidelines as to how to conduct the revision of electoral rolls in the Chakma areas. As earlier, the local electoral officials who are also employees of the State Government of Arunachal Pradesh did not comply with the guidelines and instead they imposed their own directions to ensure that even the 1,497 previously enrolled voters were deleted. As many as 36 out of 326 enrolled voters were deleted from 14-Chowkham Assembly Constituency even before beginning of the Special Summary Revision 2007[14].

In 49-Bordumsa-Diyun and 50-Miao Assembly Constituencies several Chakma villages were not even officially informed about the revision process and were informed only after the Election Commission of India issued specific instructions following complaints from the Committee for Citizenship Rights of the Chakmas of Arunachal Pradesh. The Chakma claimants were subjected to harassment, humiliation and were openly discriminated by electoral officers led by the Deputy Commissioner of Changlang district Hage Batt, who has been designated as Electoral Registration Officer of 49-Bordumsa-Diyun and 50-Miao Assembly Constituencies. Instead of conducting the hearing of claims and objections at Diyun, Mr. Batt sat at Bordumsa, which is 60 kilometers away from Diyun. As there were no means of transportation between Bordumsa and Diyun, none out of 7,311 Chakma claimants from Diyun Circle could appear for hearing. The hearings were re-held at Diyun only after the Election Commission intervened on complaints from the CCRCAP. Taking cognizance of these violations of its guidelines by the local Electoral Officials, the Election Commission of India deputed two teams to the four Chakma inhabited Assembly Constituencies. But justice continues to elude the Chakma citizens as the Election Commission has again failed. In February 2008, the Election Commission ordered the publication of final rolls in three of the four Assembly Constituencies (14-Doimukh, 46-Chowkham, and 50-Miao). 49-Bordumsa-Diyun remained in abeyance until further orders. Out of about one thousand eligible voters, the names of only 201 claimants were included in the electoral rolls in 14-Doimukh while in 46-Chowkham, out of more than 1400 new claimants the names of only 14 were enrolled and names of 44 previously enrolled voters deleted. Similarly in 50-Miao, only 1 out of about 4500 new claimants was included in the electoral roll[15]. The Election Commission of India assured the CCRCHAP that it would send 2 more teams to Itanagar to examine claimants' documentation from 49-Bordumsa-Diyun. At the end of the year, the Election Commission of India had failed to enforce its guidelines[16].

Incidence of Discrimination

Here the discrimination largely connected to the term *'adequate'* means that these services are available, accessible, acceptable, and adaptable. Availability means that the goods and services are made available to the affected population in sufficient quantity and quality; Accessibility requires that the goods and services (a) granted without discrimination to all in need, (b) within safe reach and can be physically accessed by everyone, including vulnerable and marginalised groups, and (c) known to the beneficiaries; (iii) Acceptability refers to the need to provide goods and services that are culturally appropriate and sensitive to gender and age; (iv) Adaptability requires that the goods and services be provided in ways flexible enough to adapt to the change of needs in the different phases of emergency relief, reconstruction[17].

During the immediate emergency phase, food, water and sanitation, shelter, clothing, and health services are considered adequate if they ensure survival to all in need of them. The concerned authorities after reasonable verification shall issue to the affected and displaced persons all documents necessary for the enjoyment and exercise of their legal rights, such as passports, personal identification documents, birth certificates, death certificates and marriage certificates. Any lack of access to such legal documents or not having such legal documents shall not disentitle them for recompense[18]. But none of the concepts applies here when it comes to Chakmas proved during my field work. I found a large list of intentional discrimination by the AAPSU as well as State Regime. But let me bring few point and analysis which I experienced in my field work when I interacted with these excluded peoples:

1. Election Commission of India sent K.R. Prasad as the representatives from Centre to see and verify the candidature of Chakmas particularly in the Changlang Districts of Arunachal Pradesh in 9th February, 2006 for the inclusion of Chakmas in the electoral role as well to grant citizenship. State Government of Arunachal Pradesh with the help of AAPSU took that representative to the different route and shown non Chakma community as well as other area and said that this is Diyun of Changlang and not informed to a single Chakma that some one came from Delhi to meet Chakmas. Finally, the Indian government representatives made a report that not a

single Chakmas came to meet me and the condition is that there is no problem with the Chakmas and the Arunachalees.

2. There is not a single case registered in the Kokila, Papumpare police station on the violence done by the AAPSU, in many occasion. When I asked about the views of the AAPSU, one of the senior Chakma told that, *"I do not understand what criminalization is! And how Chakmas are criminal"*. He was asking the definition of crime. He told one small boy of his village below the age of 18 years just stole four bananas and for that he was kept in prison for at least four years without trial and order of the court. It was largely supported by the AAPSU and the state government officers. And such many more similar examples he gave with full tears in his eyes.

3. Gayanjoti Chakmas one of the old Chakma heads share why Chakmas being popularised by Arunachalees as criminals, generally Khamptis, Shinkpos and Adis are the people who forcefully compel Chakmas to work in the field, go for hunting with them, and do other things as they order. For them Chakmas is 1. nothing but bounded labourers. They engaged Chakmas to cut timbers, kill elephants, and many more. Once upon a time one Shingpo leader of the area engaged few Chakmas forcefully and told that you all have to come with me for hunting elephant. He told that you Chakmas just have to help me for capturing elephant. When Chakmas reached to the jungle, Shingpo leader told that you have to kill the elephant because I need the teeth of the elephant, but Chakmas refused to do so. Then Shingpo started fooling innocent Buddhist Chakmas by saying that, the teeth are very costly in the market and if you help to kill this wild animal you will get your share and at least you earn some thing to get food. Finally Chakmas accepted to help him but not to kill. Shingpo told that I will kill just you have to arrange all the things. As according to plan things went positive. With the help of Chakmas Shingpo killed that wild elephant and as plan taken both the big teeth. Shingpo took that teeth to his house and was planning to sell in the market. Next day Chakmas went to his house and started one tooth as the deal was accepted, but Shingpo refused to give the teeth to the innocent Chakmas by saying that you people do not know any thing about the market and also it is very risky to take teeth out side because it is a crime to do this. So you all just go back to your house I

know how to sell, I do it and once I get the money I will inform you. You all just come and collect your money. Chakmas believe Shingpo and return back with the hope that they will very soon get their reward. But the things changed very differently. Shingpo sold two teeth and got good money but did not inform any of the Chakmas. Chakmas after many days went once again to ask their share, but as I said things got very different, Shingpo when he saw Chakmas got angry started beating Chakmas with his other family members and called upon police to catch. Shingpo told police that these Chakmas are criminals these six Chakmas killed my domestic elephant, taken teeth and sold in the market. Police also belongs to their community supported Shingpo and arrested all the six Chakmas and jailed for many years and declared that Chakmas are criminal. After this case many AAPSU activist took the opportunities to unite local Arunachalees against the Chakmas. In that case many Chakmas were killed; their houses were burnt, their property being looted. After ward Chakmas started living fearfully. After this incidence, Chakmas finally declared in the state that Chakmas are criminals. After this incidence all the opportunities have been blocked. Complete economic blockage, education stopped, basic health facilities being suspended and many more explained by saying as one of the biggest black spots on human civilisation in the 21st century.

4. Many AAPSU activists and state government officials told me that the Chakmas are now days engaged in robbery and recently they looted SBI bank in Itanagar. When I enquired I found it was completely false rather I found SBI being looted by the Arunachalees (Government officials, news appeared in the Times of India, January, 2009).

5. First Chakmas allowed settling in Ledu (Changlang), the hilliest and dense forest areas. Over a period of time Chakmas with their hard work made it a place to live like. Latter, many Shingpo came from others parts of Arunachal Pradesh and started claiming that the Chakmas settled areas are ours and started torturing Chakmas to leave the land. Finally conflict become more violent in the area and by looking all this situation the Deputy Commissioner of the District Mr. Lokhande (IAS) in October, 2007 mediated between the Chakmas and the All Arunachal Mismi Student Union (AMSU) and drawn the boundary by saying that this is the

area given to Chakmas and these are the areas where Mismis can used for their purpose. Finally both the groups accepted to solve the problem but latter after a few months AMSU started creating problems to the Chakmas by saying that we don't accept the solution given by Mr. Lokhande and this is our land we can do any thing without asking any one. Even what ever Chakmas produces in their field has been taken by the Mismis forcefully. By looking all these many conflicts took place in between the Chakmas and the Mismis over a period of time.

6. In November 2005 Zila Parisad Member (ZPM) Mr. Ongla an Singhpo leader kidnapped by the AAPSU activists demanded 10 lakhs from his family and latter murdered brutally after taking money and told entire every one that it has been done by the Chakmas to bring an anti-Chakmas feeling in the local populations.

7. As per Arunachal Panchayati Raj Institution is concerned, head of the village is called '*Gam Bura*' but in Chakma village is '*Head Man*'.

8. Chakma students are not getting admission after 8th because there is only 15 primary 2 secondary and only 1 higher secondary school in Changlang, which is 10 kilometer from Diyun (Chakma settled area). And over all it is 25 to 30 kilometers from all the primary and secondary school if we take an average of all the Chakma settled areas.

9. There are no roads at all in all the three districts where Chakmas are settled.

10. Chakmas are facing flood situation in their areas and Government have not initiated a single programme to control even after four decades.

11. There are no electricity facilities.

12. Not a single Chakmas found as a government employee in the state.

13. No Security from any side of the government/non government organisation of their life and property.

14. Generation which is born in India as per the rule of the constitutional provisions to be the citizens of India is not being included to be the Indian citizens.

15. No response either from the UNHRCR, under any migration provisions as well as any civil societies.

16. Many primary schools where Chakma children's are studying have complete shortage of regular teachers, even in these schools Chakmas themselves managing teachers by paying money.

17. All the central, as well as UNCEF/International organization programmes have been suspended in all the three Chakma settled districts, Anganwadi Programmes, Sarva Siksha Abhiyan, National Rural Grantee Scheme, National Health Mission Scheme, and many more.

Categorisation of Chakmas

Chart: 4 (H)

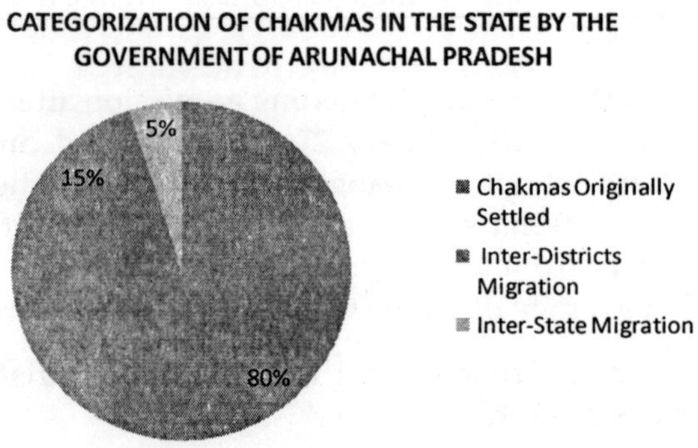

So far Chakmas of Arunachal Pradesh are concerned they are concentrated to the three districts particularly in Papumpare (Urban), Changlang and Tirap respectively, Government of Arunachal Pradesh violating all the basic rules and laws defining in their own way by categorizing these Chakmas into three categories[20]:

(a) Chakmas those who settled originally in the year 1964.

(b) Inter-Districts migration and settled in Papumpare, Changlang and Lohit

(c) Inter-state migration and settled in Tripura, Mizoram, Assam, West Bengal, Mizoram.

In its first part Chakmas who directly migrated in the year 1964 and settled in various parts of India and latter brought to NEFA (present Arunachal Pradesh) originally. Secondly, inter-state migration from within the state because of the situations like floods, life threat, livelihood etc. They generally migrated within the state and mixed with the other Chakmas in the districts particularly the Changlang, Lohit and Papumpare. And lastly, intra-district migration for example the first Chakma exodus happen in the year 1947 just after independence and they granted citizenship as well as scheduled tribes status and mainly settled in the states of Assam, Tripura, West Bengal, Mizoram etc. but latter migrated for job, education and some other purposes and married and settled in Arunachal Pradesh over a period of time.

The Tapun Area Welfare Society (TAWS) an Arunachalees civil society group has accused the Centre of being soft on Chakma refugees, which had allegedly encouraged them to destroy forests at Diyun range under Lohit district. The society alleged that the refugees were violating the prescribed norms fixed during their resettlement from Mizo district to Tirap Division of the then NEFA. The administrative blessings in one form or other by the State Government have further accelerated their (refugees), well-planned intention of encroaching the entire Dihing Valley, including Mishmi land in Kathan, New Kathan, Tumba and Tilangkiong villages under Wakro circle of Lohit district. They alleged that owing to the administrative backing the refugees have resorted to extreme steps against the indigenous people of the said villages in way of theft, looting and taking away mithuns and other domestic cattle.

"Last year, the refugees, in large numbers, marched to Kathan village and destroyed the altar of the community's Tamla rituals, the society said, adding the refugees also took hostage six youths of All Mishmi Students' Union. "In February, the refugees once again walked into the village and torched a house"[21]

The society also questioned the state government as to why it was not initiating any measures against the Chakmas who had been killing and torturing the locals.[22] But so far my field survey is concerned I did not find any thing in which Chakmas were involved in killing and torturing locals. There is no proving of such cases in any of the Chakma settled districts. It is all rumors created by the Arunachalees particularly the AAPSU and other student organizations as well as local based civil society groups for their political or economic gain.

Response of Civil Society Groups

Avoipur is a small Chakma inhabited village in the district of Changlang. Elderly Chakmas remember that they had come to India in the year 1965 and they term it as the year of *Borporang* since they came as refugees. They took refuge in the states of Bihar, Mizoram, Tripura and Arunachal Pradesh. According to the judgment of the supreme court of India Chakmas are entitled to be the citizens of India[23]. Arunachal Pradesh government has been unable to accept the Supreme Court judgment and they still consider them as foreigners. Chakmas living here have been deprived of accessing resources from the state govt. The Chakmas living in other states are in a more comfortable position than them. The situation worsened in the year 1995 when the Chakma students were not allowed to attend classes in the schools run by the Arunachal Pradesh Government and it is still continuing. The well to do families could send their children to other states but in Avoipur and its nearby villages consisting of very poor families, the children remained at home. By looking all these problems SNEHA, a Delhi based NGO then took up the initiative to start a school for these deprived children. They named the school as SNEHA School, a Pali name meaning '*Love*'.

It was established in the year 2003 with 109 children in the village of Dumpani in Changlang. The school is presently located in the village of Avoipur. It started following the Central Board of Secondary Education (CBSE), New Delhi, India with the aim of preparing the children for the class X and Class XII examinations. The medium of instruction is Hindi and English. NFI-SDTT nucleus made a visit to the school from 10th to 13th of April 2007. The Nucleus had a meeting with the teachers and guardians separately and also with a handful of students. The nucleus also made visits to the surrounding villages and spoke to people of different ages, backgrounds and also religious leaders. The specific observation has been made like, the school has been upgraded to Class VII, *pucca* office building has been inaugurated by State Health and Family Welfare Minister of Arunachal Pradesh[24].

The guardians of the area stated that SNEHA is providing good education to their children and have good future if they sent their children. The villagers have started owning up the school as the guardians provide physical support and labour if there are any infrastructure works. The guardians have also built a thatched hut in the school premises so that SNEHA could accommodate more students dividing the classes into sections. The teachers are committed for the cause of Chakmas as most of them are members or have been members of the Arunachal Pradesh Chakma Students Union (APCSU). The Teachers give attention to each and everyone student as weak students are kept after school for extra Classes. Reference books for the teachers are being accumulated. Majority of the Chakma students are the first generation learners. It is also reported that they have more then 85 percent pass put in each and every classes starting from nursery to class VIII. Students of this school speak good English as well as Hindi. Apart from English and Hindi, Chakma language also introduced by Arindam Dewan, head master of SNEHA. The school has been divided into four houses to install in them a sense of healthy competition. Students from far away villages are staying in the houses of teachers. A parent-teacher association (PTA) has been formed for addressing the grievances of the teachers and the guardians[25].

Over a period of time Mahabodhi School and St. Judes English medium schools come up in the areas to accommodate Chakma children including other ethnic groups and started providing good education with hostel facilities in the areas[26].

Chart: 4 (I)

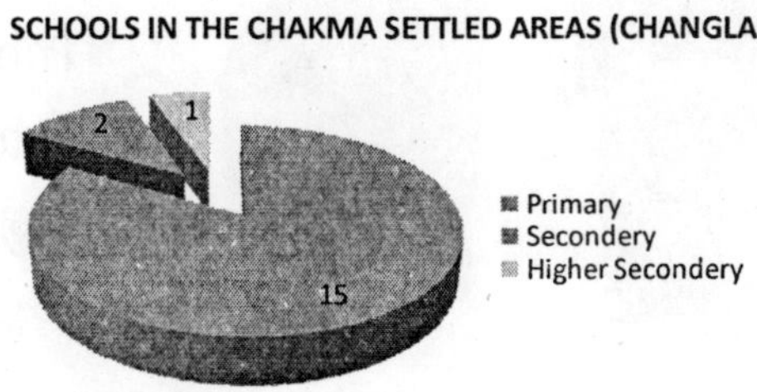

Chart: 4 (J)

SCHOOLS IN THE CHAKMA SETTLED AREAS (LOHIT)

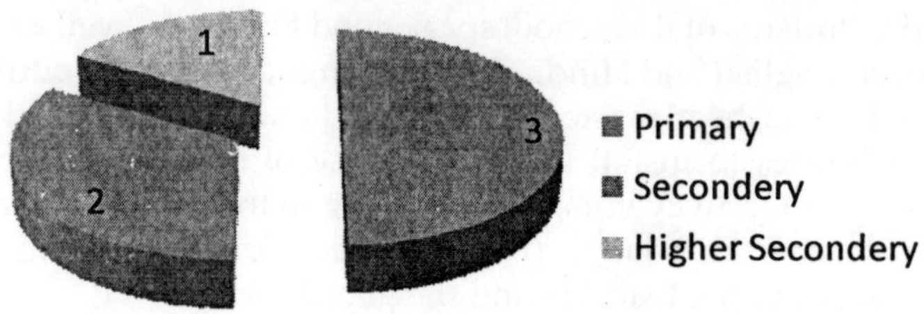

Chart: 4 (K)

SCHOOLS IN THE CHAKMA SETTLED AREAS (PAPUMPARE)

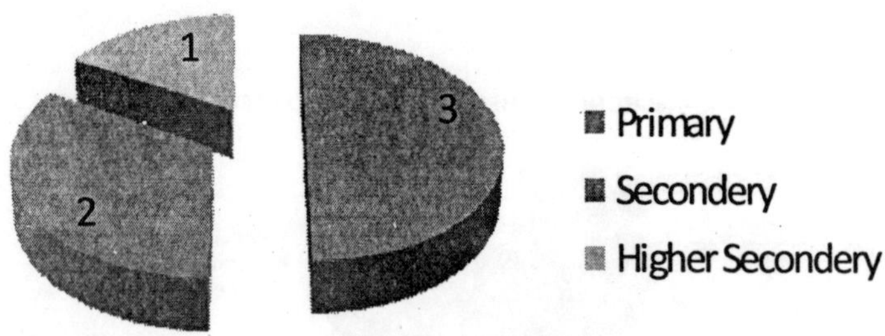

Basic Relief and Rehabilitation Policy Recommendations

The basic principles in the National Relief and Rehabilitation Policy (NRRP) must be incorporated in the Rehabilitation and Resettlement Bill, 2007 (R & R Bill). For instance, the five year residence limit[27] is higher than the one in the NRRP, which only specifies three year residence[28]. Given that inter-state and intra-state migration for work occurs at a large scale in India and that the beneficiaries of these provisions are among the most poor and vulnerable sections of our society, it would be appropriate to lower the limit of number of years to three. There should be a mechanism to ensure equitable sharing of project benefits with the displaced people. This may be in terms of providing direct or indirect employment or reservation of a quota of shares etc[29]. The conditional availability of certain resettlement provisions in the Relief and Resettlement Bill are a matter of concern (S.36(1) reads

> *"Each affected family owning agricultural land in the affected area and whose entire land has been acquired or lost shall be allotted to agricultural land or cultivable wasteland if Government land is available in the resettlement area"*. S.41(i) provides, *"In case of a project involving land acquisition on behalf of a requiring body-(i) the requiring body shall give preference to the affected families in providing employment in the project, at least one person per family, subject to the availability of vacancies and suitability of the affected person for the employment"*. S.49(4) says, *"Each affected family of Scheduled Tribe followed by Scheduled Caste categories shall be given preference in allotment of land-for-land, if Government land is available in the resettlement area"*[30]

Alternatives should be spelt out if these conditions are not met. The Bill should be in line with other existing legislations such as those related to lands of tribal peoples or forest lands. Time limit should be defined for various stages in the process for acquisition of the land. Besides, where land has been acquired and has not been used for the intended purpose or any other public purpose, then instead of auctioning the land, option should be given to the original owner to take it back on laid down terms[31]. There shall be no arbitrary displacement of individuals from their home or place of habitual residence by state authorities. In particular, public interest should justify any large-scale development project. In all cases of large-scale development projects, authorities should hold public consultation with people likely to be displaced. The concept of *'eminent domain'* should be in line with constitutional obligations and the proposed amendments to the land acquisition act and the relief and resettlement bill should provide for more scope for consultation/participation of affected people both in the acquisition as well as relief and rehabilitation process.[32] Under the Rehabilitation and Resettlement Bill, 2007, a multiplicity of authorities is sought to be created. In several cases, modalities relating to their operation are *'as may be prescribed'* by the Government. It is impetrative to define their roles so that they are complementary and there is synergy in their functions[33]. The guiding principle in cases of development related displacement should be minimal displacement. Where agricultural land is sought to be acquired, it should be mandatory that area of wasteland equal to double the area acquired will have to be acquired and reclaimed for public purpose or at least funds for the same should be deposited in a special fund to be created for the purpose of rehabilitation of displaced persons or in the Central Relief and Rehabilitation Fund (CRRF). People who are displaced due to development projects include not only property owners but also others such as tenants, farm labourers or others whose livelihood may be dependent on the land even though they may not have legal title to it. Therefore protection of their rights must be ensured[34]. It shall be mandatory for all local bodies to formulate land use plans and building rules so as to minimise and regulate conversion of agricultural lands for other uses. No non-agricultural activity should normally be allowed in areas marked for agriculture unless there are overriding and compelling reasons in public interest.

It has been the experience that where infrastructure projects likehighways, roads are planned, the land values of the adjoining areas go up. Appropriate legislation should be put in place to charge additional duty/tax for such enhanced value, at least at the time of the subsequent transfers of the land and sums so collected should be transferred to the Central Relief and Rehabilitation Fund or any special fund created for the purpose of rehabilitation of displaced persons. Social impact assessment and understanding local aspirations are best captured through continuous dialogue with local people who are affected and NGOs. Hence while carrying out social or environment impact assessment, local people especially those who are likely to be displaced or some expert NGOs may be consulted. Norms of social impact assessment should be laid down and at least three alternatives should be examined in the same or different areas[35]. Where there are multiple displacements, it is necessary to compensate the displaced people appropriately e.g. by enhancing the solatium amount provided for in the bill or otherwise. Regarding service of notice under the LA Act, Section 45(3) provides:

"When such person cannot be found, the service may be made on any adult male member of his family residing with him, and, if no such adult male member can be found, the notice may be served by fixing the copy on the outer door of the house in which the person therein named ordinarily dwells". The reference to '*adult male member*' is in violation of gender equality and autonomy of women and the term '*adult male member* may be replaced with '*adult member*''[36].

Other Recommendations on displacement on account of natural and man made disasters including conflicts particularly the Rehabilitation and Resettlement Bill, 2007 must explicitly cover persons displaced due to violence as also due to natural or other man-made disasters. The NRRP as well as the R & R Bill, 2007 have to be comprehensive. The reference to any *'involuntary displacement due to any other reason'* is very vague. It does not specifically cover conflict induced and disaster induced displacement. Also the definition of disaster has to be widened taking into account the environmental vagaries in different parts of out country. For instance, soil erosion does not fall within the category of natural disaster[37].

In disaster related displacement, rehabilitation is the biggest challenge. There is a need to address as to how one rehabilitates displaced persons in locations similar to their former residence. In instances relating to displacement on account of conflicts, there is a need to focus on what assurances would displaced persons require in order repatriating to former place of residence voluntarily? People displaced on account of conflicts or natural disasters should be able to return to their former places of residence voluntarily in safety and dignity. Authorities should ensure that their property is protected against destruction and arbitrary and illegal appropriation when they are displaced. When they return to their places of habitual residence, they shall not be discriminated against. Authorities shall assist the returnees to recover, to the extent possible, their property that they left behind or were dispossessed of upon their displacement. Where it is not possible to recover property and possession, then authorities shall be responsible for providing just reparation to them. Temporary Settlement should not be long drawn and there should be a time frame for the completion of relief and resettlement of people displaced on account of conflict and natural disasters. In the case of conflict, natural or human-made disasters, there is a need for a larger vision, which emphasizes the *'prevention'* aspect of displacement. The Central Relief Fund (CRF) should be renamed as CRRF and funds should be set aside for rehabilitation of displaced individuals. All affected and displaced persons have the right to security for their physical well being and their property. Security agencies functioning under the administrative control of the States/Central Government must be geared towards preventing looting and other anti-social activities, and instilling a sense of security amongst the affected and displaced persons.

All affected and displaced persons have the right to immediate humanitarian assistance. In particular, they have right to food, shelter, healthcare (including mental health care) and education. To ensure smooth rescue, relief and rehabilitation, lists of person dead or missing as also property damaged fully or partially etc should be prepared in a transparent manner at the earliest and authenticated by appropriate authority. Such lists should be given wide publicity so that people can easily have access to the same. Special attention should be given to the vulnerable groups, e.g. disabled persons, women, children and the elderly in this regard. All affected persons have right to information about their missing relatives, friends, colleagues etc. Authorities concerned should put in place appropriate arrangements to collect information about missing persons and keep their kin/relatives informed about progress in the matter. Similar efforts should be made and arrangements put in place about identification of dead and dissemination of information about them, and handing over their mortal remains to their kin after following all procedures. Till then, the mortal remains shall be preserved properly. If the dead are not identified within reasonable time, their last rites may be performed after obtaining appropriate orders and with full respect for dignity as per customs of religion to which she/he is believed to belong based on prima facie evidence. The concerned authorities after reasonable verification shall issue to affected and displaced persons all documents necessary for the enjoyment and exercise of their legal rights, such as passports, personal identification documents, birth certificates, death certificates and marriage certificates. Any lack of access to such legal documents or not having such legal documents shall not disentitle them for recompense[38].

After my widespread field work I come to the conclusion that Arunachal Pradesh is no more the *'land of peace'* rather it is the *'land of discrimination'* and one of the most worse state then any other states of the republic of India in terms of human security and representation is concerned. The states Inner Line Regulation Act (ILRA) is also creating lots of problems not only to the Chakmas but also to all the Indians who are more than 40 percent and working for the welfare and development of the state. State Government using the ILP as the easy tools to harass Chakmas in many occasions by asking, even not required. Some time state government does not issue the ILP and demand from the Chakmas and put in the jail and harass. The Government of India should take a necessary step and remove all the British policies so that its citizens should live freely without discrimination in any part of Indian Territory. I personally do not understand why Government of Indian is following all the British policies even after sixty two years of independence. All these inhumane policy, harassing Indians should be removed.

References

1. P. Oberoi (2006), Exile and Belonging: Refugees and State Policy in South Asia, Oxford University Press, New Delhi, pp. 77–103.

2. Advisory Service, on International Humanitarian Law, ICRC, 07/2004, the International Association of Refugee Law Judges, Netherlands.

3. The propaganda generally Arunachalees so far making is not correct on the issue related to Chakmas. It is India Government who granted land to the Chakmas and made it clear to make it the place of living. Chakmas cleaned only some of the areas where they allowed resettling. So far my field work is concerned; largely the Arunachalees are involved in deforestation and smuggling of timber and other natural resource with the neighboring states. Arunachalees engaging Chakmas and illegal Bangladeshis for the purpose of smuggling particularly timbers, elephant teeth, and other natural resource. The Bangladeshis are bounded labourers in Arunachal Pradesh who works only for food.

4. As per report by various NGO's like SNEHA in New Delhi as well as Government of India and Arunachal Pradesh in its 2001 census report, also reported by South Asia Human Rights Documentation Centre (SAHRDC).

5. These are the villages where Chakmas are resettled in Arunachal Pradesh. All these villages and Districts are in the official list of Government of Arunachal Pradesh as well as Government of India.

6. SNEHA is the only effective NGO working in Arunachal Pradesh for Chakmas.

7. Arunachalees here I mean the tribals (settlers) of Arunachal Pradesh.

8. This information is mainly part of my field work conversation with the head man and other most senior members of the Chakma communities.

9. Ajit, Rana (2004), Election Commission throws Chakma spanner, The Pioneer, 23 January.

10. Basti here refers to the villages. It is the local dialects used in all the states of India's Northeast.

11. SNEHA stands here for love, it is a Pali word.

12. See website, http://news.oneindia.in, urges-centre-to-resolve-contentious-refugee-issue, February 1, 2008.

13. *Ibid.*

14. See website, http://ceoarunachal.nic.in, for detail information on the voter list in Chakma settled districts (constituencies), Office of the Chief Electoral Officer Arunachal Pradesh.

15. *Ibid.*

16. See website http://www.achrweb.org, article published by the Asian Centre for Human Rights.

17. *Ibid.*

18. See website, http://nhrc.nic.in, NHRC Recommendation on Relief and Rehabilitation of Displaced Persons, New Delhi August 22, 2008. The following important recommendations and suggestions emerged at the National Conference on Relief and Rehabilitation of Displaced Persons organised by the National Human Rights Commission on 24-25 March 2008 in New Delhi.

19. GAM is the head of the village and representative of the community as per Arunachal Pradesh Panchayati Raj Institution is concern. Arunachal Pradesh have their own training centers for all these GAM's called Gam Training Centers (GTC), but it has reported and my survey proved that there is not a single GTC in these three districts where Chakmas are settled.

20. This information is mainly part of my field work conversation with the head man and other most senior members of the Chakma communities.

21. It is reported by the Tapun Area Welfare Society (TAWS) an Arunachalees civil society group, See for detail information published by webindia123, www.news.webindia123.com.

22. *Ibid.*

23. Judgment of Supreme Court of India (1996), Original Civil Jurisdiction, Writ Petition (Civil) No. 720 of 1995, Between NHRC versus State of Arunachal Pradesh, 9th January, New Delhi.

24. See website, http://www.sneha.org.in, the report published by the SNEHA, New Delhi.

25. *Ibid.*

26. Explored during my field work in the districts of Chakma settled areas of Changlang and Lohit.

27. See in detail sections 3(n), 3(d), 3(iii), 21(2)(vi) 35(2) of Relief and Resettlement Bill, 2007.

28. See in detail Sections 6.4(vi), 3(o),7.3, 3.1(d), 3.1(b)(iii) of NRRP.

29. See Reports by United Nations High Commissioner for Refugees, 14th Annual Tripartite Consultations on Resettlement, Geneva; 30 June-2, July 2008, pp. 4-57.

30. See website, http://www.nhrc.in, address by Mr. Justic S. Rajendra Babu, Chairperson, National Right Commission, India, at National Human Right Commission, India, at National Conference on Relief and Rehabilition of Displaced Person, Organized by National Human Right Commission, India, 24 March, 2008, India Habital Centre, New Delhi.

31. See in detail the section 22 of the Land Acquisition Bill.

32. According to Section 6(2) of the Relief and Resettlement Bill, 2007, the public hearing undertaken in the project affected area for the environmental impact assessment shall also cover issues relating to social impact assessment. The Bill does not envisage public hearing for social impact assessment where no environment impact assessment is required. Public hearing should be held during all instances of social impact assessment.

33. See sections 9, 11,12,13,14,16 and 19 of the Relief and Resettlement Bill, 2007, envisage creation of various administrative authorities.

34. Reading Section 3(b)(ii), 3(c) and Section 20(i) of Relief and Resettlement Bill, 2007, it appears agricultural or non-agricultural labourers, landless person, rural artisan, small trader or self-employed person will be covered under this Act only in cases where there is likely to be involuntary displacement of four hundred or more families on masse in plain areas, or two hundred or more families en masse in tribal or hilly areas, DDP blocks or areas mentioned in the Fifth

Schedule or Sixth Schedule to the Constitution. An explicit provision to this effect should be provided in the R & R Bill to guarantee the rights of this category of people. LA Bill also should reflect the interest of people who do not have legal title to the land.

34. See website, http://www.nhrc.nic.in, address by Mr. Justice S. Rajendra Babu, Chairperson, National Human Rights Commission, India, at National Conference on Relief and Rehabilitation of Displaced Person, Organised by National Human Rights Commission, India, 24 March, 2008, India Habitat Centre, New Delhi.

35. See in detail the section 22 of the Land Acquisition Bill.

35. Section 4 of the Relief and Rehabilitation Bill should be appropriately amended to reflect this.

36. *Ibid.*

37. According to Section 2 of the Relief and Resettlement Bill, 2007, the provisions of this Act shall apply to the rehabilitation and resettlement of persons affected by acquisition of land under the Land Acquisition Act, 1894 or any other Act of the Union or a State for the time being in force; or involuntary displacement of people due to any other reason.

38. See website, http://nhrc.nic.in, NHRC Recommendation on Relief and Rehabilitation of Displaced Persons, New Delhi August 22, 2008. The following important recommendations and suggestions emerged at the National Conference on Relief and Rehabilitation of Displaced Persons organised by the National Human Rights Commission on 24-25 March 2008 in New Delhi.

5

Citizenship An issue Between Two Nations

Regime is a mode or system of rule or government or a ruling or prevailing system or a government in power or more specific the period during which a particular government or ruling system is in power[1]. It is not easy for any one simply to conceptualize the refugee regime in India. For this the very simple reason is India's historical recognition of human value based on strong Buddhist principles. As we know India is the country of without proper refugee law and policy but even having all this the largest refugee population are concentrated and it is only due to the India's strong belief in humanity.

The refugees in any country is nothing but based on full cleavages and contradiction within their group, with the local of the area, recognition by international organisation, civil societies as well center and states respectively. And this is what Chakmas of Arunachal Pradesh are facing today largely for their survival. Any society cannot move forward unless, if not have belief on humanity and brotherhood. The problem of Chakmas in Arunachal Pradesh is nothing but the lack of proper coordination between the two regimes one the Government of India and another Government of Arunachal Pradesh. As per my field work is concerned in the Chakmas settled areas of Arunachal Pradesh particularly three districts where Chakmas largely concentrated viz. *Papumpare, Lohit* and *Changlang* and I found the problem of Chakmas are completely a political problem. It is largely a political agenda of all the political parties in the state with the help of AAPSU. As per the history of Arunachal is concerned it said that the Arunachal Pradesh is the state of rising sun but today Arunachal Pradesh is not the state of rising sun rather the land of discrimination. This is not with the case of Chakmas but other Indians who are living in the state before independence. AAPSU and other student organisations with the help of State Government fully engaged in torturing, looting and all other anti-social activities in the region[2].

So far Indian Human Rights Commission Report 2007 is concerned it has been reported that the ruling Indian National Congress, the State Government of Arunachal Pradesh continued to practice racial discrimination against the Chakmas[3]. The State Government of Arunachal Pradesh and the Government of India have been blatantly violating the judgment of the Supreme Court of 9 January 1996 by not processing the citizenship applications of those Chakmas who had migrated to Arunachal Pradesh between 1964 and 1969[4]. The state Government also dishonored the direction of the ECI to enroll all the eligible Chakmas into electoral rolls as per the Section 3(1) (a) of the Citizenship Act, 1955[5].

The basic facilities and amenities such as educational and healthcare facilities and the right to employment earlier withdrawn by the State Government have not been restored. As a result, the socio-economic conditions of the Chakmas remained highly pathetic. Many false cases have also been filed against the activists of the CCRCAP, which has been leading a democratic struggle for the citizenship rights of the Chakmas. As per the State Police records, a total of 2,262 crimes were committed during 2006. These included 60 murders, 34 attempt to murder, 75 kidnapping and abduction, 93 crimes against women including 37 rapes, 181 grievous hurt and nine under the Arms Act, among others[6]. The very unfortunate to be made public is that all has been done by the Arunachalees who claim to be the highly educated and best among the entire northeast India[7].

Despite the establishment of the Arunachal Pradesh State Commission for Women in January 2005, the conditions of the women and children remained miserable in the State. The National Family Health Survey III (2005-2006) found that 38.8 per cent women in the State were victims of domestic violence,[8] and 41 per cent women were married off under the age of 18 years[9]. In a significant judgment on 7 December 2006, a Sessions Judge in *Kurung Kumey* district ruled that minor girls could not be married off as per the existing customs of the tribals[10]. Arunachal Pradesh remained the only State in the country with no prison. There were 18 convicts by the end of July 2006. They were kept in prison of *Asom*, thereby contributing to the problem of overcrowding[11]. There was no separation of the judiciary from the executive. As on 30 June 2006, there were a total of 5,220 cases pending with the District and Subordinate Courts in the State[12].

On 9 January 1996, the Supreme Court of India in its historic judgment in the case of National Human Rights Commission Vs State of Arunachal Pradesh and Anr (Civil Writ Petition 720 of 1995) directed the State government of Arunachal Pradesh to process the citizenship applications of those who migrated between 1964 and 1969[13]. But not a single application out of 4,677 applications submitted since 1997 had been processed by the end of 2006[14].

In 2004, 1,497 Chakmas who were born in India were enrolled in the State's electoral rolls pursuant to the directions of the Election Commission of India (ECI). Yet, there had been no further progress to the process of enrolling other Chakmas who are citizens of India by birth under Section 3(1) (a) of the Citizenship Act, 1955 due to the apathy and racial discrimination being practiced by the State Government against the Chakmas.

On 23 March 2005, the ECI issued an order for conduct of intensive revision in Arunachal Pradesh. The ECI also issued detailed guidelines to be complied with by the electoral officers during the conduct of the revision exercise. As stated in India Human Rights Report 2006, in clear violations of the above guidelines, from day one of the revision process, the Electoral Registration Officers (ERO) and Assistant Electoral Registration Officers (AEROs) prescribed birth certificate as the only document for enrolment. Ignoring clause (e) the EROs and AEROs arbitrarily and illegally subjected all eligible Chakma voters who have been issued electoral cards to undergo local verification irrespective of whether linkage as required under Guideline (d) (i) was established or not. The CCRCAP, an organisation representing the Chakmas, complained to the ECI against gross and willful violations of the ECI Guidelines of 23 March 2005 by the EROs, AEROs and other concerned electoral officials of Arunachal Pradesh during the revision exercise. Taking cognisance of such gross violations of its guidelines, the ECI suspended publication of Draft Rolls in 46-Chowkham; 49-Bordumsa-Diyun and 50-Miao Assembly Constituencies inhabited by the Chakmas till the ECI decides on the issue. At the end of the year, the issue remained pending before the ECI. By the end of 2006, ECI failed to take a final decision. On 9 August 2006, the Gauhati High Court (Itanagar Permanent Bench) dismissed the three writ petitions [WP(C) No. 154 (AP) 2006], [WP(C) 155(AP) 2006] and [WP(C) 156(AP) 2006] challenging the order of the ECI of 2 January 2004 directing the concerned Electoral Registration Officers to include names of 1,497 Chakma voters in the electoral rolls[15].

In January 2005, Arunachal Pradesh State Commission for Women (APSCW) was formed. But there had been little improvement in the plight of women in the State. They were subjected to cruel and degrading treatment, most particularly sexual exploitation in the name customs and traditions. As per the state police records, 93 crime against women including 37 rapes were registered during 2006[16]. The National Family Health Survey III (2005-2006) found that 38.8 per cent women were victims of domestic violence in the State[17]. Child marriage was common. According to the National Family Health Survey III (2005-2006), 41 per cent women were married off under the age of 18 in Arunachal Pradesh. The figure was 28 per cent during its earlier survey of 1998-99[18]. In a significant judgment delivered on 7 December 2006, a Sessions Judge in *Kurung Kumey* district ruled in favour of a Class XII girl, Yumbam Yaku who had moved the court asking to be freed from her marriage. Sessions Judge Repo Ronya ruled that the girl was not a party to the betrothal agreement as neither her consent was sought nor was she in a position to give consent at the time of her wedding. The court was also of the opinion that marriage could not be solemnized against the will of one of the concerned parties, citing the provisions of the Child Marriage Restraint Act, 1929. The petitioner, Yumbam Yaku was married off as a child to Bengia Kami in return for a bride price in the form of mithuns[19], cows and pigs, according to tribal practice[20].

In Arunachal Pradesh, regulations prohibit non-locals and non-residents from acquiring interests in land or land produce. Due to these regulations, the Arunachal Pradesh authorities felt that the decision to settle the Chakmas was wrong. Here, we find the conflict generating due to the possession of land. The Arunachal authorities felt that other states should also share the burden of settling these refugees. At present, these refugees are settled in Lohit, Changlang and Papumpare in Arunachal Pradesh. The present population of Chakmas in Arunachal Pradesh is approximately around 60,000. The growth in the last three decades has been phenomenal. Since their resettlement, the Chakmas have been illegally denied Indian citizenship and systematically deprived of other fundamental rights[21].

Settlers claim that the Chakmas are occupying land so they had to be removed. Here we see that to remove them, they were tortured, forcibly evicted after burning their houses. This conflict was mainly over land. The AAPSU launched *'Refugee Go back'* movement to evict Chakmas from Arunachal Pradesh. In 1980, the government of Arunachal Pradesh banned employment of Chakmas, seized their trade licenses in 1994. Thus, their employment options were reduced, which would force them to leave, locked in a vicious cycle of poverty. Basic social infrastructure like schools and hospitals were dismantled in areas inhabited by Chakmas[22]. The Government of Arunachal Pradesh kept on insisting that the Chakmas were foreigners and so, they were not entitled to fundamental rights and could be asked to quit the state at any time. In 1996, the Supreme Court observed that the Government of Arunachal Pradesh should protect the life and liberty of the refugees in the region. But till date, few steps have been taken to implement the directives of the Supreme Court. Moreover, the state government remained a silent spectator while the situation worsened for the refugees. The AAPSU began a *'detect and deport'* foreigner's programme. The main motive behind all this, one can see, is the desire to acquire the land occupied by the Chakmas. In 1994, all official facilities for the Chakmas were withdrawn. Economic blockades were organized around Chakma refugee camps. Facing a hostile administration and hostile political parties, the Chakmas have survived over the years. They have faced institutionalized discrimination under different regime under the various Chief Ministers. They have become permanent victims of xenophobia[23].

India Needs Refugee Policy and Laws

The present demand for the grant of citizenship and Scheduled Tribe status by the Chakmas clearly shows that they are not only unwilling to move out of the state, but also they are politically conscious and quite determined to stay permanently in the state. Unable to bear the atrocities and faced with displacement on account of the construction of the Kaptai Hydel Project about 30,000 Chakmas migrated to India in 1964[24]. They were settled in Arunachal Pradesh after due consultation with the local leaders by the Central Government of India under a *'Definite Plan of Rehabilitation'*. The Government of India extended all possible kind of helps including financial aids, employment, trade, license, book grants etc for proper establishment of their shattered life. After the partition of India, the Government's policy was to grant citizenship to those who originated from areas that were part of Undivided India. The rest of the migrants were accorded Indian citizenship. However the Chakmas were not granted Indian citizenship. In the wake of the anti-foreigner agitation in Assam, the State Government of Arunachal Pradesh undertook a series of repressive measures beginning in 1980. The State Government vide its letter no. POL–21/80 dated 29th September 1980 banned public employment for the Chakmas in the State.

In 1991, the CCRCAP was formed to demand for citizenship rights of the Chakmas of Arunachal Pradesh. Starting in 1992, the State Government of Arunachal Pradesh became more hostile and started inciting sectarian violence against the Chakmas. The AAPSU served a *'Quit Arunachal Pradesh'* notice to the Chakmas to leave the State by 30 September 1994. As a result, a large number of Chakmas fled from

Arunachal Pradesh and took refuge in the neighboring Indian State of Assam. However, the State Government of Assam issued shoot at sight orders against the fleeing Chakmas. The CCRCAP approached the NHRC about the deadline set by the AAPSU and the threat to the lives and property of the Chakmas. The NHRC treated it as a formal complaint and asked the state government and central government to report on the issue[25].

On 7 December 1994, the NHRC directed the state government of Arunachal Pradesh and Central Government to provide information about the steps taken to protect the Chakmas. This was ignored till September 1995. In the meantime, the harassment, intimidation, arrests and detention continued and increased. The issue became critical following the meeting of all-party leaders and the AAPSU held at Naharlagan, Itanagar on 20 September 1995. Political leaders of Arunachal Pradesh led by former Chief Minister Mr. Gegong Apang passed a unanimous resolution to resign *en masse* from the national party membership if the Chakmas are not deported by 31 December 1995. The resolution also prohibited any social interactions between the local Arunachalees and the Chakmas. The CCRCAP approached the NHRC again on 12 and 28 October 1995 to seek protection of their lives and liberty in view of the deadline and support extended to the AAPSU by the State Government[26]. As the state government was inordinately delaying the transmission of information regarding the steps taken to protect the Chakmas, the NHRC, headed by Justice Ranganath Mishra, approached the Supreme Court to seek appropriate relief and filed a writ petition (720/1995). The Supreme Court in its interim order on 2 November 1995 directed the State Government to, *"ensure that the Chakmas situated in its territory are not ousted by any coercive action, not in accordance with law"*[27].

As the 31st December 1995 deadline approached, then the former Prime Minister Late. Shri PV Narashima Rao formed a high-level committee headed by the Home Minister SB Chavan to look forward the issues in details. Despite the clear and unambiguous order of the Supreme Court, the State Government of Arunachal Pradesh has not taken any measure to implement the court's directions. Rather, the State Government has undertaken various measures to undermine and violate the Supreme Court judgment. The State Government has been making the conditions of the Chakmas untenable by denying them fundamental rights such as right to education and other basic facilities such as health care, employment facilities. Other measures included a complete halt to any development activities, refusal to provide trade licenses, refusal to deploy teachers in the schools located in the Chakma areas, withdrawal of all preprimary (*Anganwadi*) centres and finally forcible eviction by claiming the lands of the Chakmas as forest lands[28].

After the Supreme Court judgment, the AAPSU and State Government of Arunachal Pradesh began inciting communal hatred. The State Government, however, became more tactful, calculated and deliberate in its anti-Chakma activities. With a view to repel any move to submit citizenship applications to the Deputy Commissioners, the State Government attempted to provoke communal passions by calling a state-wide *bandh* on Disseminated by Asian Indigenous and Tribal Peoples Network for public information on 22 January 1996. Mr. Gegong Apang, went to the extent of describing the Supreme Court judgment as the *'step-motherly attitude of the Centre and calling it biased judgment'*[29].

On 26 January1997 the AAPSU also called a state-wide *bandh*. On 4 May 1998, 27 Chakmas went to submit the citizenship applications to the DC of Changlang District. The citizenship applications were verified by the First Class Magistrate of Margarita, Assam. However, the DC of Changlang refused to accept the applications. Due to the pervasive fear and the hostile situation engineered by the State Government, the Chakmas were unable to submit applications to the Deputy Commissioners. It was after discussions with the officials of Union Home Ministry that the Chakmas started submitting citizenship applications to the DC through the Union Home Ministry in February 1997. Over the years, around 4000 citizenship applications have been submitted. However, the concerned DC's have been blocking the said applications by not verifying them and not forwarding them within a reasonable period of time in spite of an amendment in the Citizenship Rules, 1956. Under Rule 9 of the Citizenship Rules (Amended), 1998 the deputy commissioner/state government is required to forward the citizenship application within a period of six months. The blocking of citizenship applications in this manner is a clear contempt of Supreme Court order in which the apex court clearly held that the DC are bound to forward the applications received by them, with or without inquiry, as the case may be, to the Central Government for consideration. It has been learnt that the State Government has forwarded around 260 citizenship applications in January 2000 after due verification. However, until today the Union Home Ministry has not taken any decision on these applications despite the fact that all the applicants have provided documentary proof (such as identity cards issued by the state government) that can stand judicial scrutiny to prove their migration in 1964 and continuous stay in Arunachal Pradesh. Justice delayed is justice denied. The refusal of the Central

Government to grant citizenship to 260 applicants whose applications have been verified is further denial of justice[30].

Incidents of Human Rights Violation

On 28 January 1996, Pularam Chakma of Udaipur village under Diyun Circle of Changlang district, and Maratsa Chakma, of Vijoypur village under Bardumsa circle of Changlang district went for harvesting the mustard crop. They were working for Chandra Kri and Pyola Kri of Namgo village under Chowkham circle of Lohit district. Pularam Chakma and Maratsa Chakma were attacked by about 20 AAPSU activists and beaten up mercilessly at Medo Bazar of Lohit district in full public view. Pularam Chakma was beaten to death on the spot. Maratsa Chakma, who was left for dead, however later gained consciousness and was able to get assistance at a nearby Chakma house. On CCRCAP had approached the NHRC on the issue[31].

On 6 June 1998, Bimal Kanti Chakma was arrested by the Arunachal Pradesh Police because he is an assistant *Gaon Bura* (village headman) of Jyotipur village under Diyun circle of Changlang district and a CCRCAP leader. He has been providing help to several Chakmas of the M.pen area under the Miao circle of Changlang district, attempting to obtain bail for those who are detained[32].

The State Government of Arunachal Pradesh has adopted various policies to evict the Chakmas by issuing orders for eviction to show that its actions were being done legally without violating the Supreme Court judgment. On 8 December 1997, the State Government of Arunachal Pradesh issued eviction notices to 66 Chakma families in Kamakhyapur and Raj Nagar areas under Changlang district. Earlier, on 11 November 1997, the Circle Officer (CO) of Diyun, D Riba served quit notices (memo No. Diyun/LR/EVC/97) to 109 families of Jyotsnapur village under Changlang district and directed them to proceed to their original settlement areas. D. Riba did not give any explanation for such eviction notice. In his notice, D. Riba simply stated,

"You are hereby directed to proceed to your original settlement Jyotipur village with family latest by 20 November 1997 without fail. Failing which legal action will be initiated against you"[33]

The Chakmas have been living in Jyotsnapur village for the last two decades. They have settled in Jyotsnapur village after the Diyun River flooded their areas and destroyed their houses during monsoon. For about 40,000 Chakma population there is only one Government

Secondary School at Diyun. In the absence of any middle school in the whole Diyun circle, this school has to accommodate all the Chakma students passing out every year from more than 10 primary schools operating in the Chakma areas. Around 1,400 (12 teachers) are enrolled in this school with virtually no infrastructural facilities.

Many of the Chakma villages in Changlang district are without even primary schools. The existing schools, which had 2-3 teachers each, are left behind with one or no teachers since 1994. The following villages do not have primary schools. The state government of Arunachal Pradesh in a circular on 31 October 1991 (No FPSO -3/90-91) had ordered all the Chakmas to surrender their ration cards under the public distribution system (PDS) to the CO. Thousands of Chakmas were forced to surrender their ration cards to the State Government. Despite the Supreme Court judgment the State Government has not returned the ration cards. The Chakmas are very poor and rely to a large extent on the PDS. Ration card facilities are indispensable for the daily labourers. By denying the ration card facilities, the State Government of Arunachal Pradesh has condemned them to poverty. As stated above, the Chakmas are not even issued permission to sell their cash crops in neighboring Assam. They are not issued licenses for trade in the local markets. At the same time, hundreds of families were rendered landless due to soil erosion caused by the Dihang River and its tributaries. More than 90 percent of the Chakmas are below poverty line[34].

The victims filed a petition before the Guwahati High Court. The Guwahati High Court in its judgment (Civil Rule No 5255 of 1997) stated, "Whenever trade is regulated by licence, the licence is entitled for renewal of the license as a rule and non-renewal of the licence is exception since granting or refusing of licence regarding trade or business is intrinsically connected with the livelihood of a person, a right rooted in the Indian Constitution. The licensing power is bristled with enormous ramification immensely affecting the rights and liberties of citizens and livelihoods of citizens in particular and thus require a fair procedure"[35]

In the light of the Supreme Court judgment in the *National Human Rights Commission Vs the State of Arunachal Pradesh,* the Guwahati High Court directed the State Government of Arunachal Pradesh "to consider the case of the petitioners for renewal of their licenses as per law. The Deputy Commissioner, Changlang, Arunachal Pradesh shall also ensure and to see that the original documents which were seized from the petitioners on 22 October 1997 by the Circle Officer, Circle Diyun along with the Officer-in-Charge, Diyun Police Station and Second Officer of the said police station are returned to the petitioners. In the meantime, the Respondents are directed to allow the Petitioners to run their business and shops"[36]

While the State government has restored the trade licenses of the above victims, no fresh licenses have been issued since 1991. The State Government vide circular dated 29th September 1980 and circular dated 31st October 1997 has banned employment in government service, agricultural field, contract work and business etc. for the Chakmas in the state, resulting in the Unemployment among a large number of educated youths. The ban on employment continues until today[37].

The entire Chakma area consisting of 30 villages, there is only one Primary Health Centre (PHC) at Diyun circle, whereas, in other local areas PHC has been provided in almost all villages. The PHC of Diyun hardly able to cater to the needs of Chakmas as it has only one doctor, five nurses and eight beds. The patients often remain unattended and therefore people prefer to give their own treatment gained by way of experience. Instances of malarial deaths and other simple and serious diseases otherwise not fatal are numerous. Though it is claimed that the Chakmas are provided medical facilities, in effect they are still denied treatment. Nurses also charge money to give injections. Some Chakma villages such as Dharmapur, circle Miao, Bijoypur, circle Bordumsa and Deban area (eight villages) in Changlang district are located far away from the nearest PHC. As there are rivers, which are sometimes flooded, people remain cut off sometime for a month from rest of the places. Therefore, even simple fever often proves fatal in these places[38].

On 23 August 1995, a petition was filed before the Rajya Sabha Committee. After extensive visits to several places where the views of the local people, the Chakmas, experts, the State Government and the Central Government were taken into account, the Committee in its 105th Report of 14 August 1997 recommended the speedy granting of Indian citizenship to the Chakmas of Arunachal Pradesh. It was also recommended that, "All the old applications of Chakmas for citizenship which have been either been rejected or withheld by Deputy commissioners or the state government continue to block the forwarding of such applications to central government, the central government may consider to incorporate necessary provision in the Rules (or the Act if so required) whereby it could directly receive, consider and decide the application for citizenship in the case of Chakmas of Arunachal Pradesh"[39]

The Committee further recommended that the Chakmas be also considered for granting them the status of Scheduled Tribe at the time of granting the citizenship. Although, the Government of India has submitted Action Taken Report, practically none of the recommendations of the Rajya Sabha Committee on Petitions have been implemented until today.

After the Arunachal Pradesh government threatened that all members of State Assembly would resign en masse if the Chakmas were not expelled by 31 December 1995, a committee headed by the Prime Minister of India was established. A Sub-committee under the chairmanship of the Union Home Minister was formed to find an amicable solution to the Chakma problem. The Home Ministry officials headed by Mr. P. D. Shenoy, Additional Secretary and the MHA representing the said Sub-Committee visited the Chakma and Hajong inhabited areas on 6 and 7 March 1999. The Sub-Committee in January 2000 submitted the report to the union home minister, who is currently the chairman, containing specific recommendations to resolve the Chakma problem. Unfortunately, no decision has been taken for implementation of the recommendations of the Home Ministry team[40].

In addition to the Chakmas who migrated in 1964, there are about 5,000 Chakmas who are born after the migration of their parents in 1964. They are Indian citizens by birth under Section 3(1) (a) of the Indian Citizenship Act, 1955 which states that, *"Except as provided in sub-section (2), every person born in India, (a) on or after the 26th day of January, 1950 but before the commencement of the Citizenship (Amendment) Act, 1986" is a citizen by birth"*[41]

The CCRCAP filed a complaint with the NHRC on 12 December 1997 against the denial of franchise rights to the Chakmas. The NHRC issued notice to the State Government of Arunachal Pradesh and the Union Government of India on the issue. In their replies to the NHRC, both the Central Government and the state government of Arunachal Pradesh recognized that, *"as per the provisions of the Citizenship Act 1955, every person born in India on or after 26th January 1950 and before 1st July 1987 are citizens of India by birth and therefore eligible for electoral rolls"*[42]

However, when the Chakmas who were born after their parents' migration and are citizens under Section 3(1)(a) of Indian Citizenship Act, 1955, went to the Assistant Electoral Registration Officer of Diyun under Changlang District of Arunachal Pradesh, the officer refused to accept their Form 6 Application for inclusion of name in electoral rolls. The CCRCAP approached the Ministry of Home Affairs (MHA). The MHA informed it that the Election Commission had been requested to include all the Indian citizens into the electoral rolls. But the Election Commission took no action. Since no action has been taken to ensure that the Chakmas are enrolled in the voters' list, the PUCL and the

CCRCAP filed a writ petition (CPR No. 886 of 2000) before the Delhi High Court. In its judgment on 28 September 2000, the Delhi High Court ordered the registration of all eligible voters. This order, too, was flouted on various pretexts. Till date, not a single Chakma has been included in the electoral rolls. During the revision of electoral roll 2001 around 2000 Chakmas filed claim applications enclosed therewith their proof of age, residence etc. All the claim applications were, however, rejected for not specifying house enumeration number and due to lack of polling station in the Chakma areas. It may be stated that the allotment of house enumeration number and setting up of polling station are tasks of EC and the Chakma applicants cannot be punished for omission on the part of the officials of the EC. The repeated representations to the EC failed to elicit any positive result[43].

One of the concerns of the Central Government that unfortunately prevailed over the need to uphold the rule of law by processing citizenship applications has been the perceived opposition to the grant of citizenship to the Chakmas of Arunachal Pradesh by the local tribal communities. The CCRCAP has consistently stated that it was nothing but a creation of the then State Government of Arunachal Pradesh to deny the Chakmas the right to citizenship. The Chakmas since their migration enjoyed excellent relationship with the neighboring communities. Even the Central Team that visited in 1982 to study the problems of the Chakmas had submitted in its report that, *"No reports have been received regarding involvement of these refugees in anti-national activities. The presence of these refugees in the area has not resulted so in any major law and order problem though some isolated instances of friction between the locals and these refugees have come to our notice. The grant of citizenship would introduce an element of responsible social behavior in these refugees"*[44]

Therefore, the plea of the State Government that opposition by local tribal people against grant of citizenship to the Chakmas is unfounded. In fact, many leaders of the local Shingpo and Thangsa community leaders including ex-Members of Legislative Assembly have written to the former Union Home Minister, Mr. Lal Krishna Advani on various occasions supporting the grant to citizenship rights of the Chakmas of Arunachal Pradesh.

The root cause of the suffering of the Chakmas of Arunachal Pradesh ranging from denial of educational facilities including withdrawal of all pre-primary *Anganwadi* centers with a view to keep the Chakmas illiterate is the denial of citizenship rights in clear contempt of the supreme court order. While the CCRCAP admits that the NHRC and the MHA have applied the necessary pressure, the state government often gets away by providing false information. Unless the NHRC takes measures to monitor the implementation of the recommendations by assigning a Special Rapporteur for the task, the Chakmas may be continuously denied all other rights. In order to bring an end to untold sufferings and denial of fundamental rights to the Chakmas for the last four decades and to uphold the majesty of the rule of law and respect for the highest court of the country and the NHRC[45].

Sadly, every time there is a problem, a violent tactic is the only one used. Violence never produces a stable political goal. Finally, everyone gets hungry, tired and uprooted, at which time peace negotiations are started. When relative peace comes, adequate reforms to deal with the problems are not put into place, and the cycle repeats itself. Court orders have filled legislative gaps and in many cases provided a humanitarian solution to the refugee's problem. In India courts have allowed refugees intervening NGOs to file case before them, further they have interpreted provisions of the Indian Constitution, exiting law, and in the absence of seekers[46]. Given below is a summary of the type of protection that Indian courts have provided to refugees. Indian courts have decided in a number of cases that the Constitutional protection of life and liberty must be provided to refugees.[47]

The Supreme Court of India and the National Human Rights Commission versus State of Arunachal Pradesh case restrained forcible expulsion of Chakma Refugees from the state[48]. The Supreme Court in its interim order on November 2, 1995 directed the State Government to ensure that the Chakmas situated in the territory are not ousted by any coercive action, and should be treated in accordance with law. The Court directed the state government to ensure that the life and personal liberty of each and every Chakma residing within the state shall be protected. Any attempt to forcibly evict them out the state by organised groups shall be repelled by using Para-military or police force and if additional forces are required then the state should take the necessary steps. The court also decided that the Chakmas shall not be evicted from their home except in accordance to the law; the quit notices and ultimatums given by other groups should be dealt with in accordance with the law; application for their Citizenship be forwarded and processed expeditiously; the pending decision on these application shall not be evicted[49].

In a number of cases in India, courts have protected the rights of refugees where there was substantial ground to believe that their life would be in danger. There are cases where the courts have ordered the life of refugees who are in danger be safeguarded and have allowed them to be granted status by UNHCR. In Zothansangpui versus State of Manipur (C.R No. 981 of 1989) The Gauhati Imphal Bench, Guahati High Court ruled that refugees have the rights not to be deported if their life was in danger[50].

The case of U.Myat Kyaw vs State of Manipur has contributed substantially to India's refugee policy[51]. It involved eight Burmese, aged 12 to 58 years, who were detain for illegal entry at Manipur central jail, Imphal. These persons had participated in the democratic movement, voluntarily to the Indian authorities and taken into custody. Cases were registered under section 14 of the Foreigners Act for illegal entry into India. They petitioned for their release to enable themselves to seek refugee status before the UNHCR in New Delhi. The Gauhati High Court, under Article 21 ruled that asylum seekers who enter India (even if illegally) should be permitted to approach the Office of the United Nation[52].

The Court has upheld a refugee's right to leave the country, in Nuang Maung Mye Nyant versus Government of India and Shar Aung versus Government of India of 1998, the courts ruled that even those refugees against whom cases were pending for illegal entry should be provided exit permits to enable them to leave the country for third country resettlement[53]. This included conformity with International Conventions and Treaties, although not enforceable, the government was obliged to respect them. But the power of the government to expel a foreigner is still absolute. Article 21 guarantees the right to life for non-citizens. International Covenants and Treaties which effectuate the fundamental rights can be enforced. The principal of non-refoulement is encompassed in articles so long as it is not prejudicial to national security[54].

For many years India has not applied its mind to the world of refugees, their problems and discontents. It is the time now that India recognizes the constitutional values in the shape of a national refugee policy. The refugee problem has assumed an unprecedented dimension in the international sphere. Some scholars have viewed present century as the century of uprooted people. The total number of refugees is believed to be twenty million. Refugees policy is quite complex involving many countries and so many issues. The Constitution of Indian contains just a few provisions on the status of international law in India. Leading among them is Article 51 (c), which states that, *"the State (India) shall endeavor to foster respect for international law and treaty obligations in the dealings of organised peoples with one another"*[55]

As for the minimum standard of treatment of refugees, India has undertaken an obligation by ratifying the International Covenant on

Civil and Political Rights and the International Covenant on Economic, Social and Cultural Rights to accord an equal treatment to all non-citizens with its citizens wherever possible. India is presently a member of the Executive Committee of the UNHCR and it entails the responsibility to abide by international standards on the treatment of refugees[56].

As early as 1953 the then prime minister of India, Mr Jawaharlal Nehru informed Parliament that India would abide by international standards governing asylum by adopting similar, non-binding domestic policies. Since then, the Indian government has consistently affirmed the right of the state to grant asylum on humanitarian grounds. Based on this policy, India has granted asylum and refugee status to Tibetans and Tamils from Sri Lanka. The 1971 refugees from Bangladesh were officially called evacuees, but were treated as refugees requiring temporary asylum. No other community or group has been officially recognized as refugees. India claims to observe the principles of non-refoulement and thus never to return or expel any refugee whose life and liberty were under threat in his/her country of origin or residence. Refuting this claim, Indian human rights groups do point to specific cases of refoulement, where clear evidence and refugee testimony prove that forcible repatriation has taken place. A closer examination of India's refugee policy reveals a number of intricate problems.

The plight of refugees in India generally depends upon the extent of protection they receive from either the Indian government or the UNHCR. Below is brief definition of the three primary categories followed by a description of the living conditions faced by each refugee category like

(a) Refugees who receive full protection according to standards set by the Government of India;

(b) Refugees whose presence in Indian Territory is acknowledged only by UNHCR and are protected under the principle of non-refoulement;

(c) Refugees who have entered India and have assimilated into their communities. Their presence is not acknowledged by either the Indian Government or UNHCR.

India plays host to more then 300,000 refugees from neighbouring countries, the country has a completely ad hoc system of refugee determination, deportation and protection. Within the refugee regime the move away from States and adherence to States are two sides of the same coin. First, the new refugee regime reflects the trend away from the State and strict notions of sovereignty. At the same time, however, the new regime exposes the staying power of the statist paradigm: The role of States has indeed been altered, but States retain their role as important and often essential actors. States still hold the key to asylum and to permanent, durable solutions and, it follows; States are most often essential actors in efforts to protect the human rights of the uprooted. India has a completely *ad hoc* system of refugee determination, deportation and selective protection. So, people fleeing persecution and ending up in India are left at the mercy of the government's *ad hoc* policies and the limited operations of the UNHCR. All this, despite a Supreme Court judgment (NHRC vs State of Arunachal Pradesh) that categorically states that all 'refugees' within Indian territory are guaranteed the right to life and personal liberty enshrined under Article 21 of the Constitution[57].

The crisis of refugee protection in India in general and Arunachal Pradesh in particular is often a failure of the international as well as national regime. The processes by which regime norms and practices are shaped locally, rather than inter-state bargaining or summit-level negotiation, fundamentally determine regime effectiveness, and, importantly, condition regime change over time. The adaptation of international norms and policies regarding refugees is determined by various factors, including the relative indeterminacy of international guidelines and policies; the degree of delegation to third actors, as well as their availability; the nature of the host-state and the character.

From an anthropological perspective on the fact that, by taking the category of refugees as both the primary focus and the boundary for its research, refugee Studies is underpinned by definitions that originate from policy. It contends that the definitions of categories of people like Internally displaced peoples, Migrants and Refugees arising from the refugee and humanitarian regime are not necessarily meaningful in the academic field from an analytical point of view. Empirical research has demonstrated that in practice it is not possible to apply these definitions to separate discrete classes of migrants. They are policy related labels, designed to meet the needs of policy rather than of scientific enquiry. Moreover, as products of a specific system, they bear assumptions which reflect the principles underlying the system itself. For these reasons refugee studies need to maintain analytical independence from the refugee regime. This would require inter-alia disentangling the analysis from policy categories and including policy as one of the objects of study[58].

These factors in turn shape the capacity of increasingly heterogeneous inter-organisational networks and decision-making procedures to define and institutionalise practices within particular refugee situations. The resulting local regime configurations literally shape the ground rules of the international regime by establishing the non-contractual basis of contract such as degrees of trust for international or summit-level negotiations regarding refugee policies. In this sense a feedback loop exists between local configurations and the global regime that goes beyond images of learning to include both positive and negative features of socialisation. Empirically the study draws on specific fieldwork in long-standing refugee situations in Arunachal Pradesh, using the methodological tools of both quantitative and qualitative network analysis[59].

Refugee Policy in India Motivated by Religion

Afghan refugees mainly of communities like Hindus, Sikhs and Muslims fled to India and it is almost twenty years. India is home to 8,400 Afghan refugees of whom 7,560 are Hindu and Sikhs refugees. According to the United Nations High Commissioner for Refugees about 4,000 of the Hindu and Sikh refugees have shown interest in applying for Indian citizenship and as on date more than 510 are now Indian nationals[60]. Only Hindus and Sikhs applications have been granted and given citizenship but none of the Muslim who migrated at the same time has been entertained by the India's refugee regime. In December, 2010 Bharatiya Janata Party (BJP) favoured Hindu Bangladeshi who settled over a period of time in the Indian State of Assam for their citizenship and voting rights, but BJP was very much against the Muslim Bangladeshi who settled at the same time with other Bangladeshi settlers[61].

The AAPSU has filed a Public Interest Litigation (PIL) in Gauhati High Court terming the Election Commission's guidelines to include the names of Chakma refugees in the electoral roll for the Lok Sabha elections as illegal. They also demanded re-election in the constituencies dominated by Chakmas. The PIL stated that the Election Commission has tried to include not only the names of those refugees who had entered India in 1964-65 and their descendants, but also those who have come thereafter to the state. The students' union has also questioned the Dorjee Khandu-led state government's silence over the matter and accused it of clandestinely trying to help the Chakmas[62].

The apex students' organisation of Arunachal Pradesh stated in the PIL that anyone who is found to have entered the state without valid inner line permit cannot be allowed to be a voter in any election. The people of Arunachal Pradesh have long been protesting against the attempt to include the names of Chakma refugees from Bangladesh who migrated to India in 1964-65 in the electoral rolls. The Chakmas, on their part, approached the Supreme Court, which directed that no action shall be taken against the community and that both the Union and the State Governments shall ensure that the lives and property of Chakmas remain safe. The PIL challenged the legality and validity of various guidelines issued by the Election Commission in respect of the revision of electoral rolls in the state[63]. The organisation also stated that though the state governments in the past had taken a strong stand against inclusion of names of Chakmas in the electoral roll, it was surprising that the present government has done nothing. The attitude of the state government is causing a lot of resentment among the indigenous people of the state[64].

Ideas of *the refugee* in India, long integrated with concepts of the nation through the partition experience, have significantly contributed to India's lack of formal refugee legislation. The present article argues that the resultant vague conceptual basis or '*script*' for refugee treatment has allowed India to deal relatively successfully with refugee situations of great variation and huge scale in the past when refugees were largely integrated into an existing narrative of '*minorities*', a vital component of India's national identity and political landscape. However, recent pressures from within and from the international community to standardise refugee treatment and introduce a formal refugee law have combined with political events of recent years to disadvantage some refugee groups. This article seeks to understand the changes in refugee treatment in India today and focuses on Tibetans, who appear to suffer increasingly from association with a changing narrative that links refugees, penetration by outsiders, and threats to national security, arising partly as a result of the activities of refugee Tamils from Sri Lanka, and non-refugee incomers from Pakistan[65].

Contradiction on Refugee Laws in India

India's diversity, stability and relatively well established rule of law have made it a natural destination for people fleeing persecution and instability in their own countries. Within the South Asian region, India stands out as an exception of tolerant, democratic and secular government in a neighborhood of unstable and volatile states. India has historically faced numerous influxes over many millennia and the ability of these peoples to integrate into a multi-ethnic society and contribute peacefully to local cultures and economies has reinforced the perception of India being a country traditionally hospitable to refugees. India shares seven land borders and one sea border with countries in varied states of strife and war; and, over the years, has hosted large refugee populations from neighbouring countries.

There are no authoritative statistics on the number of people who have fled persecution or violence in their countries of origin to seek safety in India[66]. However, because of India's porous borders and accommodative policies, it was estimated that India hosted approximately 3,30,000 such people in 2004. According to the Convention Relating to the Status of Refugees, 1951, a refugee is a person who flees across an international border because of a well-founded fear of being persecuted in his country of origin on account of race, religion, nationality, membership of a particular social group, or political opinion. Therefore, refugees and asylum seekers are externally displaced people[67].

The refugee problem was acknowledged as having international dimensions and requiring global cooperation as far back as 1921- 22 in the aftermath of the First World War, the break up of the Austro Hungarian empire and the Russian revolution. However, real movement to protect refugees began only with the 1948 Universal Declaration of Human Rights which proclaimed basic rights for all human beings irrespective of their nationality or citizenship. This declaration was an important first step since refugees face unique hardships and are particularly vulnerable in foreign countries. It is therefore incumbent upon the international community to protect their rights both in countries of origin and asylum[68].

None of the South Asian countries are party to the 1951 Convention Relating to the Status of Refugees which currently is ratified by 134 nations. This may reflect the unwillingness of South Asian governments to submit to international scrutiny. Though India is not a party to the Refugee Convention, the general principle prohibiting forced repatriation called non-refoulement has risen to the level of customary law, such that they bind even non-signatories.

Since the matter (entry and regulation of aliens) falls under the Union List, the Central Government is empowered to deal with refugees[69]. Traditionally, the Union Cabinet has made reactive decisions with each particular refugee influx, often taking action only when the particular refugee influx went beyond the control of the Border Security Force, and the matter became political. India thus lacks a cohesive national policy for handling refugee inflows. The lack of a national Indian policy limits the ability of the state governments and Border Security Force to deal with refugees instantly, resulting in mass rejections at the frontier while policy directions are awaited or non-recognition of refugees sneaking into Indian Territory[70].

Although India is not a party to the 1951 UN Convention on Refugees, asylum-seekers who are not offered direct protection by the Indian government can get refugee status from the UNHCR in a de facto system of refugee protection in India. But in the recent past, refugees under UNHCR protection have begun losing faith in a system plagued by insensitivity and inefficiency. India, along with all the other South Asian states, is not a party to the United Nations Convention Relating to the Status of Refugees 1951 (1951 Convention) and the Protocol Relating to the Status of Refugees 1967 (1967 Protocol). India maintains that the 1951 Convention is Euro-centric and cannot be effectively implemented in the South Asian region. India also believes that it has always been generous towards refugees, even without being party to the 1951 Convention. However, critics argue that India is hesitant to accept the financial responsibility that ensues from undertaking the obligations of the 1951 Convention. The World Refugee Survey 2007, which rates refugee protection in countries on four categories of rights — physical protection, freedom from illegal detention, freedom of movement and the right to earn a livelihood — has rated India 'D' in three categories, signifying 'a level of treatment marginally above the rest' and 'C' with regard to freedom from illegal detention, signifying that refugees have reasonable access to the Indian judiciary[71].

After the Second World War and the shared European experience of massive displacement, the Refugee Convention was adopted with restricted geographical and temporal conditions to apply to post-War Europe. In 1967, in an effort to give the Convention universal application, a Protocol relating to the Status of Refugees [1967 Protocol] that removed the restrictions of the Convention was added. Together, these two key legal documents provide the basic framework for refugee protection across the world. As of February 2006, 146 countries were states parties to either the Convention or its Protocol or both. However, India has repeatedly declined to join either the Refugee Convention or its 1967 Protocol. In addition, India has resisted demands for a national legislation to govern the protection of refugee[72].

The judicial basis of the international obligations to protect refugees, namely, non-refoulement including non-rejection at the frontier, non-return, non-expulsion or non-extradition and the minimum standard of treatment are traced in international conventions and customary law. The only treaty regime having near universal effect pertaining to refugees is the 1951 Refugee Convention and its 1967 Protocol on the Status of Refugees which is the magna carta of refugee law. Since India has not yet ratified or acceded to this regime its legal obligation to protect refugees is traced mainly in customary international law. An examination of this aspect raises the basic question of relation and effect of international law with the Indian municipal law.

The Constitution of Indian contains just a few provisions on the status of international law in India. Leading among them is Article 51 (c), which states that, *"the State [India] shall endeavour to foster respect for international law and treaty obligations in the dealings of organised peoples with one another"*[73].

Leaving a little confusion, this provision differentiates between international law and treaty obligations. It is, however, interpreted and understood that *'international law'* represents international customary law and *'treaty obligations'* represent international conventional law. Otherwise the Article is lucid and directs India to foster respect for its international obligations arising under international law for its economic and social progress. Article 51 (c) is placed under the Directive Principles of State Policy in Part IV of the Indian Constitution, which means it is not an enforceable provision. Since the principle laid down in Article 51 is not enforceable and India has merely to endeavour to foster respect for international law, this Article would mean prima facie that international law is not incorporated into the Indian municipal law which is binding and enforceable. However, when Article 51(c) is read in the light of other Articles and judicial opinion and foreign policy statements, it suggests otherwise[74].

Refugee Categories

The plight of refugees in India generally depends upon the extent of protection they receive from either the Indian government or the UNHCR. Below is brief definition of the three primary categories followed by a description of the living conditions faced by each refugee category:

I. Refugees who receive full protection according to standards set by the Government of India;

II. Refugees whose presence in Indian Territory is acknowledged only by UNHCR and are protected under the principle of non- refoulement;

III. Refugees who have entered India and have assimilated into their communities. Their presence is not acknowledged by either the Indian Government or UNHCR[75].

Category (I) Refugees

The Tamils

Tamil refugees have fled to India in several waves. When the conflict in Sri Lanka between the Sinhalese majority community and the Tamil minority took a violent turn in 1983, the Tamils fled to India on their tiny boats from the northern peninsula of Sri Lanka. During the first wave 134,053 Tamil refugees were reported to have come to India in between 1983 to 1987[76]. Following the 1987 Accord with Sri Lanka and the Indian Government, which sought to create a power sharing agreement between the two warring communities, the Indian Government repatriated 25,885 Tamil refugees from 1987-1989[77]. India had to stop the repatriation program in 1989 when its shores were flooded again with another refugee wave fleeing Sri Lankan violence[78].

During this second phase of Tamil flight in search of a safe haven (1989-1991), 122,037 Tamil refugees reportedly reached India but 113,298 of them are held in 298 camps along the coastal Indian states of Tamil Nadu and Orissa[79]. Once again, the Indian Government repatriated a large number of Tamil refugees with the cooperation of UNHCR. About 31,000 refugees have been returned to Sri Lanka in between 1992-1995[80]. As a result of these repatriations, roughly half of the original 110,000 refugees remain in Tamil Nadu, India. There have been no new returns to Sri Lanka from Tamil Nadu since the breakdown of peace talks and resumption of hostilities between the LTTE in 1996.

Today, those remaining Tamils, suffer from poor living conditions in India. Camp conditions vary from district to district, depending on the sympathies of local officials. The camps closest to Madras are, for the most part, well-maintained, while in Pooluvapatti camp near Coimbatore, 4700 refugees use eight latrines. Accumulated waste, cramped quarters, lack of electricity and poor sanitation all contribute to the miserable state of the camps.

Additionally, the Indian Government restricts the movement of the Tamils in Tamil Nadu. Members of the police and notorious 'Q' branch of the state intelligence agency are stationed at the gates of many of the camps, including the camp in Coimbatore, Tamil Nadu and carefully monitor their activities[81]. One government official claimed that the police protect the refugees, but the Tamils themselves believe that the guards are more concerned with controlling their movement[82]. Camp authorities employ indirect measures to restrain the Tamils. Refugees in the Poolvapatti, Tamil Nadu camp were told by the village administrative official that they could leave the camp to visit other areas if they wanted to, but that their daily allowances would be cut if they did. Obtaining permission to leave the camp often depends on the vagaries of the camp authorities. Moreover travel restrictions make visits to the offices of the UNHCR or the Sri Lankan Deputy High Commissioner (DHC) in Madras virtually impossible for refugees confined to outlying camps.

In addition to the regular camps, the State Government has converted jails into so-called Special Camps to hold Tamils with suspected terrorist links. Since 1990, 100 of refugees have been detained in these facilities. The South Asian Human Rights Documentation Centre (SAHRDC) and the NHRC of India have compiled numerous reports of non-militant refugees, particularly young Tamil males, being arrested and detained under the Foreigners Act. Many of these individuals have been languishing in detention facilities for more than three years and still do not know why they were arrested. When pressed, the government justifies these Special Camps as necessary measures to deal with alleged LTTE terrorists.

On the Sri Lanka repatriation, the UNHCR states that, "Between 1992 and 1 January 1996, 54,059 persons returned from India and benefited from UNHCR's Special Programme in Sri Lanka. Of this number, 7464 persons were staying in government centres as of 30 April 1996, while the remainder had returned to their home areas. A total of 10,013 persons returned in the first quarter of 1995. The UNHCR statistics on the voluntary repatriation of refugees from India are not supported by evidence. The UNHCR has allegedly connived with the Government of India in hastily repatriating the Sri Lankan Tamil refugees. Many of these refugees who could not reach their native places but live in the refugee camps back in Sri Lanka are fleeing back to India[83].

By October 1996, 2000 reached the Indian State of Tamilnadu to seek refuge again[84]. As a part of its protection mandate, UNHCR is expected to share the information on the conflict situation in the country of origin but failed to do so for the last five years to the Tamil refugees. Rather, it was informing the refugees that "certain liberated zones" were available for the refugees to return to. Refugees shifted to the Pesalai camps in Sri Lanka from India in 1994 could not go to their places and languished in UNHCR transit camps till 1996 when conflict broke out. Many of them returned to India consequently[85].

These are some 56,000 Sri Lankan Tamil refugees accommodated in Indian camps and another 45,000 reportedly living outside the camps. A court order forced the government to halt the repatriation program and gave the UNHCR the right to interview the returnees[86]. However, the UNHCR is not allowed access to the camps and cannot speak to the refugees until they have already consented to leave India. It is clear that the token presence of UNHCR in Madras only provides respectability to what is essentially a program of involuntary repatriation.

The fact that the Indian Government has not acceded to the international Refugee Convention has adverse effects upon the Tamil refugees. The Convention established basic rights such as food, water and shelter that the host country should provide its refugees. Since India is not a signatory, Tamil refugees are subject to the whims of the political party in power. The State Government in Tamil Nadu, though originally sympathetic to the refugee's cause, consistently failed to maintain the refugee camps in accordance with well-recognised international standards[87]. Thus, the policies of India and the State of Tamil Nadu directly contravene conventional human rights laws as well as customary international law regarding non-refoulement[88]. The SAHRDC recommends that if the Indian Government is serious about maintaining the camps it should allow NGOs to resume their former duties. Furthermore, the UNHCR, accustomed to treading lightly in India where it is not an officially recognised UN agency, should arm it with the international conventions to which it owes its creation and take a more pro-active role in the protection of the Sri Lankan Tamil refugees[89].

The Jumma

The Jumma peoples from the Chittagong Hill Tracts of Bangladesh are another example of category I refugees. The Buddhist Jumma have been fleeing religious harassment from the Muslim Government of Bangladesh. In a country with scarce arable land, the Bangladesh Government has been trying to settle the fertile Chittagong Hill Tracts. Since 1978, the Indian Government has provided temporary shelter for these people in the neighbouring Indian states of Mizoram and Tripura[90]. Following a series of massacres by Bangladesh security forces in 1986, nearly 70,000 Jumma refugees sought shelter in six camps established by the Indian Government in Tripura[91]. Their presence in India has been a source of embarrassment for the Bangladesh Government.

As part of its effort to improve relations with Bangladesh in 1992, the Indian Government began to pressurize the Jumma to return to Chittagong Hill Tracts, thus seemingly shifting the status of these refugees from Category I to Category II. The approximation of geo-political and economic relationship caused the change of attitude towards the refugees. As part of its effort to improve relations with its Muslim neighbour, Bangladesh, the Indian Government began to pressure the Jumma to return to the Chittagong hill tracts. India has been encouraging "voluntary" repatriation by making living conditions in the Tripura camps untenable. The Government of India has denied food to the Jumma as a means of forcing them to return to their homeland. Ration supplies to the Jumma refugees sheltered in Tripura State have been suspended since mid 1992[92].

SAHRDC most recently received information about the discontinued supply of rice and salt from 21 November 1995 in a fresh attempt to force the refugees out[93]. Food provisions are given in 10 days cycles but the quantity given normally suffices for only eight days. Often, even those meagre rations are delayed. A delay of two days means that indigent tribal refugee families must go hungry. Still, delays of over five days in the supply of rations are not uncommon. The Humanity Protection Forum, a Tripura based civil liberties organization reported one week later that hunger had engulfed the Jumma refugee camps and many refugees were facing starvation. Medical facilities and other basic amenities are non-existent[94].

The State Government of Tripura, in concert with the Central Government of India, also denies educational facilities to Jumma refugee students. This is an element of India's non-violent pressure policy, designed to encourage refugees who want their children to be educated, to return to the Chittagong Hill Tracts as their own risk. The SAHRDC conducted a study on camp conditions in 1993 and 1994 which revealed that the Jumma refugees have been systematically denied access to education[95].

In 1994, about 5,000 Jumma refugees returned *'under duress'* to the CHT after bilateral discussions between India and Bangladesh. Though the Government of Bangladesh promised to return them to their lands, many are still dislocated. Following the return of this first refugee group in February 1994, human rights groups in Dhaka, Bangladesh conducted a survey indicating that 37 percent of the 42 families interviewed had not reclaimed their original lands[96]. One month later, the Jumma refugee welfare association, after visiting the Chittagong Hill Tracts, reported that more than 103 families had still not received the land they originally left[97].

The Returnee Jumma Refugees' 16 Points Implementation Committee states that out of the 1027 families consisting of 5186 individual refugees, 25 returnee Jummas refugees who had earlier been employed in various government jobs were not reinstated in their previous jobs, 134 returnee Jumma refugee families could not settle in their own lands due to the misappropriation of their lands by the security forces and Bengali illegal settlers and 79 families were not given back their lands as it was under forcible occupation of the illegal settlers from the plains. The Bangladesh Government also registered false cases against 23 returnee refugees[98]. The SAHRDC filed a complaint with the Indian National Human Rights Commission about the involuntary repatriation of the Jumma refugees in 1994. The NHRC asked the MHA, the MEA and the Tripura Government to reply to SAHRDC's allegations of forced repatriation[99]. the visit, the team found that many of the tube wells were out of order and that the inmates of the camps were bringing water from far-off places. The camps were also unclean and bore signs of neglect. The report noted that refugee children were suffering from malnutrition, water-borne diseases and malaria, while there was no visible effort to improve their living conditions[100]. The investigation team attributed the problems faced by the refugees, to the callousness and hostility of the officials towards the refugees, accumulated over the years, as they are not keen to go back[101].

Although the complaint of SAHRDC relating to the involuntary repatriation of the Jumma refugees in 1994 is still under the consideration of NHRC, the Government of India decided to repatriate 6,172 Jumma refugees without consulting the NHRC. The SAHRDC in a complaint on 7 March 1997 drew the attention of the NHRC about the undue duress being brought to bear upon the refugees. The NHRC failed to take any positive action to ensure voluntary repatriation exposing once again its ineffectiveness on human rights issues having geo-political dimensions[102].

Category (II) Refugees

In addition to the refugees under the care of the Government of India, there are about 20,800 Category II refugees comprised of Afghan, Iranian, Somali, Sudanese and Burmese refugees as of 1 January 1996. This includes 19,900 Afghan refugees, 200 Iranian refugees, 300 Somali refugees, 300 Burmese refugees and 100 sudanese refugees[103]. Their presence in India is acknowledged and protected under the principle of non-refoulement by the United Nations High Commissioner for Refugees. However, the condition of these refugees who receive protection and subsistence allowance from the UNHCR is no better than that of Category I refugees receiving protection from the Government of India[104].

There have been allegations that the UNHCR in Delhi has been arbitrary in its cancellation of refugee status and allowances for certain individuals. After receiving numerous complaints to this effect, SAHRDC conducted a study of the conditions of refugees protected by the UNHCR in Delhi[105]. The report about the the Status of Refugees under the Protection of the UNHCR in New Delhi, released on 1 May 1995 to examined services offered by the UNHCR to refugees in Delhi; the relevance of services available; the accessibility of such services; the UNHCR's services with regard to their attention to refugee rights and human rights and problems faced by refugees in Delhi[106].

SAHRDC found that UNHCR's New Delhi office has become a fortress. The services offered by the UNHCR were inadequate. The report stated that communication between the refugees and the UNHCR has reached an all time low. The SAHRDC has conveyed its concerns over this deterioration of relations to UNHCR officials in New Delhi on more than one occasion. The refugees view the UNHCR officials with suspicion, and do not believe that they have refugee interests at heart. UNHCR officials claim that the global policies of its organization have led to a virtual freeze on the refugee subsistence allowance in India. This has exacerbated resentment and tension in the refugee community. SAHRDC feels that there is an urgent need for a more positive financial input from the UNHCR headquarters in Geneva.

SAHRDC made recommendations to improve the conditions of the refugees and the report was forwarded to both the New Delhi Office of UNHCR and its headquarters in Geneva. SAHRDC has not received any comments as yet. SAHRDC also has good reasons to believe that the situation has not improved. Meanwhile, in a callous attempt at reduction of the case load, UNHCR arbitrarily terminated the subsistence allowance of over 2000 refugees. Destitution has allegedly led to two suicides in the refugee community. SAHRDC also has specific cases of human rights abuses on the asylum seekers from arbitrariness in determination of refugee status and suspension of subsistence allowance to beating by UNHCR security guards of asylum seekers. Though the UNHCR is only as effective as the government permits, these actions indicate a general disregard for the plight of the refugees[107].

Category (III) Refugees

A large number of ethnic Chin and other tribal refugees have escaped repression from the Burmese military and entered the Indian state of Mizoram. The presence of Chin refugees from the Chin State of Burma, Nagas from Burma, Rakhain refugees from Arakan State in Burma, and ethnic Nepalese of Bhutanese nationality is not acknowledged by the Government of India. The largest among these refugees groups is the Chins, numbering about 40,000. While the Burmese Nagas have sought refuge in the Indian State of Nagaland, the Chins and Rakhains have sought refuge in Indian State of Mizoram[108].

Though they have generally assimilated into Indian society, their living standards are still poor. They can be described as Category III refugees since neither the Indian Government nor UNHCR recognize their presence. Moreover, the Chin does not receive state assistance or international assistance because of their ambiguous status. They have been left unto themselves in a foreign land where they have no means for survival[109].

The Mizoram State Government has forcibly repatriated many Chin refugees since 1994. While it was not reported in the press, a senior official of the Mizoram State Government confirmed to a SAHRDC representative that a large number of Chin refugees indeed had been forcibly returned to Burma by the State Government in 1994[110]. The practice of the Indian Government has been to deal with refugees in three main ways:

(a) Refugees in mass influx situations are received in camps and accorded temporary protection by the Indian Government including, sometimes, a certain measure of socio-economic protection.

(b) Asylum seekers from South Asian countries, or any other country with which the government has a sensitive relationship, apply to the government for political asylum which is usually granted without an extensive refugee status determination subject, of course, to political exigencies.

(c) Citizens of other countries apply to the Office of the UNHCR for individual refugee status determination in accordance with the terms of the UNHCR Statute and the Refugee Convention.

The ambivalence of India's refugee policy is sharply brought out in relation to its treatment of the UNHCR. While no formal arrangement exists between the Indian government and the UNHCR, India continues to sit on the UNHCR's Executive Committee in Geneva. Furthermore, India has not signed or ratified the Refugee Convention. This creates a paradoxical and rather baffling situation regarding the UNHCR where India sits on its Executive Committee and allows the UNHCR to operate on its territory, but refuses to sign the legal instrument that brought the organisation into existence[111].

Given the legal vacuum with regard to refugees, the process of addressing large-scale refugee inflows over the years has been *ad hoc*, mainly through executive action. This process is far from appropriate and is often governed by 'political instinct' based on India's diplomatic relations with the country of origin at the time[112].

The Foreigners Act 1946 is an outdated and draconian piece of legislation that defines a foreigner as any person who is not a citizen of India, and includes refugees. A similar provision was also introduced through an amendment to the Indian Citizenship Act in 2003 which fails to make any distinction between refugees and their special circumstances and other foreigners and illegal immigrants.

Under Section 3 (2) of the Act, the Indian government has wide discretionary powers to regulate the entry and movement of foreigners within India. The Foreigners Order 1948 also restricts the entry of foreigners into Indian Territory at given entry points without proper authorisation. Every foreigner should be in possession of a valid passport and visa at the time of entry into India, unless exempted. Most often, refugees are not in possession of these documents and thus are refused entry into India. Article 51 (c) of the Indian Constitution provides that.

"India shall endeavour to foster respect for international law and treaty obligations in the dealings of organised peoples with one another" and Article 253 of the Constitution gives the Indian Parliament the *"power to make any law for the whole or any part of the territory of India for implementing any treaty, agreement or convention with any other country or countries or any decision made at any international conference, association or other body"*[113].

The Indian judiciary has also ruled in favour of harmonious construction of international and domestic law when it is consistent with fundamental rights (Visakha vs. State of Rajasthan, 1997 [6] [SCC] 241). The scope and ambit of Articles 14 and 21 of the Indian Constitution, through progressive judicial interpretation, extends to non-citizens including refugees. In the landmark judgment of the Chakma refugee case, the Supreme Court clearly held that the State was under a constitutional obligation to protect refugees (National Human Rights Commission vs. State of Arunachal Pradesh, AIR 1996 SC 1234)[114]. In Malvika Karlekar vs. Union of India (Criminal Writ Petition No 243 of 1988), the Supreme Court stayed the deportation of Burmese refugees in the Andaman and Nicobar Islands, as their applications for refugee status were pending with the UNHCR[115].

A national model refugee law for granting statutory protection to refugees has long been considered in India but is yet to be implemented. The model law aims to harmonise norms and standards on refugee law, establish a procedure for granting refugee status and guarantee them their rights and fair treatment[116].

In India, refugees are placed under three broad categories. Category I refugees receive full protection from the Indian government (for example, Tamil refugees from Sri Lanka); Category II refugees are those who are granted refugee status by the UNHCR and are protected under the principle of *non-refoulement* (for example, Burmese and Afghan refugees); and Category III refugees who are neither recognised by the Indian government nor the UNHCR but have entered India and assimilated into the local community (for example, Chin refugees from Burma living in the state of Mizoram)[117].

In the absence of a concrete domestic refugee policy in India, the refugee certificate of the UNHCR is of utmost importance. However, refugees complain that the UNHCR refugee determination process is arbitrary, complicated and full of delays. The SAHRDC reports that refugees and their representative NGOs do not understand the UNHCR's criteria for refugee status determination and often complain of unfair treatment during the interview process. Language barriers between refugees and the UNHCR authorities serve as a severe constraint in effective communication, despite the presence of Burmese interpreters. Those whose applications are rejected are not given reasons for the same and yet they have the right to appeal the decision before the same authorities, rendering the appeals process practically meaningless. Delays in the refugee determination process, with interviews being rescheduled, cancelled or interview letters not reaching on time further jeopardise the refugees' conditions.

Given the fact that even recognised refugees do not have the legal right to work in India and are not issued a valid work permit, these vocational training courses are futile as they do not lead to self-reliance, as unrealistically envisaged by the UNHCR. Even those refugees who do complete the vocational training courses on offer have no guarantee of employment or a regular source of income. Lack of legal protection over identity and employment subject them to workplace and pay-related discrimination. They can seek employment in the informal job market and their employers can hire and fire them without too much difficulty. According to noted human rights activist Ravi Nair, many recognised refugees cannot avail of this scheme as they are unable to provide the necessary documents such as a residential permit and address proof establishing their identity as refugees, to the UNHCR[118].

Most refugees living in India do not see 'local integration' as a viable solution to their problems. This is primarily attributable to their antagonistic relationship with the local community. As foreigners, they are often treated as outsiders by the local population and language barriers further deepen the divide between the two. Burmese refugees living in west Delhi face discrimination at the hands of their host community. Landlords evict refugee families on a regular basis on the pretext of late rent payments and other related problems. Given their poor financial position, refugees are forced to live in small, overcrowded apartments with no electricity, water, cooking or sanitation facilities. Although the YMCA conducts home visits to assess the real living conditions of refugees, the infrequent nature of these visits and insensitivity of staff conducting the visits hurt rather than help refugee interests. With respect to Afghan refugees, the SAHRDC reported that inconsistent needs assessment surveys conducted by the YMCA, and lack of understanding of refugee problems, led to the SA cut-offs[119].

The Socio-Legal Information Centre (SLIC) is authorised by the UNHCR to provide legal assistance to recognised refugees. Refugees are required to obtain a Residential Permit (RP) from the Foreigners Regional Registration Office (FRRO) of the MHA which has to be renewed on a bi-annual basis. Refugees are harassed by the FRRO officials who refuse to issue or renew RPs or unnecessarily delay the process.

Refugees also face the constant threat of illegal arrest, detention and deportation[120]. According to the World Refugee Survey 2007, a number of Burmese nationals were deported from Mizoram and the UNHCR could not intervene due to lack of access. Some Bhutanese refugees were also deported to Nepal. Four refugees were detained in West Bengal on illegal immigration charges, of whom three were subsequently released. Similar cases of detention were also reported from New Delhi[121]. Despite the high number of illegal arrests and detention of refugees, the SLIC has been of limited assistance. Despite its limitations, however, the UNHCR is often the last beacon of hope for many refugees who flee to India in search of a secure refuge. However, in the recent past, refugees under UNHCR protection have been losing faith in a system that is plagued by insensitivity and inefficiency. To redeem itself in the eyes of those it seeks to protect, the UNHCR must engage directly with refugee communities to better understand their problems rather than delegate all responsibility to its implementing partners. It must also strengthen the refugee status determination process and ensure effective monitoring and implementation of its health, education and legal services. At the same time, it must exert pressure on the Indian government to ratify the 1951 Convention and enact domestic legislation for refugee protection[122].

In the absence of a specialised statutory framework, India relies on the Foreigners Act, 1946 to govern the entry, stay and exit of foreigners in India. However, the Foreigners Act is an archaic legislation that was enacted by a colonial government in response to the needs of the Second World War (3) Section 2(a) of the Act defines as, thus covering all refugees within its ambit as well. Without a specialised governance regime for country of his former habitual residence as a result of such events, is unable or, owing to such fear, is unwilling to return to it. The unrestricted power of the executive to remove foreigners was first confirmed by the Supreme Court in1955[123].

However, foreigners are entitled to some degree of constitutional protection while in India. These include the protection of the equality clause (Article 14) and the life, liberty and due process provisions (Article 21) of the Indian Constitution. While Article 14 guarantees equality before the law and the equal treatment of the law, classifications of persons into separate and distinct classes based on intelligible differentia with a nexus to the object of the classification are allowed. Article 21 protects any person from the deprivation of his life or personal liberty except according to procedure established by law. From a rather staid interpretation of this provision, the Supreme Court has radically reinterpreted Article 21 to include a substantive due process of law to be foll[124]. Foreigners enjoy the protection of Article 21 in two ways:

(a) They are equally entitled to the right against deprivation of life or bodily integrity and dignity.

(b) To a certain extent, the right against executive action sans procedural due process accrues to them.

India has received and accommodated mass influx refugees from Tibet and Sri Lanka in special camps with varying facilities for health, education and employment. Asylum seekers who enter India individually after a mass influx has taken place are granted asylum after a preliminary screening mechanism. This process continues in the case of Tibetans and Sri Lankans who enter India in small numbers and must fulfill certain criteria before they are registered by the Indian Government. In 2003, the UNHCR handled, inter alia, 10,283 refugees from Afghanistan and 940 refugees from Myanmar. The UNHCR also handles refugees from Iran, Somalia, Sudan and other countries[125]. Indian courts, while generally strictly interpreting the stringent legislation on foreigners by refusing to interfere with the powers of the executive, have, on occasion, evolved a wider and more humane approach to protect the rights of refugees in India.

In 1996, the Supreme Court in National Human Rights Commission Versus State of Arunachal Pradesh[126] intervened with a liberal interpretation of the law to suggest that refugees are a class apart from foreigners deserving of the protection of Article 21 of the Constitution[127]. The need for a stable and secure guarantee of refugee protection in India led to the establishment of an Eminent Persons Group (EPG), chaired by former Chief Justice P. N. Bhagwati, to suggest a model law for refugee protection. However, the process of drafting appropriate refugee protection legislation began earlier at the Third South Asian Informal Regional Consultation on Refugee Migratory Movements, where a five-member working group was constituted to draft a model refugee protection law for the South Asian region[128]. The India-specific model law was born out of this regional consultative process to provide statutory protection to refugees in the diverse South Asian region. Despite technical or specific misgivings about the model law, there has been unanimity about its necessity and widespread acceptance of its use as a framework for future protection[129].

With this conclusion one hopes to examine the question as to whether international refugee law is in conflict in any way with Indian legislations or, in the absence of such legislations, with Indian attitude and policy on refugees[130]. India never had a clear policy as to whom to grant refugee status. When the question of adoption of a Convention and establishment of an agency for the international protection of refugees came for discussion in the Third Committee of the UN General Assembly, in 1949, the Indian delegation expressed its views on these issues. India would have voted for the establishment of a High Commissioner's Office if it had been convinced that there was a great need to set up an elaborate international organisation whose sole responsibility would be to give refugees legal protection. It was believed that at a time when its own refugees were dying of starvation, India felt obliged to vote against all the resolutions submitted, and hoped that its stand would not be misinterpreted[131]. After the Convention was adopted India did not ratify or accede, and the reasons for not doing so are never disclosed except that it was stated in the Parliament by the former External Affairs Minister, B R Bhagat that since the government had come up with certain basic difficulties, the implications, if India ratifies these Conventions, were under study. In other words, India's initial stand on the treaty regime of the refugee law was declared to be a subject of review[132]. Refuting this claim, Indian human rights groups do point to specific cases of refoulement, where clear evidence and refugee testimony prove that forcible repatriation has taken place. A closer examination of India's refugee policy reveals a number of intricate problems[133].

India no doubt reasonably have a good record of providing protection and hospitality to refugees, while pointing out the contradictions in the relation between these positive aspects and the manner in which state power has been exercised in post-colonial India. In examining the varied encounters between the state and refugees, the contributors demonstrate that India's story of providing care is simultaneously one of limiting care. It reveals the power of the state to decide whom to extend hospitality to and whom to deny it to. Thus, the issue of affording asylum becomes one of exercising power on the part of India's political establishment. Providing protection and humanitarian assistance to those seeking refuge, argue the contributors, should not be a question of dispensing kindness. What is required in place of a regime of charity is a regime of rights and policy.

References

1. G. Loescher (1993), The Origins of the International Refugee Regime, in *Beyond Charity: International Co-operation and the Global Refugee Crisis,* Oxford University Press, Oxford, pp. 32–55.

2. See website, http://www.achrweb.org, Indian Human Rights Report 2007.

3. *Ibid.*

4. Judgment of Supreme Court of India (1996), Original Civil Jurisdiction, Writ Petition (Civil) No. 720 of 1995, Between NHRC versus State of Arunachal Pradesh, 9th January, New Delhi.

5. See for detail information on the provisions of citizenship, Constitution of India.
6. Crime Statistics of Arunachal Pradesh State police, The Telegraph, 13 December 2006.
7. NHRC Vs State of Arunachal Pradesh and Anr (720/1995) and the present plight of the Chakmas of Arunachal Pradesh, 16th December 2002, Committee for Citizenship Rights of the Chakmas of Arunachal Pradesh.
8. 37 percent women face domestic violence; Bihar tops list, *The Hindu*, 4 March 2007.
9. Nearly 45 percent women married off before 18: NFHS, *The Hindu* 24, February 2007.
10. The Telegraph, 13 December 2006.
11. Arunachal is the only state with no prison, The Asian Age, 3 August 2006.
12. See for detail Court News, July-September 2006, Supreme Court of India.
13. Judgment of Supreme Court of India (1996), Original Civil Jurisdiction, Writ Petition (Civil) No. 720 of 1995, Between NHRC versus State of Arunachal Pradesh, 9th January, New Delhi.
14. During my field visit it has been explored that many of the applicants have already died and this is nothing but contempt of the highest court of the country.
15. The Hindu, 4 May, 2004.
16. See for detail the Crime Statistics of Arunachal Pradesh State police.
17. See for detail Court News, July-September 2006, Supreme Court of India.
18. Nearly 45 percent women married off before 18: NFHS, The Hindu, 24, February 2007.
19. Wild Buffalo; Mithun is the state animal of Arunachal Pradesh.
20. The Telegraph, 13 December 2006.
21. *Boddhi Times*, No. 6, June 2009.

22. *Ibid.*

23. NHRC Vs State of Arunachal Pradesh and Anr (720/1995) and the present plight of the Chakmas of Arunachal Pradesh, 16 December 2002, Committee for Citizenship Rights of the Chakmas of Arunachal Pradesh.

24. Deepak K. Singh (2001), Refugee question in Arunachal Pradesh: Some conflicting currents' Journal of Anthropological Survey of India, 50(4), December, pp. 95-102.

25. NHRC Vs State of Arunachal Pradesh & Anr (720/1995) and the present plight of the Chakmas of Arunachal Pradesh, 16 December 2002, Committee for Citizenship Rights of the Chakmas of Arunachal Pradesh.

26. *Ibid.*

27. *Ibid.*

28. *Ibid.*

29. Deepak K. Singh (2001), Refugee question in Arunachal Pradesh: Some conflicting currents, Journal of Anthropological Survey of India, 50(4), December, pp. 95-102.

30. NHRC Vs State of Arunachal Pradesh and Anr (720/1995) and the present plight of the Chakmas of Arunachal Pradesh, 16 December 2002, Committee for Citizenship Rights of the Chakmas of Arunachal Pradesh.

31. *Ibid.*

32. *Ibid.*

33. *Ibid.*

34. *Ibid.*

35. *Ibid.*

36. *Ibid.*

37. *Ibid.*

38. *Ibid.*

39. See India Human Rights Report 2007, (www.achrweb.org/reports/india/AR07/arunachal.htm).

40. Rajya Sabha, committee on petition, hundred and fifth, report,

(presented on the 14th august 1997), Rajya Sabha secretariat, New Delhi, august 1997, New Delhi: (O. Rajagopal), 14 august 1997 chairman, Committee on petition.

41. D.D, Basu (2004), The Introduction to the Constitution of India, See the articles related to the Citizenship rights, pp. 54-58.

42. *Ibid.*

43. NHRC Vs State of Arunachal Pradesh & Anr (720/1995) and the present plight of the Chakmas of Arunachal Pradesh16th December 2002 Committee for Citizenship Rights of the Chakmas of Arunachal Pradesh.

45. In the cases of Luis de Readt (1991) 3 SCC 554 and Khudiriam (nos. 1994 Supp. (1) SCC 615, the Supreme held that Article 21 of the Constitution of India, which protects the life, and liberty of Indian citizens are extended to all, including aliens.

46. P. Oberoi (2006), Exile and Belonging: Refugees and State Policy in South Asia, Oxford University Press, New Delhi, pp. 77–103.

47. Tapan K. Bose (2000), India: Policies and Laws towards Refugees, Vol, 10, No. 10, October, Article appeared on the website of Human Rights Solidarity, www.hrsolidarity.net.

44. *Ibid.*

48. Supreme Court Civil WP No. 720/95: 1996 (1) Supreme, 295.

49. Tapan K. Bose (2000), India: Policies and Laws towards Refugees, Vol, 10, No. 10, October, Article appeared on the website of Human Rights Solidarity, www.hrsolidarity.net.

50. *Ibid.*

51. Supreme Court Civil Rule No. 516 of 1991.

52. Tapan K. Bose (2000), India: Policies and Laws towards Refugees, Vol, 10, No. 10, October, Article appeared on the website of Human Rights Solidarity, www.hrsolidarity.net.

53. B.S, Chimni (1999), From Resettlement to Repatriation: Towards a Critical History of Durable Solutions to Refugee Problems, UNHCR.

54. *Ibid.*

55. See Constitution of India for detail information on the article related to the protection of individuals.

56. The Hindu, 24 June, 2004.

57. See Judgment of Supreme Court of India (1996), Original Civil Jurisdiction, Writ Petition (Civil) No. 720 of 1995, Between NHRC versus State of Arunachal Pradesh, 9 January, New Delhi.

58. B.S.Chimni (2005), Outside the Bounds of Citizenship: The Status of Aliens, Illegal Migrants and Refugees in India in edited book by Rajiv Bhargava and Helmut Reifeld, Civil Society, Public Sphere and Citizenship, Dialogues and Perceptions, Sage Publication, New Delhi, pp. 277-313.

59. *Ibid.*

60. The Hindu, 20 June, 2009.

61. The Hindu 27 December, 2010.

62. The Hindu 27 December, 2010.

63. The Telegraph, June 11, 2009.

64. See website, http://news.oneindia.in, urges-centre-to-resolve-contentious-refugee-issue, February 1, 2008.

64. *Ibid.*

65. P. Oberoi (2006), Exile and Belonging: Refugees and State Policy in South Asia, Oxford University Press, New Delhi, pp. 77–103.

66. B.S.Chimni (2005), Outside the Bounds of Citizenship: The Status of Aliens, Illegal Migrants and Refugees in India in edited book by Rajiv Bhargava and Helmut Reifeld, Civil Society, Public Sphere and Citizenship, Dialogues and Perceptions, Sage Publication, New Delhi, pp. 277-313.

67. See website, http://www.legalserviceindia.com, article by Isha Bothra on refugees in India.

68. P. Oberoi (2006), Exile and Belonging: Refugees and State Policy in South Asia, Oxford University Press, New Delhi, pp. 77 – 103.

69. Under the Constitution of India, powers and functions are

divided into Union List (Federal Government) and State List (Provincial Government or State Government).

70. See website, http://www.hrdc.net, article published on the issue related to refugees by South Asian Human Rights Documentation Centre, New Delhi, October, 1997.

71. See website, http://infochangeindia.org, article by Ipshita Sengupta on UNHCR 's role in refugee protection in India

72. See website, http://www.legalserviceindia.com, article by Isha Bothra on refugees in India.

73. See for detail, Constitution of Indian Article 51C.

74. See website, http://www.hrdc.net, article published on the issue related to refugees by South Asian Human Rights Documentation Centre, New Delhi, October, 1997.

75. V.T. Patil and P.R. Trivedi (2000), Migration, Refugees and Security in the 21st Century, Authors Press, Delhi, pp. 8-31.

76. Sri Lankan Tamil Refugees in Tamilnadu Camps, Voluntary Repatriation or Subtle Refoulment, South Asia Human Rights Documentation Centre, New Delhi, January 1996.

77. *Ibid.*

78. South Asian Human Rights Documentation Centre (1997), Refugee Protection in India, Report, October, New Delhi.

79. *Ibid.*

80. *Ibid.*

81. *Ibid.*

82. The "Q" branch is the Special Branch of the Tamil Nadu Police. It is known for illegal arrests, unacknowledged detention, torture, harassment and intimidation of Tamil refugees. It is also used against political opponents and trade union activists.

83. Sri Lankan Tamil Refugees in Tamil Nadu Camps - Voluntary Repatriation or Subtle Refoulement, South Asia Human Rights Documentation Centre, New Delhi, January 1996.

84. South Asian Human Rights Documentation Centre (1997), Refugee Protection in India, Report, October, New Delhi.

85. Sri Lankan Tamil Refugees in India: Accords, People and the

UNHCR, presented by the Jesuit Refugee Service, South Asia in a seminar on Refugees, migrants and displaced peoples in South Asia, organised by South Asia Forum for Human Rights in Katmandu, Nepal, October 1996.

86. *Ibid.*

87. SAHRDC News, New Delhi, July-August 1995, Volume 1, Number 2.

88. B.S. Chimni (2005), Outside the Bounds of Citizenship: The Status of Aliens, Illegal Migrants and Refugees in India in edited book by Rajiv Bhargava and Helmut Reifeld, Civil Society, Public Sphere and Citizenship, Dialogues and Perceptions, Sage Publication, New Delhi, pp. 277-313.

89. Sri Lankan Tamil Refugees in Tamil Nadu Camps - Voluntary Repatriation or Subtle Refoulement, South Asia Human Rights Documentation Centre, New Delhi, January 1996.

90. Ibid.

91. No Secure Refuge, South Asia Human Rights Documentation Centre, New Delhi, 14 February 1994.

92. The Hindustan Times, New Delhi, 28 November 1995.

93. Private communication, from the CHTs Jumma Refugees Welfare Association to the SAHRDC in November 1995.

94. *Ibid.*

95. *Ibid.*

96. Returnee Refugees: Frustrated for not getting promised help - a report of Bangladesh Manab Adhikar Sammanay Parishad, National Committee for the Protection of Fundamental Rights in CHTs, Jatiyo Mahila Ainjibi Samiti, Ain-O-Salish Kendra and Human Rights Journalist Forum, Dhaka, Bangladesh, 27 May 1994.

97. Report on the visit of Jumma refugee team to the Chittagong Hill Tracts, Bangladesh on 14 & 15 March 1995", Takumbari, Tripura, India, 4 April 1995.

98. Memorandum of Returnee Jumma Refugees 16 Points Implementation Committee, Khagrachari, Bangladesh, 15 October 1996.

99. South Asian Human Rights Documentation Centre (1997), Refugee Protection in India, Report, October, New Delhi.

100. Human Rights Newsletter, National Human Rights Commission, New Delhi, July 1996.

101. Letter of the National Human Rights Commission on 13 August 1996.

102. Complaint of the South Asia Human Rights Documentation Centre on 7 March 1997.

103. Draft Report of the 47th Session of the Executive Committee of the UNHCR, Geneva, 7-11 October 1996.

104. B.S.Chimni (2005), Outside the Bounds of Citizenship: The Status of Aliens, Illegal Migrants and Refugees in India in edited book by Rajiv Bhargava and Helmut Reifeld, Civil Society, Public Sphere and Citizenship, Dialogues and Perceptions, Sage Publication, New Delhi, pp. 277-313.

105. The Status of Refugees under the Protection of UNHCR in New Delhi, SAHRDC/0131/1/95 of 1 May 1995, New Delhi.

106. South Asian Human Rights Documentation Centre (1997), Refugee Protection in India, Report, October, New Delhi.

107. *Ibid.*

108. SAHRDC News, New Delhi, Jul-Aug 1995, Volume 1, Number 2.

109. *Ibid.*

110. This was stated by the Chief Secretary of Mizoram State Government in a hearing on the harassment of the Chakmas at the National Human Rights Commission on 8 November 1996.

111. See website, http://www.legalserviceindia.com, article by Isha Bothra on refugees in India.

112. See website, at http://news.indlaw.com, Bhairav Acharya, the Law, Policy and Practice of Refugee Protection in India' 2004.

113. P. Oberoi (2006), Exile and Belonging: Refugees and State Policy in South Asia, Oxford University Press, New Delhi, pp. 77–103.

114. Judgment of Supreme Court of India (1996), Original Civil

Jurisdiction, Writ Petition (Civil) No. 720 of 1995, Between NHRC versus State of Arunachal Pradesh, 9th January, New Delhi.

115. See website, http://www.uscr.org, India Scores Low on Refugee Protection', SAHRDC press release, July 11, 2007.

116. Trakroo, A. Bhat, and S. Nandi (eds.) (2006), Refugees and the Law, Human Rights Law Network, Delhi, pp. 68–76.

117. See website, http://www.hrdc.net, SAHRDC, 'Refugee Protection in India', October 1997.

118. See website, http://www.himalmag.com, Ravi Nair, 'The UNHCR Refugee Agency has been Oddly Listless in Addressing the Problems Faced by Burmese Refugees in Delhi', Himal South Asian, December 2006.

119. SAHRDC, 'Abandoned and Betrayed: Afghan Refugees Under UNCHR Protection in New Delhi', November 1999.

120. See website, http://www.refugees.org, World Refugee Survey 2007, Country Report: India.

121. See website, http://infochangeindia.org, article by Ipshita Sengupta on UNHCR's role in refugee protection in India.

122. See website, http://infochangeindia.org, article by Ipshita Sengupta on UNHCR's role in refugee protection in India.

123. The Foreigners Act confers the power to expel foreigners from India. It vests the Central Government with absolute and unfettered discretion and, as there is no provision fettering this discretion in the Constitution, an unrestricted right to expel remains. The untrammeled right of the executive to remove foreigners from India has been upheld by the Supreme Court in a number of subsequent decisions.

124. Rajeev, Dhavan (1996), Rajeev, Treaties and People: Indian Reflections, 44 JILI, pp. 362-376.

125. See, the UNHCR Statistical Yearbook India , 2003, UNHCR Geneva.

126. Indian Constitution confers certain rights on every human being and certain other rights on citizens. Every person is entitled to equality before the law and equal protection of the laws. So also, no person can be deprived of his life or personal

liberty except according to procedure established by law. Thus the State is bound to protect the life and liberty of every human being, be he a citizen or otherwise, and it cannot permit anybody or group of persons, e.g., the AAPSU, to threaten the Chakmas to leave the State, failing which they would be forced to do so, 1996, 1 SSC, 742, we are a country governed by the Rule of Law.

127. The Eight Annual Report of the National Human Rights Commission, 2002-2003 at pp. 5.20-5.21.

128. The first draft of this proposed law was presented at the 1997 SAARC LAW Seminar in New Delhi, modified and then adopted by the Fourth Annual Meeting of the Regional Consultation at Dhaka in 1997.

129. See website, http://www.legalserviceindia.com, article by Isha Bothra on refugees in India.

130. Trakroo, A. Bhat, and S. Nandi (eds.) (2006), Refugees and the Law, Human Rights Law Network, Delhi, pp. 68–76.

131. Summary Records of the third Committee meeting 259 (10 November 1949), GAOR, Sixth Session, p. 8143; and Mrs. Kripalani, *Ibid.*, mtg 263 (15 November 1949), p. 8144.

132.. India, Lok Sabha Debates, Vol. XVII, 7 May 1986, Col. 32.

133. *Ibid.*

Conclusion

India is a largest country experiencing refugeehood. During her liberation in 1947, an estimated 10 million people took refuge from neighbouring countries. India has been hosting refugees for a long time, however it is not a state party to the UN Convention relating to the status of refugees 1951 or its Protocol of 1967. There is also no domestic legal framework to deal with the issue of asylum and refugees. Although there are few provisions in the Indian Constitution, which could be translated for the protection of refugees, however there is a lack of common understanding on those. In this backdrop, there is a point for India for accession to the UN Convention relating to the status of refugees 1951 and adoption of a normative legal framework. The Refugee Convention was adopted at a special UN conference on 28 July 1951. The convention is the basic instrument of Refugee Laws that defines a refugee, and sets out the rights of them and the responsibilities of states that grant asylum.

The convention also sets out which people do not qualify as refugees, such as war criminals or having involved on serious non-political crimes among others. Protection of refugees forms the core of all Human Rights Law and Humanitarian Law. However, since its inception there have been many objections to the provisions of the Convention. It is said that the Convention mandates protection for those whose civil and political rights are violated. However, it does not protect persons whose socio-economic rights are at risk. For example, the Convention is unable to cover the need of the IDP and the latest consequences of the global warming, the climate refugees. Apart from that, the Convention needs for further revisions due to increased complexities in the process of refugee generation, protection and due to advance in the field of refugee studies.

The Convention has been the point of contention for the developed and developing countries. While developed countries are bidding for a rights-based approach; developing countries on the other hand have been voicing their incomprehension as to why they would be expected to abide by the standards that the North no longer seems to accept. It is likely that now the Northern countries assume only a fraction of the responsibilities for refugees. It mainly finds four dilemmas in the Convention with regard to refugee for example; definition, material assistance, shared responsibilities, and unravelling consensus in observing standards of international law. Developed countries have already developed and implemented the concept of *'third country protection'* or *'offshore asylum system'*. These types of initiatives are contradictory to the spirit of the Convention. Even senior officials of the UNHCR openly support modifications in the Convention. Ms. Carol Batchelor, Chief of Mission of UNHCR in India says,

"the Convention has to be looked into from different angles or perspectives considering the present scenario,"[1]

In this scenario, none of the South Asian Countries is a signatory to the Refugee Convention, few citing certain biases in the provisions of the Convention. B.S. Chimni feels that before acceding to the 1951 Convention or 1967 Protocol, South Asian States should go ahead for adoption of a rights-based national legal framework to deal with asylum and refugee issues. Enacting a comprehensive national legislation from the above discussion, it is clear that given the drawbacks in the Convention, it is very unlikely that South Asian Countries should sign the instrument in near future[2].

Therefore, adoption of national legislation will be a more viable option for the countries including Bangladesh. The benefits of national legislation are manifold. These include dissolution of adoption of ad-hoc measures; permanent mechanisms for determination and treatment of refugees; ensuring judicious, fair and accountable procedures; enhancement of administrative control of the state; achieving concerted search for durable solution; co-ordination among concerned agencies; reducing frictions and conflicts among states. These hardly consider protection needs of an individual, especially in case of women and children. Again, due to lack of any explicit legal regime, asylum seekers and refugees are dealt under ad-hoc administrative arrangements, which by their very nature could be arbitrary and discriminatory, and do not accord any right to the refugees. Therefore, the government should be serious on the matter. It is a high time that Government of India adopts a comprehensive policy on Chakma refugee issues in particular and others in general with a view to resolve the problem through bilateral and multi-lateral means. It largely requires pro-active diplomacy. A rights-based approach as to domestic legislation is to give weight within a framework that recognizes the distinctive essence of humanitarian problems and gives legal recognition to the fact that every person, alien or national, is of equal moral worth, and worthy of treatment that does not violate his/her dignity. The law should have provisions, among others, on the definition of refugees, asylum procedure, rights and obligation, status of mixed-mirages, cancellation and cessation processor of refugee status etc.

The Ministry of Home Affairs formulates the policies and programmes for relief and rehabilitation of people of Indian origin displaced from other countries. It has also been entrusted with the work of providing relief to the Tibetan and Srilankan refugees. Various relief and rehabilitation schemes are being implemented by the Ministry of Home Affairs through the State Governments and Union Territory Administrations. A wide range of measure was taken for resettlement of *'old migrants'* during the period 1948 to 1961. These included agricultural schemes, vocational and technical training schemes and rehabilitation loans for small traders, businessmen and professionals and provision of housing, medical and educational facilities. Another measure was taken to resettled *'new migrants'* who arrived between January 1, 1964 and March 25, 1971. All these migrants largely resettled in the eastern and north-eastern states of India. The settlement wing functions as a subordinate office of the Rehabilitation Division of the Ministry of Home Affairs and deals with residuary matters of resettlement of displaced persons from former West Pakistan under the Displaced Persons Compensation and Rehabilitation Act, 1954 and the rules framed there under.

So far the India's refugee regime is concerned she should frame its refugee law and has to put her refugees in different categories, reason due to their historical divide and injustice. Chakmas are such a category who comes under it. Chakmas, who settled in 1964, is almost more than five decades from now, are reclaiming their basic human dignity which they were denied on various occasions by the State Government as well as civil society groups. My field work explored that the socio-economic and political conditions of the Chakmas in the settled districts of Papumpare, Lohit, and Changlang are very poor and no one is concerned about the problems of these people. The whole debates on the issue of Chakmas are largely related to the question of citizenship and survival with dignity.

Marshallian theory of citizenship focuses on interest groups and the states creation of citizenship rights. Cultural rights focuses on identity and are much more concerned with the formation and operation of social movements, and skipping a level of globalisation and national civil society. Along with the citizenship rights as being concentrated to the state, theories of civil society also need to be developed to provide the informal aspects of citizenship integrating both the public and private spheres. In the 1967 Protocol, there is no procedural mechanism for providing official protection or benefits to refugees living in India. UNHCR, however, does have a presence in India and continues to register, recognize and resettle Chakma refugees.

Arunachalees have the misconception that Chakmas look like Bengalis, since they were from Bangladesh so they are not tribals like them which is not true at all. The Chakmas were given land in Arunachal Pradesh by the Indian government with the intention of permanently settling them. They thought that the Chakmas can again build their shattered life in the state. Chakmas were settled in the state on humanitarian basis. Also, the government thought that they will be comfortable living in the state as they were also tribal and Buddhist by religion. That was one of the reason they were settled near the Khamtis and Singphos, who were also Buddhist and tribals. From the time the Chakmas were settled in the state, they were given employment opportunities like in paramilitary forces. Some were also given government jobs. There were no problem and no question of citizenship as they were given equal opportunities like any other Indian citizen. There was no discrimination towards them since Arunachal Pradesh was union territory (NEFA) at that time. But the problem started after it was made a full fledge state.

Under the chief ministership of Gegong Apang, slowly all the facilities given to the Chakmas by the Union Government were withdrawn like ration cards, free books for the students, drinking water, electricity etc. After some time, the Circle Officer of Diyun gave a circular ordering the Chakmas to surrender their ration cards, which added more miseries to the life of the community. Since almost all the Chakmas were dependent on agriculture, even after toiling days after days they don't get enough rice to sustain them throughout the year. So they depended on the PDS for rice and kerosene oil for lighting their home at night. Thus, snatching away of those facilities resulted in hunger among the community. This was not only a crime against the helpless Chakmas but also a crime against humanity. In order to add more miseries to the already piled mountain of miseries, the Arunachal Pradesh Government ordered the closure of most of the schools in Chakma areas. The Chakma children were also prevented from looking for admission in other nearby schools in Chowkham. This inhumane step taken by the State Government had resulted to a generation of illiterate children among the Chakmas and till date the middle school is lying vacant to be re-opened.

The injustice was not only done to the Chakmas of Lohit but also to their fellows of Changlang and Papumpare districts. In Changlang district, the Chakma students were prevented to take admission in any of the government schools. Some of the students studying in Miao Senior Secondary School, Innao Senior Secondary School, Namsai Senior Secondary School, etc. had to leave the school in the middle of the academic session rendering hundreds of students' school-less. Till now Chakma students are denied admission in any of the government run schools after primary. The only school open to the Chakmas in Changlang district is the Diyun secondary school where more than 150 students study in a single class room. In grade six, more than 250 students sit in a single class room. The pressure in grade six is more since the entire student from various villages comes to take admission in Diyun. Since there is no other school to accommodate the student, the Head Master is bound to give admission to the entire student. Also all the schools in Chakma areas were dying from lack of teacher, proper school building. Only one teacher is allotted for a primary school which is very difficult for a single teacher to maintain discipline in five classes at the same time. Such is the pathetic condition of the Chakma students only because they are born in Chakma community of Arunachal Pradesh they have to go through this ordeal.

Letter the Chief Minister of Arunachal Pradesh requested the Prime Minister Manmohan Singh to constitute a high-level committee to solve the Chakma problems in the state.[3] It is really difficult to understand whether the committee will be made from the Centre or from the State Assembly. As already a high power committee had been constituted in the state few months back with Setong Sena as the Chairman. The problem can only to be solved if the willingness comes from the politician as it is a political problem. Only constituting high level committee will take the problem to nowhere.

The question that is persisting in the minds of all those who believe in humanity is that being born and brought up in India, according to the Citizenship Act, 1955 and also the Citizenship (Amendment) Act, 2003 of section 3-1(a) every person born in India on or after the 26th day of January, 1950, but before the 1st day of July, 1987, shall be citizen of India by birth. Then, why is this not applicable to the Chakmas of Arunachal Pradesh? Why they have to go through the trauma of leveling them as refugees? Also according to International Convention a person should not be denied a citizenship on the basis of caste, community, religion. But then why the Arunachalees Chakmas are denied nationality? It's been almost five decades and still Chakmas in Arunachal Pradesh living with a doubt, that whether they are Indian or refugees. Ironically, all other Chakmas who were settled in other parts of India are leading a normal life like any other Indian citizen. Then, why is injustice being done to the Arunachalees Chakmas? Because of this injustice the future of thousands of Chakma children is hanging in balance. They are not getting education. The youth are not getting any jobs. But one thing is clear that "For every action, there is an equal and opposite reaction". This is not only Newton Third law motion but it is equally applicable to our daily life.

Chakmas don't have any source of employment, as the Arunachal Pradesh Government stops providing employment to the Chakma. It is also difficult to find job outside the state. Chakmas are frustrated when they see their friends from other communities when they get jobs just after passing Class 10 or 12; they are unemployed even after doing graduation. Is not this pure *'discrimination'*? Despite being more educated and qualified they are being ignored in job opportunities even in their place of birth. The state government should find a solution to the Chakma citizenship issue as soon as possible otherwise; the situation may go out of control. Nobody wants Arunachal Pradesh to be another Manipur. It is important to remember that the educated militants are more dangerous than the uneducated ones. The Chakma society as a whole is a non-violent society. Also they are Buddhist by religion. Nobody supports any type of violence, because once any community take up arms, that society is bound to be doomed, unless any good leader is there to guide the whole community. Look at the example of Pakistan; they are violent society, now Pakistan is almost a failed state. The Chakma youth who joined those militant groups must have done without the consent of their parents and society and they must have done out of their frustration in life. So, it is the responsibility of both the society and the state government to bring them into the mainstream. The State Government should start giving employment opportunities to all the youth without discrimination base on community, caste, religion, tradition, sex, ethnicity, nationality etc.

Now a day there are lots of talks about the issue of development in Arunachal Pradesh. Chief Minister Dorjee Khandu has taken the oath to root out corruption, streamlining of the PDS, time-bound accelerated implementation of power projects and other critical on-going schemes related to developmental activities which have direct bearing on the life of rural poor of the state. Now, people got very high expectation from Dorjee's regime and changes are expected to be seen very soon. But, what ever developmental activities and project are going on are mainly centered in western and central part of the state. There are no development projects slated for Changlang and Lohit districts and not realizing that the development of the three districts is as equally important as any other districts. And this is so because Chakmas are largely concentrated in these districts.

Indian's refugee regime represents a particularly salient case for exploring the role of interconnections between issue-areas as an independent variable in cooperation. This is because the absence of a binding normative framework on burden-sharing, and the fact that states have few interests in contributing to burden-sharing for its own sake, mean that the prospects for international cooperation have been determined largely by the ability of UNHCR to use linkages to connect refugee protection to states' interests in issue-areas outside the immediate scope of the regime.

Two conceptual conclusions of particular relevance for the role of complexity emerge from this case study. Firstly, structural interconnections between issue-areas play a role in cooperation because they enable and constrain the ability of actors to appeal to linked interests within bargaining. Secondly, institutional interconnections (such as nesting, parallel and overlapping institutions) are but one special case of structural interconnections.

It is surprising that the India's refugee regime has not been given greater prominence in international relations. There was a fundamental contradiction between the principles of sovereignty and human rights, but argued that this conspiracy is mitigated by the practice of granting rights of asylum to foreign political refugees? Refugees actually buttressed a territoriality-based conception of sovereignty because states could allow unwanted populations to flee without taking more extreme actions, and the international community could assist refugees without direct intervention. Refugees were, in essence, a necessary relief valve for the system of sovereign states.

The plight of the refugees irrespective of whether they are looked after either by the UNHCR or the Government of India is abominable to say the least. The condition of the refugees who are not recognized either by the UNHCR or the Government of India is the worst. The lack of legal mechanisms and policies on refugees is one of the fundamental flaws of refugee protection in India. But the courts in

India have awarded judgments to abide by international principles on refugee protection including non- refoulement.

However, the cardinal problem arises when both the UNHCR and the Government of India violate their own standards and principles. While it is possible to bring the Government of India under the scrutiny of the quasi-judicial bodies like the NHRC and judiciary, there is no such mechanism to scrutinize the UNHCR in New Delhi. Official rules and procedures have become an excuse to raise the *'veil of secrecy'* and to resort to arbitrariness at the expense of the refugees. It is a well known fact that none of the regions of South Asia including India, Bhutan, Maldives, Nepal, Myanmar, Sri Lanka and Bangladesh is a party to the 1951 convention or to its 1967 protocol as stated before. It is also true, that there are no national refugee legislations and administrative provisions related to the protection of refugees. Despite the positive example set by India's generous naturalisation of Afghan refugees of Sikh or Hindu ethnic background in 2007 and 2008. For those countries hosting refugees, local integration continues to remain a very limited option.

The ratification of 1951 Convention relating to the status of refugees is a statement of intent unless it is enforceable in domestic courts. Since, the Government of India is not even considering the ratification of the 1951 Refugee Convention, its enforcement in domestic legislation or development of a refugee legal regime is a far cry. A consistent legal framework is vital to the prevention of political ad-hocism, which often translates into forcible repatriation for refugees. The issue is not only development of domestic legislation but how to ensure that both the UNHCR and the Government of India strictly abide by their own standards and principles. For the refugees, the latter remains the immediate concern and the UNHCR has manifestly failed to address the issue of protection[4].

As voluntary repatriation still remains elusive in these situations, UNHCR will continue, as in 2007 and 2008 to promote resettlement as a durable solution for most of the refugee camp population in Bangladesh, Thailand and Nepal. Within the context of strategic resettlement, special attention is also given to the protracted refugee situation in Malaysia and India. The UNHCR also hopes that in 2009 resettlement countries will provide support to address the protracted situation of Afghan refugees in Iran and Pakistan, the two countries hosting the largest number of refugee's world-wide. It is hoped that considerable progress in strategic resettlement of these caseloads will open new opportunities for increased asylum space.

The basic findings of the research suggest that their should be right to life with dignity and access to uniform treatment to all the refugees so far settled in India over a period of time. Civil societies need to work independently without any pressure. India required immediate implementation of national migration and refugee laws and policies with the support of the NHRC and International Organisations. What ever the case may be, so far as my understanding is concerned I have a firm belief that in coming days India's refugee regime would be more loyal towards the refugees who settled in India in general and Chakmas in particular. It also plays more important role in the entire South Asia and bring some of the very effective policies and laws to minimize the gap of denial of the refugee rights. So far my hypothesis is concerned it has been proved through my field work that India's refugee regime is yet to evolve a transparent framework linking rights, laws and policies and results in great prevarication between policies and practices. The treatment of refugees by the refugee regime widely differs in India from state to state and is subject to much pressure from civil society groups.

So far migration is concerned, to my mind, it is in human nature and every one has to migrate. The only thing is who comes first, settle and claims to be the original settler. The Chakma problem is nothing but the political and policy problem in Arunachal Pradesh in particular and northeast in general. This can only be solved once both the state and center sit together and think over it deeply in a sense to solve the problem without doing any politics over it. My extensive field work resulted that the Chakmas are the legal migrants particularly the second and third generation is concerned. Chakmas fall on the ambit of the citizenship rights acts of the constitution of India. They should be given citizenship rights as well as Scheduled Tribes status so that they should live with dignity. The refugee regime of India should also keep in mind that the solution should be democratic which not only satisfy the Chakmas but also the tribals of Arunachal Pradesh in particular & north east in general so that the situation like conflict should not arise in future.

References

1. Former head of agency's stateless unit in Geneva in an international workshop on Forced Migration in Kolkaka, India last year. The writer was one of the participants of the workshop.

2. B.S, Chimni (2000), International Refugee law: A Reader, Sage Publication, New Delhi, pp. 146-152.

3. Dorjee Khandu was the Chief Minister of Arunchal Pradesh between 9th April 2007 to 30th April 2011, from Indian National Congress.
4. See website, http://www.hrdc.net, article published on the issue related to refugees by South Asian Human Rights Documentation Centre, New Delhi, October, 1997.

Appendices

Appendix-I

Text of Indo-Pak Agreement 1973

Following is the full text of the agreement between India and Pakistan signed in New Delhi on August 28, 1973.

1. The special representative of the Prime Minister of India, P.N. Haksar, and the Pakistan Minister of Defense and Foreign Affairs His Excellency Aziz Ahmed, held talks in Rawalpindi from July 24 to July 31, 1973, and in New Delhi from August 18 to August 28, 1973. P.N. Haksar was assisted by Foreign secretary, Kewal Singh, Secretary to the Prime Minister; P.N. Dhar, Joint Secretaries in the Ministry of External Affairs; K.P.S. Menon; A.S. Chib and S.P. Jagota and Deputy Secretaries, K.N. Bakshi and Naraesh Dayal. The Leader of the Pakistani delegation was assisted by the Foreign Secretary, Agha Shahi; Director General in the Ministry of Foreign Affairs; Abdus Sattar and Directors, Abul Waheed and Khalid Saleem. These talks were held in the context of solving the humanitarian problems set out in the joint Indo-Bangladesh Declaration of April 17, 1973.

2. During the course of the talks both at Rawalpindi and New Delhi, which were marked mutual understanding, the delegation of India and Pakistan reviewed the progress so far made in the implementation of the Simla Agreement since they met last in New Delhi in August 1972. The special representatives reaffirmed the resolve of their respective governments expressed in the Simla Agreement that "the two countries put an end to the conflict and confrontation that have hitherto marked their relations and work for the promotion of a friendly and harmonious relationship and the

establishment to durable peace in the sub-continent". In this connection the Special Representatives were confident that the repatriation of prisons of war and nationals of Bangladesh and Pakistan would generate an atmosphere of reconciliation and thus contribute to the building of a structure of a durable peace in the sub-continent.

3. Desirous of solving the humanitarian problems resulting from the conflict of 1971, and thus enabling the vast majority of human beings referred to in the Joint Indo-Bangladesh Declaration to go to their respective countries, India and Pakistan have reached the following agreement.

(i) The immediate implementation of the solution of these humanitarian problems is without prejudice to the respective positions of the parties concerned relating to the case of 195 prisoners of war referred to in clause;

(ii) Subject to the clause (i), repatriation of all Pakistani prisoners of war and civilian internees will commence with the utmost dispatch as soon as logistics arrangements are completed and from a date to be settled by mutual agreement;

(iii) Simultaneously, the repatriation of all Bangalees in Pakistan and all Pakistanis in Bangladesh referred to in clause (v) below, to their respective countries will commence;

(iv) In the matter of repatriation of all categories of persons the principle of simultaneity be observed through out as far as possible;

(v) Without prejudice to the respective position of Bangladesh and Pakistan on the question of non-Bangalees who are stated to have "opted for repatriation to Pakistan", the government of Pakistan, guided by considerations of humanity, agrees, initially, to receives a substantial number such non-Bangalees from Bangladesh. It is further agreed that the prime ministers of Bangladesh and Pakistan or their designated representatives will thereafter meet to decide what additional number of persons who may wish to migrate to Pakistan may be permitted to do so, Bangladesh has made it clear that it will participate in such a meeting only on the basis of sovereign equality;

(vi) Bangladesh agrees that no trials of the 195 prisoners of war shall take place during the entire period of repatriation and that pending the settlement envisaged in clause (vii) below these prisoners of war shall remain in India;

(vii) On completion of repatriation of Pakistani prisoners of war and civilian internees in India, Bangalees in Pakistan and Pakistanis in Bangladesh referred to in clause (v) above, or earlier if they so agree, Bangladesh, India and Pakistan will discuss and settle the question of 195 prisoners of war;

Bangladesh has made it clear that it can participate in such a meeting only based on sovereign equality;

The special representatives are confident that the completion of repatriation provided for in this Agreement, would make a signal contribution to the promotion of reconciliation in the sub-continent and create an atmosphere favorable to a constructive outcome of the meeting of the three countries;

(vii) The time schedule for the completion of repatriation of the Pakistani prisoners of war and civilian internees from India, the Bangalees from Pakistan, and the Pakistani referred to in clause (v) above from Bangladesh and Pakistan will be worked out by India in consultation with Bangladesh and Pakistan as the case may be. The Government of India will make the logistic arrangements for the Pakistani prisoners of war and civilian internees who are to be repatriated to Pakistan. The Government of Pakistan will make logistic arrangements within its territory up to agreed points of exit for the repatriation of Bangladesh nationals to Bangladesh. The Government of Bangladesh will make logistic arrangements within its territory up to agreed points of exit for the movements of the Pakistani referred to in clause (v) above who will go to Pakistan. The Government of Pakistan will make necessary arrangement for the transport of these persons from such agreed points of exit to Pakistan. In making logistic arrangements the Government concerned may seek the assistant of international humanitarian organisations and others;

(viii) For the purpose of facilitation the repatriation provided for in this agreement, the representatives of the Swiss

Federal Government and any international humanitarian organization entrusted with this task shall have unrestricted access at all times to Bangalees in Pakistan and to Pakistanis in Bangladesh referred to in clause (v) above. The Government of Bangladesh and the Government of Pakistan will provide all assistance and facilities to such representatives in this regard including facilities for adequate publicity, for the benefit of the persons entitled to repatriation under this agreement.

(ix) All persons to be repatriated in accordance with the Agreement will be treated with humanity and consideration.

4. The Government of India and the Government of Pakistan have concurred in this Agreement. The Special Representative of the Prime of India, having consulted the Government of Bangladesh has also conveyed the concurred of Bangladesh Government in this Agreement.

DONE in New Delhi on August 28, 1973 in three Originals, all of which is equally authentic

P.N. Haksar	Aziz Ahmed
Special Representative of the Prime Minister of India	Minister of State for Defense and Foreign Affairs, Government of Pakistan

Appendix-II

Text of The Tripartite Agreement of Bangladesh-Pakistan-India 1974

Following is the full text of tripartite agreement signed in New Delhi on 9 April 1974:

1. On 2 July 1972, the President of Pakistan and the Prime Minister of India signed an historic agreement at Simla under which they resolved that "the two countries put an end to the conflict and confrontation that have hitherto marred their relations and work for the promotion of a friendly and harmonious relationship and the establishment of durable peace in the subcontinent." The agreement also provided for the settlement of "their differences by any other peaceful means mutually agreed upon".

2. Bangladesh welcomed the Simla Agreement. The Prime Minister of Bangladesh strongly supported its objective of reconciliation, good neighborliness and establishment of durable peace in the subcontinent.

3. The humanitarian problems arising in the wake of the tragic event of 1971 constituted a major obstacle in the way of reconciliation and normalisation among the countries of the subcontinent. In the absence of recognition, it was not possible to have tripartite talks to settle the humanitarian problems, as Bangladesh could not participate in such a meeting except on the basis of sovereign equality.

4. On 17 April 1973, India and Bangladesh took a major step forward to break the deadlock on the humanitarian issues by setting aside the political problem of recognition. In a declaration issued on that date, they said that they "are resolved to continue their efforts to reduce tension, promote friendly and harmonious relationship in the sub-continent

and work together towards the establishment of a durable peace."

Inspired by this vision and "in the larger interest of reconciliation, peace and stability in the subcontinent", they jointly proposed that the problem of the detained and stranded persons should be resolved on humanitarian considerations through simultaneous repatriation of all such persons except those Pakistani prisoners of war who might be required by the Government of Bangladesh for trial on certain charges.

5. Following the declaration, there were a series of talks between India and Bangladesh and India and Pakistan. These talks resulted in an agreement at Delhi on 28 august 1973, between India and Pakistan with the concurrence of Bangladesh, which provided for a solution of the outstanding humanitarian problems.

6. In pursuance of this agreement, the process of three-way repatriation commenced on 19 September 1973. So far nearly three lakh persons have been repatriated which has generated an atmosphere of reconciliation and paved the way for normalization of relations in the sub-continent.

7. In February 1974, recognition took place thus facilitating the participation of Bangladesh in the tripartite meeting envisaged in the Delhi Agreement, on the basis of sovereign equality. Accordingly, Dr. Kamal Hossain, Foreign Minister of Government of Bangladesh, Mr. Swaran Singh, Minister of External affairs, Government of India, and Mr. Aziz Ahmed, Minister of State for Defense and Foreign Affairs of the Government of Pakistan, met in New Delhi from 5 April to 9 April 1974 and discussed the various issues mentioned in the Delhi Agreement, in particular the question of the 195 prisoners of war and the completion of the three-way process of repatriation involving Bangladesh and Pakistani prisoners of war in India.

8. The Ministers reviewed the progress of the three-way repatriation under the Delhi Agreement of 28 August 1973. They were gratified that such a large number of persons detained or stranded in the three countries had since reached their destinations.

9. The Ministers also considered steps that needed to be taken in order expeditiously to bring the process of three-way repatriation to a satisfactory conclusion.

10. The Indian side stated that the remaining Pakistani prisoners of war and civilian internees in India to be repatriated under the Delhi Agreement, numbering approximately 6,500, would be repatriated at the usual pace of a train on alternate days and the likely shortfall due to suspension of trains from 10 April to 19 April 1974, on account of the Kumbh mela, would be made up by running additional trains after April 19. It was thus hoped that the repatriation of prisoners of war would be completed by the end of April 1974.

11. The Pakistan side stated that the repatriation of Bangladesh nationals from Pakistan was approaching completion. The remaining Bangladesh nationals in Pakistan would also be repatriated without let or hindrance.

12. In respect of non-Bengalis in Bangladesh, the Pakistan side stated that the Government of Pakistan had already issued clearances for movement of Pakistanis in favour of those non-Bengalis who were either domiciled in former West Pakistan, were employees of the Central Government and their families or were members of the divided families, irrespective of their original domicile. The issuance of clearances to 25,000 persons who constitute hardship cases was also in progress.

    The Pakistan side also reiterated that all those who fall under the first three categories would be received by Pakistan without any limit to numbers. In respect of persons whose applications had been rejected, the Government of Pakistan would, upon request, provide reasons why any particular case was rejected. Any aggrieved applicant could at a time, seek a review of his application provided he was able to supply new facts or further information to the Government of Pakistan in support of his contention that he qualified in one or other of the three categories. The claim of such persons would not be time-barred. In the event of the decision of review of a case being adverse, the Government of Pakistan and Bangladesh might seek to resolve it by mutual consultation.

13. The question of 195 Pakistani prisoners of war was discussed by the three Ministers in the context of the earnest desire of

the Governments for reconciliation, peace and friendship in the sub-continent. The Foreign Minister of Bangladesh stated that the excesses and manifold crimes committed by those prisoners of war constituted, according to the relevant provisions of the UN General Assembly resolutions and international law, war crimes, crimes against humanity and genocide, and that there was universal consensus that persons charged with such crimes as 195 Pakistani prisons of war should be held to account and subjected to the due process of law. The Minister of State for Defense and Foreign Affairs of the Government of Pakistan said that his Government condemned and deeply regretted any crimes that may have been committed.

14. In this connection, the three Ministers noted that the matter should be viewed in the context of the determination of the three countries to continue resolutely to work for reconciliation. The Ministers further noted that following recognition, the Prime Minister of Pakistan had declared that he would visit Bangladesh in response to the invitation of the Prime Minister of Bangladesh and appealed to the people of Bangladesh to forgive and forget the mistakes of the past in order to promote reconciliation. Similarly, the Prime Minister of Bangladesh had declared with regard to the atrocities and destruction committed in Bangladesh in 1971, that he wanted the people to forget the past and to make a fresh start, stating that the people of Bangladesh knew how to forgive.

15. In the light of the foregoing and, in particular, having regard to the appeal of the Prime Minister of Pakistan to the people of Bangladesh to forgive and forget the mistakes of the past, the Foreign Minister of Bangladesh stated that the Government of Bangladesh had decided not to proceed with the trials as an act of clemency. It was agreed that the 195 prisoners of war might be repatriated to Pakistan along with the other prisoners of war now in the process of repatriation under the Delhi Agreement. 16. The Ministers expressed their conviction that the above agreements provide a firm basis for the resolution of the humanitarian problems arising out of the conflict of 1971. They reaffirmed the vital stake the 700 million people of the three countries have in peace and progress and reiterated the resolve of their Governments to work for the

promotion of normalization of relations and the establishment of durable peace in the sub-continent.

Signed in New Delhi on 9 April 1974, in three originals, each of which is equally authentic

Kamal Hossain	**Swaran Singh**	**Aziz Ahmed**
Minister of Foreign Affairs, Government of Bangladesh	Minister of External Affairs, Government of India	Minister of State for Defense and Foreign Affairs, Government of Pakistan

Appendix-III

In The Supreme Court of India Original Civil Jurisdiction Writ Petition (Civil) No. 720 of 1995

National Human Rights Commission . . . Petitioner Versus

State of Arunachal Pradesh & Anr. . . . Respondents judgment Ahmadi, CJI

This public interest petition, being a writ petition under Article 32 of the Constitution, has been filed by the National Human Rights Commission (hereinafter called "NHRC") and seeks to enforce the rights, under Article 21 of the Constitution, of about 65,000 Chakma/ Hajong tribals (hereafter called "Chakmas"). It is alleged that these Chakmas, settled mainly in the State of Arunachal Pradesh, are being persecuted by sections of the citizens of Arunachal Pradesh and the second respondent is the Union of India. The NHRC has been set up under the protection or Human Rights Act, 1993 (No. 10 of 1994). Section 18 of this Act empowers the NHRC to approach this Court in appropriate cases. The factual matrix of the case may now be referred to. A large number of Chakmas from erstwhile East Pakistan (now Bangladesh) were displaced by the Kaptai Hydel Power Project in 1954. They had taken shelter in Assam and Tripura. Most of them were settled in these States and became Indian citizens in due course of time. Since a large number of refugees had taken shelter in Assam, the State Government had expressed its inability to rehabilitate all of them and requested assistance in this regard from certain other States. Thereafter, in consultation with the erstwhile NEFA administration (North East Frontier Agency - Arunachal Pradesh), about 4,012 Chakma families were settled in parts of NEFA. They were also allotted some land in consultation with local tribals. The Government of India had also sanctioned rehabilitation assistance @ Rs. 4,200/- per family. The present population of Chakmas in Arunachal Pradesh in estimated to be around 65,000. The issue of conferring citizenship on the Chakmas was considered by the second respondent from time to time. The Minister of State for Home Affairs has on several occasions expressed the intention of the second respondent in this regard. Groups of Chakmas have represented to the petitioner that they have made representations for the grant of citizenship under Section 5(1)(a) of the Citizenship Act, 1995 (hereinafter called "The Act") before their local Deputy Commissioners but no decision has been communicated to them. In recent years, relations between citizens of Arunachal Pradesh and the Chakmas have deteriorated, and the latter have complained that they are being subjected to repressive measures with a view to forcibly expelling them from the State of Arunachal Pradesh. On September 9, 1994, the People's Union for Civil Liberties, Delhi brought this issue to the attention of the NHRC which issued letters to the Chief Secretary, Arunachal Pradesh and the Home Secretary, Government' of India making enquiries in this regard. On September 30, 1994, the Chief Secretary of Arunachal Pradesh faxed a reply stating that the situation was totally under control and adequate police protection had been given to the Chakmas. On October 15, 1994, the Committee for Citizenship Rights of the Chakmas (hereinafter called "The CCRC") filed a representation with the NHRC complaining of the persecution of the Chakmas. The petition contained a press report carried in "The Telegraph" dated August 26, 1994 stating that the All Arunachal Pradesh Students Union (hereinafter called "AAPSU") has issued "quit notices" to all alleged foreigners, including the Chakmas, to leave the State by September 30, 1995. The AAPSU had threatened to use force if its demand was not acceded to. The matter was treated as a formal complaint by the NHRC and on October 28, 1994, it issued notices to the first and the second respondents calling for their reports on the issue. On November 22, 1994, the Ministry of Home Affairs sent a note to the petitioner reaffirming its intention of granting citizenship to the Chakmas. It also pointed out that Central Reserve Forces had been deployed in response to the threat of the AAPSU and that the State Administration had been directed to ensure the protection of the Chakmas. On December 7, 1994, the NHRC directed that first and second respondents to appraise it of the steps taken to protect the Chakmas. This direction was ignored till September, 1995 despite the sending of reminders. On September 25, 1995, the first respondent filed an interim reply and asked for time of four weeks' duration to file a supplementary report. The first respondent did not, however, comply with its own deadline. On October 12, 1995 and again on October 28,

1995 the CCRC sent urgent petitions to the NHRC alleging immediate threats to the lives of the Chakmas. On October 29, 1995, the NHRC recorded a prima facie conclusion that the officers of the first respondent were acting in coordination with the AAPSU with a view to expelling the Chakmas from the State of Arunachal Pradesh. The NHRC stated that since the first respondent was delaying the matter, and since it had doubts as to whether its own efforts would be sufficient to sustain the Chakmas in their own habitat, it had decided to approach this Court to seek appropriate reliefs. On November 2, 1995, this Court issued an interim order directing the first respondent to ensure that the Chakmas situated in its territory are not ousted by any coercive action, not in accordance with law. We may now refer to the stance of the Union of India, the second respondent, on the issue. It has been pointed out that, in 1964, pursuant to extensive discussions between the Government of India and the NEFA administration; it was decided to send the Chakmas for the purpose of their resettlement to the territory of the Arunachal Pradesh for more than three decades, having developed close social, religious and economic ties. To uproot them at this stage would be both impracticable and inhuman. Our attention has been drawn to a Joint Statement issued by the Prime Ministers of India and Bangladesh at New Delhi in February 1972, pursuant to which the Union Government had conveyed to all the States, concerned, its decision to confer citizenship on the Chakmas, in accordance with Section 5(1)(a) of the Act. The second respondent further states that the children of the Chakmas, who were born in India prior to his amendment of the Act in 1987, would have legitimate claims to citizenship. According to the Union of India, the first respondent has been expressing reservations on this account. By not forwarding the applications submitted by the Chakmas along with their reports for grant of citizenship as required by Rule 9 of the Citizenship Rules, 1995, the officers of the first respondent are preventing the Union of India from considering the issue of citizenship of the Chakmas. We are further informed that the Union of India is actively considering the issue of citizenship and has recommended to the first respondent that it take all Necessary steps for providing security to the Chakmas. To this end, central para-military forces have been made available for deployment in the strife-ridden areas. The Union Government favours a dialogue, between the State Government, the Chakmas and all concerned within the State to amicably resolve the issue of granting citizenship to the Chakmas while also redressing the genuine grievances of the citizens of Arunachal Pradesh. The first respondent, in its counter to the petition, has contended before us that the allegation of violation of human rights are incorrect, that it has taken bona fide and sincere steps towards providing the Chakmas with basic amenities and has, to the best of its ability, protected their lives and properties. It is further contended that the issue of citizenship of the Chakmas has been conclusively determined by the decision of this Court in State of Arunachal Pradesh v. Khudiram Chakma (1994 Supp. (1) SCC 615 - hereinafter called "Khudiram Chakma's case"). It is therefore contended that since the Chakmas are foreigners, they are not entitled to the protection of fundamental rights except Article 21. This being so, the authorities may, at any time, ask the Chakmas to quit the state, if they so desire. According to the first respondent, having lost their case in this Court, the Chakmas have "raised a bogey of violation of human rights." The first respondent has filed a counter to the stand taken by the Union of India. The first respondent denies that the Union of India had sent the CRPF Battalions of its own accord; according to it, they were sent pursuant to its letter dated 20.9.1994 asking for assistance. It has also denied that certain Chakmas were killed on account of economic blockades affected by the AAPSU; according to it, these casualties were the result of a malarial epidemic. The first respondent reiterates that the sui qeneris Constitutional position of the State debars it from permitting outsiders to the settled within its territory, that it has limited resources and that its economy is mainly dependent on the vagaries of nature; and that it has no financial resources to tend to the needs of the Chakmas having already spent approximately Rs.100 crores on their upkeep. It has also been stated that the Union of India has refused to share its financial responsibility for the upkeep of the Chakmas. Referring to the issue of grant of citizenship it is submitted as follows:

"It is submitted that under the Citizenship Act, 1995 and the Rules made there under a specific procedure is for grant of citizenship. According to that after receiving the DC of the area makes necessary enquiries about the antecedents of the applicant and after getting a satisfactory report forwards the case to the State Government which in turn forwards it to the Central Government. It is submitted that on enquiry if the report is adverse the DC would not forward it further. It is submitted that the applications, if any, made in this regard have already been disposed of after necessary enquiry. There is no application pending before the DC."

It may be pointed out that this stand of the first respondent is in direct contravention of the stand adopted by it in the representation dated September 25, 1995, submitted by it to the NHRC where it had stated:

"The question of grant of citizenship is entirely governed by the Citizenship Act, 1995 and the Central Government is the sole authority to grant citizenship. The State Government has no jurisdiction in the matter." It is further submitted by the first respondent that under the Constitution, the State of Arunachal Pradesh enjoys a special status and, bearing in mind its ethnicity, it has been declared that it would be administered under Part X of the Constitution. That is the reason why laws and regulations applicable during the British Regime continue to apply even today. The settlement of Chakmas in large numbers in the State would disturb its ethnic balance and destroy its culture and identity. The special provisions made in the Construction would be set at naught if the State's tribal population is allowed to be invaded by people from outside. The tribals, therefore, consider Chakmas as a potential threat to their tradition and culture and are, therefore, keen that the latter do not entrench themselves in the State. Besides, the financial resources of the State without Central assistance, which is ordinarily not forthcoming, would throw a heavy burden on the State which it would find well nigh impossible to bear. In the circumstances, contends the first respondent, it is unfair and unconstitutional to throw the burden of such a large number of Chakmas on the State. We are unable to accept the contention of the first respondent that no threat exists to the life and liberty of the Chakmas guarantee by Article 21 of the Constitution, and that it has taken adequate steps to ensure the protection of the Chakmas. After handling the present matter for more than a year, the NHRC recorded a prima facie finding that the service of quit notices and their admitted enforcement appeared to be supported by the officers of the first respondent. The NHRC further held that the first respondent had, on the one hand, delayed the disposal of the matter by not furnishing the required response and had, on the other hand, sought to enforce the eviction of the Chakmas through its agencies. It is to be noted that, at no time, has the first respondent sought to condemn the activities of the AAPSU. However, the most damning facts against the first respondent are to be found in the counter affidavit of the second respondent. In the assessment of the Union of India, the threat posed by the AAPSU was grave enough to warrant the placing of two additional battalions of CRPF at the disposal of the State

Administration. Whether it was done at the behest of the State Government or by the Union on its won is of no consequence; the fact that it had become necessary speaks for itself. The second respondent further notes that after the expiry of the deadline of October 30, 1994, the AAPSU and other tribal student organisations continued to agitate and press for the expulsion of all foreigners including the Chakmas. It was reported that the AAPSU had started enforcing of economic blockades on the refugee camps, which adversely affected the supply of rations, medical and essential facilities etc. to the Chakmas. Of course the State Government has denied the allegation, but the independent inquiry of the NHRC shows otherwise. The fact that the Chakmas were dying on account of the blockade for want of medicines in an established fact. After reports regarding lack of medical facilities and the spread of malaria and dysentery in Chakma settlements were received, the Union Government advised the first respondent to ensure normal supplies of essential commodities to the Chakma settlement. On September 20, 1995 the AAPSU, once again, issued an ultimatum citing December 31, 1995 as the fresh deadline for the ousting of Chakmas. This is yet another threat which the first respondent has not indicated how it proposes to counter. It is, therefore, clear that there exists a clear and present danger to the lives and personal liberty of the Chakmas. In Louis De Raedt v. Union of India [(1991) 3 SCC 554] and Khudiram Chakma's case this court held that foreigners are entitled to the protection of Article of Article 21 of the Constitution. The contention of the first respondent that the ruling of this Court in Khudiram Chakma's case has for closed the consideration of the citizenship of Chakmas is misconceived. The facts of that case reveal that the appellant and 56 families migrated to India in 1964 from erstwhile East Pakistan and were lodged in the Government Refugee Camp at Ledo. They were later shifted to another camp at Miao. In 1996, the State Government drew up the Chakma Resettlement Scheme for refugees and the Chakmas were allotted lands in two villages. The appellant, however, stayed out and secured land in another area by private negotiations. The State questioned the legality of the said transaction since, under the Regulations then in force, no person other than a native of that District could acquire land in it. Since there were complaints against the appellant and others who had settled on this land, the State by order dated February 15, 1984, directed that they shift to the area earmarked for them. This order was challenged on the ground that Chakmas who had settled there were citizens of India and by seeking their forcible eviction, the State was violating their fundamental rights and, in any case, the order was arbitrary and illegal as violative of the principles of natural justice. On the question of citizenship, they invoked section 6-A of the Act which, inter alia, provides that all persons of Indian origin who cam before January 1, 1996 to Assam from territories included in Bangladesh immediately before the commencement of the Citizenship (Amendment) Act, 1985, and who had been ordinarily resident in Assam since their entry into Assam shall be deemed to be citizens of India as from January 1, 1996. Others who had come to Assam after that date and before March 25, 1971, and had been ordinarily resident in Assam since then and had been detected to be foreigners, could register themselves. It will thus be seen that the appellant and others claimed citizenship under this special provision made pursuant to the Assam Accord. The High Court held that the appellant and others did not fall under the said category as they had stayed in Assam for a short period in 1964 and had strayed away there from in the area now within the State of Arunachal Pradesh. On appeal, this court affirmed that view. It is, therefore, clear that in that case, the Court was required to consider the claim of citizenship based on the language of Section 6-A of the Act. Thus, in Khudiram Chakma's case, this Court was seized of a matter where 57 Chakma families were seeking to challenge an order requiring them to vacate land bought by them in direct contravention of clause 7 of the Bengal Eastern Frontier Regulation, 1873. The issue of citizenship was raised in a narrower context and was limited to Section 6-A (2) of the Act. The Court observed that the Chakmas in that case, who were resident in Arunachal Pradesh, could not avail of the benefit of Section 6A of the Act which is a special provision for the citizenship of persons covered by the Assam Accord. In the present case, the Chakmas are seeking to obtain citizenship under Section 5(1)(a) of the Act, where the consideration is entirely different. That Section provides for citizenship by registration. It says that the prescribed authority may, on receipt of an application in that behalf, register a person who is not a citizen of India, as a citizen of India if he/she satisfies the conditions set out therein. This provision is of general application and is not limited to persons belonging to a certain group only as in the case of Section 6-A. Section 5, therefore, can be invoked by persons who are not citizens of India but are seeking citizenship by registration. Such applications would have to be in the form prescribed by part II of the Citizenship Rules, 1956 (hereinafter called "The Rules"). Under Rule 7, such application has to be made to the Collector within whose jurisdiction the applicant is ordinarily resident. Rule 8 describes the authority to register a person as a citizen of India under Section 5(1) of the Act. It says that the authority to register a person as a citizen of India shall be an officer not below the rank of a Deputy Secretary to the Government of India in the Ministry of Home Affairs, and also includes such officer as the Central Government may, by a notification in the Official Gazette, appoint and in any other cases falling under the Rules, any officer not below the rank of a Joint Secretary to the Government of India in the Ministry of Home Affairs, and also includes such other officer as the Central Government may, by notification in the official Gazette, appoint. Rule 9 next enjoins the Collector to transmit every application received by him under Section 5 (1) (a) to the Central Government through the State Government or the Union Territory administration, as the case may be, along with a report on matters set out in clauses (a) to (e) thereof. Rule 10 provides for issuance of a certificate to be granted to persons registered as citizens and Rules 11 and 12 provide for maintenance of registers. These are the relevant rules in regard to registration of persons as citizens of India. From what we have said hereinbefore, there is no doubt that the Chakmas who migrated from East-Pakistan (now Bangladesh) in 1964, first settled down in the State of Assam and then shifted to areas which now fall within the State of Arunachal Pradesh. They have settled there since the last about two and a half decades and have raised their families in the said State. Their children have married and they too have had children. Thus, a large number of them were born in the State itself. Now it is proposed to uproot them by force. The AAPSU has been giving out threats to forcibly drive them out to the neighbouring State which in turn is unwilling to accept them. The residents of the neighbouring State have also threatened to kill them if they try to enter their State. They are thus sandwiched between two forces, each pushing in opposite direction which can only hurt them. Faced with the prospect of annihilation the NHRC was moved, which finding it impossible to extend protection to them, moved this Court for certain reliefs. By virtue of their long and prolonged stay in the State, the Chakmas who migrated to, and those born in the State, seek citizenship under the Constitution read with Section 5 of the Act. We have already indicated earlier that if a person satisfies the requirements of Section 5 of the Act, he/she can be registered as a citizen of India. The procedure to be followed in processing such requests has been outlined i Part II of the Rules. We have adverted to the relevant rules hereinbefore. According to these rules, the application for registration has to be made in the prescribed form, duly affirmed, to the Collector within whose jurisdiction he resides. After the application is so received, the authority to register a person as a citizen of India, is vested in the officer named under Rule 8 of the Rules. Under Rule 9, the Collector is expected to .... every application under Section 5(1)(a) of the Acts to the Central Government. On a conjoint reading of Rules 8 and 9 it becomes clear that the Collector has merely to receive the application and forward it to the Central Government. It is only the authority constituted under Rule 8 which is empowered to register a person as a citizen of India It follows that only that authority can refuse to entertain an application made under Section 5 of the Act. Yet it is an admitted fact that after receipt of the application, the Deputy Collector (DC) makes an enquiry and if the report it adverse, the DC refuses to forward the application; in other words, he rejects the application at the threshold and does not forward it to the Central Government. The grievance of the Central Government is that since the DC does not forward it to the Central Government. The grievance of the Central Government is that since the DC does not forward the applications, it is not in a position to take a decision whether or not to register the person as a citizen of India. That is why it is said that the DC or Collector, who receives the application should be directed to forward the same to the Central Government to enable it to decide the request on merits. It is obvious that by refusing to forward the applications of the Chakmas to the Central Government, the DC is failing in his duty and is also preventing the Central Government from performing its duty under the Act and the Rules. We are a country governed by the Rule of Law. Our Constitution confers certain rights on every human being and certain other rights on citizens. Every person is entitled to equality before the law and equal protection of the laws. So also, no person can be deprived of his life or personal liberty except according to procedure established by law. Thus the State is bound to protect the life and liberty of every human-being, be he a citizen or otherwise, and it cannot permit any body or group of persons, e.g., the AAPSU, to threaten the Chakmas to leave the State, failing which they would be forced to do so. No State Government worth the name can tolerate such threats by one group of persons to another group of persons; it is duty bound to protect. The threatened group from such assaults and if it fails to do so, it will fail to perform its Constitutional as well as statutory obligations. Those giving such threats would be liable to be dealt with in accordance with law. The State Government must act impartially and carry out its legal obligations. Those giving such threats would be liable to be dealt with in accordance with law. The State Government must act impartially and carry out its legal obligations to safeguard the life, health and well-being of Chakmas residing in the State without being inhibited by local politics. Besides, by refusing to forward their applications, the Chakmas are denied rights, Constitutional and statutory to be considered for being registered as citizens of India. In view of the above, we allow this petition and direct the first and second respondents, by way of a writ of mandamus, as under:- (1) the first respondent, the State of Arunachal Pradesh, shall ensure that the life and personal liberty of each and every Chakma residing within the State shall be protected and any attempt to forcibly evict or drive them out of the State by organised groups, such as the AAPSU, shall be repelled, if necessary by requisitioning the service of para-military or police force, and if additional forces are considered necessary to carry out this direction, the first respondent will request the second respondent, the Union of India, to provide such additional force, and the second respondent shall provide such additional force as is necessary to protect the lives and liberty of the Chakmas; (2) except in accordance with law, the Chakmas shall not be evicted from their homes and shall not be denied domestic life and comfort therein; (3) the quit notices and ultimatums issued by the AAPSU and any other group which tantamount to threats to the life and liberty of each and every Chakma should be dealt with by the first respondent in accordance with law; (4) the application made for registration as citizen of India by the Chakma or Chakmas under Section 5 of the Act, shall be entered in the register maintained for the purpose and shall be forwarded by the Collector or the DC who receives them under the relevant rule, with or without enquiry, as the case may be, to the Central Government for its consideration in accordance with law; even returned applications shall be called back or fresh ones shall be obtained from the concerned persons and shall be processed and forwarded to the Central Government; (5) while the application of any individual Chakma is pending consideration, the first respondent shall not evict or remove the concerned person from his occupation on the ground that he is not a citizen of India until the competent authority has taken a decision in that behalf; and (6) the first respondent will pay to the petitioner cost of this petition which we quantity at Rs.10,000/- within six weeks from today by depositing the same in the office of the NHRC, New Delhi.

The petition shall stand so disposed of. .... CJI .... J.

New Delhi; January 9, 1996.

Appendix-IV

The Passport Entry Into India Act, 1920 [Act No. 34 of 1920] [9th September 1920]

An Act to take power to require passports of pe rsons entering India Whereas it is expedient to take power to require passports of persons entering India It is hereby enacted as follows:

2. Definitions.

In this Act unless there is anything repugnant in the subject or context, - Entry means entry by water, land or air "Passport" means a passport for the time being in force issued or renewed by the prescribed authority and satisfying the conditions prescribed relating to the class of passports to which it belongs; and Prescribed means prescribed by rules made under this Act.

3. Power to Make Rules.

(1) The Central Government may make rules requiring that persons entering India shall be in possession of passports, and for all matters ancillary or incidental to that purpose.

(2) Without prejudice to the generality of the foregoing power such rules may- (a) Prohibit the entry into India or any part thereof of any person who has not in' his possession a passport issued to him; (b) Prescribe the authorities by whom passports must have been issued or renew4 and the conditions with which they must comply, for the purposes of this A4 and (c) Provide for the exemption, either absolutely or on any conditions, of any person or class of persons from any provision of such rules. Rules made under this section may provide that any contravention thereof or of any orders issued under the

authority of any such rule shall be punishable with imprisonment for a term which may extend to five years, or with fine which may extend to fifty thousand rupees, or with both.

(4) All rules made under this section shall be published in the Official Gazette, and shall thereupon have effect as if enacted in this Act.

3 A. Punishment for Subsequent Offences

[Punishment for subsequent offencesWhoever having been convicted of an offence under any rule or order made under this Act is again convicted of an offence under this Act shall be punishable with double the penalty provided for the later offence.]

1. Inserted sec.3A, Amendment the Passport (Entry into India) Act, 2000

4. Power of Arrest

(1) Any officer of police, not below the rank of a Sub-Inspector, and any officer of the Customs Department empowered by a general or special order of the Central Government in this behalf may arrest without warrant any person who has contravened or against whom a reasonable suspicion exists that he has contravened any rule or order made under Section 3.

(2) Every officer making an arrest under this section shall, without unnecessary delay, take or send the person arrested before a Magistrate having jurisdiction in the case or to the officer-in-charge of the nearest police station and the provisions of Section 1["section 57 of the Code of Criminal Procedure, 1973 (2 of 1974),", shall, so far as may be, apply in the case of any such arrest.

1. Amendment in to the Passport (Entry into India) Act, 2000

5. Power of removal

The Central Government may, by general or special order, direct the removal of any person from India, who in contravention of any rule made under Section 3 prohibiting entry into India without passport, has entered there in, and thereupon any officer of the Government shall have all reasonable powers necessary to enforce such direction.

6. Application of Act to Part B States

[Repealed by the Part B States (Laws) Act. 1951 (3 of 1951) Section 9 and Schedule.]

Appendix-V

The Passports Act, 1967

Act No. 15 of 1967

[24th June, 1967]

An Act to provide for the issue of passports and travel documents to regulate the departure from India of citizens of India and other persons for matters incidental or ancillary thereto. BE it enacted by Parliament in the Eighteenth Year of the Republic of India as follows:-

Short Title and Extent

1. Short title and extent. (1) This Act may be called the Passports Act, 1967.

(2) It extends to the whole of India and applies also to citizens of India who are outside India.

Definitions

2. Definitions. In this Act, unless the context otherwise requires,-- (a) "departure", with its grammatical variations and cognate expressions, means departure from India by water, land or air; (b) "passport" means a passport issued or deemed to have been issued under this Act; (c) "passport authority" means an officer or authority empowered under rules made under this Act to issue passports or travel documents and includes the Central Government; (d) "prescribed" means prescribed by rules made under this Act; (e) "travel document" means a travel document issued or deemed to have been issued under this Act.

Passport or Travel Document for Departure from India

3. Passport or travel document for departure from India. No person shall depart from, or attempt to depart from India unless he holds in this behalf a valid passport or travel document. Explanation.- For the purposes of this section,- (a) "passport" includes a passport which having been issued by or under the authority of the Government of a foreign country satisfies the conditions prescribed under the Passport (Entry into India) Act, 1920, (34 of 1920) in respect of the class of passports to which it belongs; (b) "travel document" includes a travel document which having been issued by or under the authority of the Government of a foreign country satisfies the conditions prescribed.

Classes of Passports and Travel Documents

4. Classes of passports and travel documents. (1) The following classes of passports may be issued under this Act, namely:- (a) ordinary passport; (b) Official passport; (c) diplomatic passport. 28

(2) The following classes of travel documents may be issued under this Act, namely:- (a) emergency certificate authorising a person to enter India; (b) certificate of identity for the purpose of establishing the identity of a person; (c) such other certificate or document as may be prescribed.

(3) The Central Government shall, in consonance with the usage and practice followed by it in this behalf, prescribe the classes of persons to whom the classes of passports and travel documents referred to respectively in sub-section (1) and sub-section (2) may be issued under this Act.

Applications for Passports, Travel Documents, etc. and Orders Thereon

Applications for passports, travel documents, etc. and orders thereon. 1*[(1) An application for the issue of a passport under this Act for visiting such foreign country or countries (not being a named foreign country) as may be specified in the application may be made to the passport authority and shall be accompanied by 2*[such fee as may be prescribed to meet the expenses incurred on special security paper, printing, lamination and other connected miscellaneous services in issuing passports and other travel documents] Explanation.- In this section, "named foreign country" means such foreign country as the Central Government may, by rules made under this Act, specify in this behalf. (1A) An application for the issue of- (i) a passport under this Act for visiting such foreign country; or (ii) a travel document under this Act, for visiting such foreign country or countries (including a named foreign country) as may be specified in the application or for an endorsement on the passport or travel document referred to in this section, may be made to the passport authority and shall be accompanied by such fee (if any) not exceeding rupees fifty, as may be prescribed. (1B) every application under this section shall be in such form and contain such particulars as may be prescribed.

(2) On receipt of an application 3*[under this section,] the passport authority, after making such inquiry, if any, as it may consider necessary, shall, subject to the other provisions of this Act, by order in writing,- (a) issue the passport or travel document with endorsement or, as the case may be, make on the passport or travel document the endorsement, in respect of the foreign country or countries specified in the application; or (b) issue the passport or travel document with endorsement, or, as the case may be, make on the passport or travel document the endorsement, in respect of one or more of the foreign countries specified in the application and refuse to make an endorsement in respect of the other country or countries; or (c) refuse to issue the passport or travel document or, as the case may be, refuse to make on the passport or travel document any endorsement. 1. Subs. by Act 31 of 1978, s. 2, for sub-section (1). 2. Subs. by Act 35 of 1993, s. 2 (w.e.f. 1-7-1993) 3. Ins. by Act 31 of 1978 s. 2, 29

(3) Where the passport authority makes an order under clause (b) or clause (c) of sub-section (2) on the application of any person, it shall record in writing a brief statement of its reasons for making such order and furnish to that person on demand a copy of the same unless in any case the passport authority is of the opinion that it will not be in the interests of the sovereignty and integrity of India, the security of India, friendly relations of India with any foreign country or in the interests of the general public to furnish such copy.

Refusal of Passports, Travel Documents

6. Refusal of passports, travel documents, etc. (1) Subject to the other provisions of this Act, the passport authority shall refuse to make an endorsement for visiting any foreign country under clause

(b) or clause (c) of sub-section (2) of section 5 on any one or more of the following grounds, and on no other ground, namely:-- (a) that the applicant may, or is likely to, engage in such country in activities prejudicial to the sovereignty and integrity of India; (b) that the presence of the applicant in such country may, or is likely to, be detrimental to the security of India; (c) that the presence of the applicant in such country may, or is likely to, prejudice the friendly relations of India with that or any other country; (d) that in the opinion of the Central Government the presence of the applicant in such country is not in the public interest.

(2) Subject to the other provisions of this Act, the passport authority shall refuse to issue a passport or travel document for visiting any foreign country under clause (c) of sub-section (2) of section 5 on any one or more of the following grounds, and on no other ground, namely :- (a) that the applicant is not a citizen of India; (b) that the applicant may, or is likely to, engage outside India in activities prejudicial to the sovereignty and integrity of India; (c) that the departure of the applicant from India may, or is likely to, be detrimental to the security of India; (d) that the presence of the applicant outside India may, or is likely to, prejudice the friendly relations of India with any foreign country; (e) that the applicant has, at any time during the period of five years immediately preceding the date of his 30 application, been convicted by a court in India for any offence involving moral turpitude and sentenced in respect thereof to imprisonment for not less than two years; (f) that proceedings in respect of an offence alleged to have been committed by the applicant are pending before a criminal court in India; (g) that a warrant or summons for the appearance, or a warrant for the arrest, of the applicant has been issued by a court under any law for the time being in force or that an order prohibiting the departure from India of the applicant has been made by any such court; (h) that the applicant has been repatriated and has not reimbursed the expenditure incurred in connection with such repatriation; (i) that in the opinion of the Central Government the issue of a passport or travel document to the applicant will not be in the public interest.

Duration of Passports and Travel Documents

7. Duration of passports and travel documents. A passport or travel document shall, unless revoked earlier, continue in force for such period as may be prescribed and different periods may be

prescribed for different classes of passports or travel documents or for different categories of passports or travel documents under each such class: Provided that a passport or travel document may be issued for a shorter period than the prescribed period- (a) if the person by whom it is required so desires; or (b) if the passport authority, for reasons to be communicated in writing to the applicant, considers in any case that the passport or travel document should be issued for a shorter period.

Extension of Period of Passport

Where a passport is issued for a shorter period than the prescribed period under section 7, such shorter period shall, unless the passport authority for reasons to be recorded in writing otherwise determines, be extendable for a further period (which together with the shorter period shall not exceed the prescribed period) and the provisions of this Act shall apply to such extension as they apply to the issue thereof.

Conditions and forms of Passports and Travel Documents

9. Conditions and forms of passports and travel documents. The conditions subject to which, and the form in which, a passport or travel document shall be issued or renewed shall be such as may be prescribed: Provided that different conditions and different forms may be prescribed for different classes of passports or travel documents or 1. Subs. by Act 35 of 1993, s. 3 (w.e.f. 1-7-1993), 31 for different categories of passports or travel documents under each such class: Provided further that a passport or travel document may contain in addition to the prescribed conditions such other conditions as the passport authority may, with the previous approval of the Central Government, impose in any particular case.

Variation, impounding and revocation of passports and travel documents

10. Variation, impounding and revocation of passports and travel documents. (1) The passport authority may, having regard to the provisions of sub-section (1) of section 6 or any notification under section 19, vary or cancel the endorsements on a passport or travel document or may, with the previous approval of the Central Government, vary or cancel the conditions (other than the prescribed conditions) subject to which a passport or travel document has been

issued and may, for that purpose, require the holder of a passport or a travel document, by notice in writing, to deliver up the passport or travel document to it within such time as may be specified in the notice and the holder shall comply with such notice.

(2) The passport authority may, on the application of the holder of a passport or a travel document, and with the previous approval of the Central Government also vary or cancel the conditions (other than the prescribed conditions) of the passport or travel document.

(3) The passport authority may impound or cause to be impounded or revoke a passport or travel document,- (a) if the passport authority is satisfied that the holder of the passport or travel document is in wrongful possession thereof; (b) if the passport or travel document was obtained by the suppression of material information or on the basis of wrong information provided by the holder of the passport or travel document or any other person on his behalf 1*[Provided that if the holder of such passport obtains another passport, the passport authority shall also impound or cause to be impounded or revoke such other passport.] (c) if the passport authority deems it necessary so to do in the interests of the sovereignty and integrity of India, the security of India, friendly relations of India with any foreign country, or in the interests of the general public; (d) if the holder of the passport or travel document has, at any time after the issue of the passport or travel document, been convicted by a court in India for any offence involving moral turpitude and sentenced in respect thereof to imprisonment for not less than two years; (e) if proceedings in respect of an offence alleged to have been committed by the holder of the passport or travel document are pending before a criminal court in India.

1. Ins. by Act 35 of 1993, s. 4 (w.e.f. 1-7-1993) 32 (f) if any of the conditions of the passport or travel document has been contravened; (g) if the holder of the passport or travel document has failed to comply with a notice under sub-section (1) requiring him to deliver up the same; (h) if it is brought to the notice of the passport authority that a warrant or summons for the appearance, or a warrant for the arrest, of the holder of the passport or travel document has been issued by a court under any law for the time being in force or if an order prohibiting the departure from India of the holder of the passport or other travel document has been made by any such court and the passport authority is satisfied that a warrant or summons has been so issued or an order has been so made.

(4) The passport authority may also revoke a passport or travel document on the application of the holder thereof.

(5) Where the passport authority makes an order varying or cancelling the endorsements on, or varying the conditions of, a Passport or travel document under sub-section (1) or an order impounding or revoking a passport or travel document under sub-section.

(3) it shall record in writing a brief statement of the reasons for making such order and furnish to the holder of the passport or travel document on demand a copy of the same unless in any case, the passport authority is of the opinion that it will not be in the interests of the sovereignty and integrity of India, the security of India, friendly relations of India with any foreign country or in the interests of the general public to furnish such a copy.

(6) The authority to whom the passport authority is subordinate may, by order in writing, impound or cause to be impounded or revoke a passport or travel document on any ground on which it may be impounded or revoked by the passport authority and the foregoing provisions of this section shall, as far as may be, apply in relation to the impounding or revocation of a passport or travel document by such authority.

(7) A court convicting the holder of a passport or travel document of any offence under this Act or the rules made there under may also revoke the passport or travel document: Provided that if the conviction is set aside on appeal or otherwise the revocation shall become void.

(8) An order of revocation under sub-section (7) may also be made by an appellate court or by the High Court when exercising its powers of revision. 33

(9) On the revocation of a passport or travel document under this section the holder thereof shall, without delay, surrender the passport or travel document, if the same has not already been impounded, to the authority by whom it has been revoked or to such other authority as may be specified in this behalf in the order of revocation.

Appeals

11. Appeals. (1) Any person aggrieved by an order of the passport Authority under clause (b) or clause (c) of sub-section (2) of section 5 or clause (b) of the provision to section 7 or sub-section (1), or sub-section (3) of section 10 or by an order under sub-section (6) of section

10 of the authority to whom the passport authority is subordinate, may prefer an appeal against that order to such authority (hereinafter referred to as the appellate authority) and within such period as may be prescribed: Provided that no appeal shall lie against any order made by the Central Government.

(2) No appeal shall be admitted if it is preferred after the expiry of the period prescribed therefore: Provided that an appeal may be admitted after the expiry of the period prescribed therefore if the appellant satisfied the appellate authority that he had sufficient cause for not preferring the appeal within that period.

(3) The period prescribed for an appeal shall be computed in accordance with the provisions of the Limitation Act, 1963, (36 of 1963.) with respect to the computation of the periods of limitation there under.

(4) Every appeal under this section shall be made by a petition in writing and shall be accompanied by a copy of the statement of the reasons for the order appealed against where such copy has been furnished to the appellant and ["by such fee as may be prescribed for meeting the expenses that may be incurred in calling for relevant records and for connected services"]

(5) In disposing of an appeal, the appellate authority shall follow such procedure as may be prescribed: Provided that no appeal shall be disposed of unless the appellant has been given a reasonable opportunity or representing his case.

(6) Every order of the appellate authority confirming, modifying or reversing the order appealed against shall be final.

Offences and Penalties

12. Offences and penalties. (1) Whoever- (a) contravenes the provisions of section 3; or (b) knowingly furnishes any false information or suppresses any material information with a view to obtaining a passport or travel document under this Act or without lawful authority alters or attempts to alter or causes to alter the entries made in a passport or travel document; or (c) fails to produce for inspection his passport or travel document (whether issued under this Act or not) when called upon to do so by the prescribed authority; or (d) knowingly uses a passport or travel document issued to another person; or (e) knowingly allows another person to use a passport or

travel document issued to him, 1. Subs. by Act 35 of 1993, s. 5 (w.e.f. 1-7-1993) 34 shall be punishable with imprisonment for a term which may extend to 1*[two years or with fine which may extend to five thousand rupees] or with both. 1*[(1A) Whoever, not being a citizen of India,- (a) makes an application for a passport or obtains a passport by suppressing information about his nationality, or (b) holds a forged passport or any travel document, shall be punishable with imprisonment for a term which shall not be less than one year but which may extend to five years and with fine which shall not be less than ten thousand rupees but which may extend to fifty thousand rupees.]

(2) Whoever abets any offence punishable under 1*[Sub-section (1) or sub-section (1A)] shall, if the act abetted is committed in consequence of the abetment, be punishable with the punishment provided in that sub-section for that offence.

(3) Whoever contravenes any condition of a passport or travel document or any provision of this Act or any rule made there under for which no punishment is provided elsewhere in this Act shall be punishable with imprisonment for a term which may extend to three months or with fine which may extend to five hundred rupees or with both.

(4) Whoever, having been convicted of an offence under this Act, is again convicted of an offence under this Act shall be punishable with double the penalty provided for the latter offence.

Power to Arrest

13. Power to arrest. (1) Any officer of customs empowered by a general or special order of the central government in this behalf and any 2*[officers of police or emigration officer] not below the rank of a sub-inspector may arrest without warrant any person against whom a reasonable suspicion exists that he has committed any offence punishable under section 12 and shall, as soon as may be, inform him of the grounds for such arrest.

(2) Every officer making an arrest under this section shall, without unnecessary delay, take or send the person arrested before a magistrate having jurisdiction in the case or to the officer in charge of the nearest police station and the provisions of 3*[section 57 of the Code of Criminal procedure, 1973 (2 of 1974) shall, so far as may be, apply in the case of any such arrest].

Power of Search and Seizure

14. Power of search and seizure. (1) Any officer of customs empowered by a general or special order of the Central Government in this behalf and any 2*[officer of police or emigration officer] not below the rank of a sub-inspector may search any place and seize any passport or travel document from any person against whom a reasonable suspicion exists that he has committed any offence punishable under section 12.

(2) The provisions of the 4*[Code of Criminal Procedure, 1973 (2 of 1974), relating to searches and seizures shall, so far as may be, apply to searches and seizures under this section.

Previous Sanction of Central Government Necessary

15. Previous sanction of Central Government necessary. No prosecution shall be instituted against any person in respect of any offence under this Act without the previous sanction of the Central Government or such officer or authority as may be authorized by that Government by order in writing in this behalf.

Protection of Action taken in Good faith

16. Protection of action taken in good faith. No suit, prosecution or other legal proceeding shall lie against the Government or any officer or authority for anything which is in good faith done or intended to be done under this Act.

Passports and travel documents to be property of Central Government. 17. Passports and travel documents to be property of Central Government. A passport or travel document issued under this Act shall at all times remain the property of the Central Government.

Passports and Travel Documents to be Invalid for Travel to Certain Countries

19. Passports and travel documents to be invalid for travel to certain countries. Upon the issue of a notification by the Central Government that a foreign country is-- (a) a country which is committing external aggression against India; or (b) a country assisting the country committing external aggression against India; or (c) a country where armed hostilities are in progress; or (d) a country to

which travel must be restricted in the public interest because such travel would seriously impair the conduct of foreign affairs of the Government of India a passport or travel document for travel through or visiting such country shall cease to be valid for such travel or visit unless in any case a special endorsement in that behalf is made in the prescribed form by the prescribed authority.

Issue of Passports and Travel Documents to Persons who are not citizens of India

20. Issue of passports and travel documents to persons who are not citizens of India. Notwithstanding anything contained in the foregoing provisions relating to issue of a passport or travel document, the Central Government may issue, or cause to be issued, a passport or travel document to a person who is not a citizen of India if that Government is of the opinion that it is necessary so to do in the public interest.

Power to Delegate

21. Power to delegate. The Central Government may, by notification in the Official Gazette, direct that any power or function which may be exercised or performed by it under this Act other than the power under clause (d) of sub-section (1) of section 6 or the power under clause (i) of sub-section (2) of that section or the power under section 24, may, in relation to such matters and subject to such conditions, if any, as it may specify in the notification, be exercised or performed- (a) by such officer or authority subordinate to the central government; or (b) by any state government or by any officer or authority subordinate to such Government; or (c) in any foreign country in which there is no diplomatic mission of India, by such foreign Consular Officer; as may be specified in the notification.

1. Omitted by Act 35 of 1993, s. 8 (w.e.f. 1-7-1993). 36

Power to Exempt

22. Power to exempt. Where the central government is of the opinion that it is necessary or expedient in the public interest so to do, it may, by notification in the official gazette and subject to such conditions, if any, as it may specify in the notification,- (a) exempt any person or class of persons from the operation of all or any of the provisions of this Act or the rules made there under; and (b) as often

as may be, cancel any such notification and again subject, by a like notification, the person or class of persons to the operation of such provisions. Act to be in addition to certain enactments. 23. Act to be in addition to certain enactments. The provisions of this Act shall be in addition to and not in derogation of the provisions of the Passport (Entry into India) Act, 1920 (34 of 1920), 1*[the Emigration Act, 1983 (31 of 1983)] the Registration of Foreigners Act, 1939 (16 of 1939), the Foreigners Act, 1946 (31 of 1946), 2* the Trading with the Enemy (Continuance of Emergency Provisions) Act, 1947 (16 of 1947), the Foreigners Law (Application and Amendment) Act, 1962 (42 of 1962), 3*[the Foreign Exchange Regulation Act, 1973 (46 of 1973)] and other enactments relating to foreigners and foreign exchange.

Power to Make Rules

24. Power to make rules. (1) The central government may, by notification in the official gazette, make rules for carrying out the purposes of this Act.

(2) In particular, and without prejudice to the generality of the foregoing power, such rules may provide for all or any of the following matters, namely :- (a) the appointment, jurisdiction, control and functions of passport authorities; (b) the classes of persons to whom passports and travel documents referred to respectively in sub-section (1) and sub-section (2) of section 4 may be issued; (c) the form and particulars of application for the issue or renewal of a passport or travel document or for endorsement on a passport or travel document and where the application is for the renewal, the time within which it shall be made; (d) the period for which passports and travel documents shall continue in force; (e) the form in which and the conditions subject to which the different classes of passports and travel documents may be issued, renewed or varied; 1. Subs. by Act 35 of 1993, s. 9 (w.e.f. 1-7-1993) 2. The words "the Foreign Exchange Regulation Act, 1947" omitted by Act 31 of 1978, s. 5. 3. Ins. by Act 31 of 1978, s. 5, ibid. 37 1*[(ee) specifying the foreign country for the purposes of the Explanation to sub-section (1) of section 5;] (f) the fees payable in respect of 2*[any application for the issue of a passport under sub-section (1) of section 5 or issue of a passport] for visiting a foreign country referred to in sub-section (1A) of section 5] or travel document or for varying any endorsement or making a fresh endorsement on a passport or a travel document and the fees payable in respect of any appeal under this Act; (g) the appointment of appellate authorities under sub-section

(1) of section 11, the jurisdiction of, and the procedure which may be followed by, such appellate authorities; (h) the services (including the issue of a duplicate passport or travel document in lieu of a passport or travel document lost, damaged or destroyed) which may be rendered in relation to a passport or travel document and the fees there for; (i) any other matter which is to be or may be prescribed or in respect of which this Act makes no provision or makes insufficient provision and provision is, in the opinion of the Central Government, necessary for the proper implementation of the Act.

(3) Every rule made under this Act shall be laid as soon as may be after it is made, before each House of Parliament while it is in session for a total period of thirty days which may be comprised in one session or 3*[in two or more successive sessions and if, before the expiry of the session immediately following the session or the successive sessions aforesaid], both Houses agree in making any modification in the rule or both Houses agree that the rule should not be made, the rule shall thereafter have effect only in such modified form or be of no effect, as the case may be; so, however, that any such modification or annulment shall be without prejudice to the validity of anything previously done under that rule. Change of short title of Act 34 of 1920. 25. Change of short title of Act 34 of 1920. In the Indian Passport Act, 1920, in sub-section (1) of section 1, for the words and figures "the Indian Passport Act, 1920," the words, brackets and figures "the Passport (Entry into India) Act, 1920" shall be substituted.

Repeal and Saving

27. Repeal and saving. (1) The Passports Ordinance, 1967 (4 of 1967) is hereby repealed.

(2) Notwithstanding such repeal, anything done or any action taken or purporting to have been done or taken under the said Ordinance shall be deemed to have been done or taken under this Act as if this Act had commenced on the 5th day of May, 1967.

Appendix-VI

The Indian Penal Code, 1860

(Act No. 45 of 1860)

[6th October 1860]

Chapter 1

Introduction

Preamble. - Whereas it is expedient to provide a general Penal Code for India; it is enacted which follows:-

1. Title and extent of operation of the Code:- This Act shall be called the Indian Penal Code, and shall extend to the whole of India except the State of Jammu and Kashmir.

Comments

History: The Indian Penal Code is the Product. Of the work of successive Law Commission constituted by the British during the 19th century, The main milestones in the work towards the preparation of the Code are as under:-

(1) Chapter Art, 1833 under which the first Indian Law Commission was constituted.

(2) Constitution of the First Indian Law Commission (1834): President Maculae Members (Commissioner): McLeod Anderson Millets.

(3) Draft Code submitted to the Governor General in Council (14th October, 1837).

(4) Constitution of Second Indian Law Commission (26th April 1845).

(5) Report of the Second Indian Law Commission on the Draft Penal Code (1846 and 1847, i.e. in two parts).

(6) Draft Code revised and presented to Governor General in Council (1856). Revision was din by Bethune and Peacock (Law Members).

(7) Passing of the Code (6th October, 1860).

2. Punishment of offences committed within India.- Every person shall be liable to punishment under this Code and not otherwise for every act or omission contrary to the provisions thereof, of which, he shall be guilty within Indian.

Comments

Foreigners: The words 'every person' are believed to have made it clear that a foreigner is subject to Indian Penal Code for an act committed within Esop.- Jilendranath Gohsoh v.Chief Secretary, Air 1932 Cal 753 : ILR 60 Cal 364,Cf Esop (1836) 7 C & p.456.

Foreign Sovereigns: Foreign Sovereigns are exempt by International Law which (in this respcct) is part of national law: The parliament Belge, (1880) 5 P D 197-207.

Territorial Waters: See Proclamation of 30th September, 1867: P.M. Bakshi, Selective Commentary on the Constitution and Rastya Rama, (1817) 8 B H C Cr CJ 63.

Within India: Section 2 focuses on operation of the Code "within India" (see the last eight words). This limits its territorial operation. But it is to be read with Section 3,4, 108A, etc. which (directly or indirectly) provided for its extra territorial preparation.

Every person: The words "every person" highlight the universal application of the Code to all persons. The expression "person" is defined in Section 11. Section 2 should, however, be read as subject to provisions to the contrary, which may be found in various enactments or sources. Principal examples are:

(a) The constitution Articles, e.g. Article 361.

(b) Excepting provisions in the Indian penal Code (e.g. Chapter 4).

(c) Excepting or limiting provisions in the Code of Criminal Procedure, 1973.

(d) Excepting provisions in special laws in the nature of protective clauses.

(e) Rules of International Law (see infra).

Rules of public International Law: Certain rules of International Law are regarded as part of the national law also. One such rule is that foreign states and foreign sovereigns are not subject to the jurisdiction of national courts. The Parliament Beige, (1889) 5 PD 197-207 (Court of Appeals per Lord justice Brett). In the U.S., the rule was first rendered authoritatively by Chief Justice John Marshall in The Schooner Exchange v. M.C Fid don, (1812) 11 U.S. (7 Crenel) 116, 136, 137, 143-146.

The Foreign Sovereign Immunities Act, 1976 (U.S.A, 28 U.S.C. Section 1604) provides that -"subject to existing international agreements to which the United States is a party at the time of enactment of this Act, a foreign state shall be immune from the jurisdiction of the courts of the United States and of the states except as provided in this Act". This expression "foreign state" is defined as including an agency or instrumentality of a foreign state. See C. Lewis, State and Diplomatic Immunity, 1980. In India, these rule continuities to apply in regard to criminal proceedings and in regard to civil proceedings; it has been slightly modified by Section 86, Code of Civil Procedure, 1908. That Section, while not totally abrogating the immunity conferred by Public International Law, provides that a foreign sovereign can not be sued except with the consent of the Central Government.

3. Punishment of offences committed beyond but which by law may be tried within India. Any person liable by any Indian law to be tried for an offence committed beyond India shall be dealt with according to the provisions of this Code for any act committed beyond India in the same manner as if such act had been committed within India.

Comments

Scope: The section provides for extra-territorial operation of Indian legislation relating to criminal law, but only if the terms of the section are satisfied. A very important ingredient of the Section is contained in the words. "Any person liable by any Indian law....". The

Section operates only where an Indian Law specifically provides that an act committed outside Indian may be dealt with under that law in India.

Indian Law: As to the expression "Indian Law", see Madhavrao v. State of M.P., AIR 1916 SC 198. The Code Itself, in Section 4, provides for extra territorial operation of the penal provisions of the Code. For extra territorial application of other, i.e. special laws, the "extent" clause (usually contained in the first Section of the special laws) should be consulted. The Child Marriages Restraint Act, 1929 does not contain any provision for its extra territorial application and , therefore, does not apply to marriage outside India. Sheikh Haidar v. Sued lssa , ILR 1939 Nag 241. At the same time, if the "Indian Law" clearly provides for its own extra territorial application then it is immaterial that the act or omission was not punishment in the foreign country.- Pheroze v. State, (1964) 2 Cr LJ 533 (Bom).

Application: Section 3, the IPC applies only to a person liable by any Indian Law to be tried for an offence committed beyond India. If the Indian Law does not have extraterritorial operation then Section 3 dies not apply: Sheikh Haidar v. Sued Issa, ILR 1939 Nag 241. At the same time if there is in force such law, it is not necessary that the act mist be punishable where it was committed: Pheroze v. Syed Issa , ILR 1939 Neg 241.

4. Extension of code to extra territorial offences.- The provisions if this Code apply also to any offence committed by-

(1) Any citizen of India in any place without and beyond India;

(2) Any person on any shop or aircraft registered in India wherever it may be.

Explanation: In this Section the word "offence" includes every act committed outside India which, if committed in India, would be punishable under this Code.

Illustration

A, who is a citizen of India, commits a murder in Uganda, He can be tried and convicted of murder in any place in India at which he may be found.

Charge

I, (name is and office of the Magistrate) hereby charge you (name of the accused) as following:-

If in the place without of beyond India:-

That you being the citizen of India on or about the ....day of...........at with the intention of or with the intention of or with the knowledge that you will hereby commit the offence in .... (Name of place) without or beyond India (specify the place thereby committed the offence (name of the offence) punishable under Section 4, I.P.C and within my cognizance.

And I hereby direct that you be tried on the said charge by the said court.

Comments

Scope: Section 4, IPC defines the extra territorial application of the Code. Procedure for securing surrender is governed by the Extradition Act, 1962. - Jugal Kishore More (1969) 3 SCR 320.

Section 4 does not apply where the offender is not a citizen of India. Central Bank of India Ltd. V. Ram Narain, (1955)1 SCR 697.

Section 4 provides for the extra territorial operation of the Penal Code. Such operation is conditioned by the nationality of the offender-clause (1), or by the place of commission-clause (2). Under clause (1), the place of commission is immaterial provided the offender is an Indian citizen.

Citizenships is governed by the Citizenship Act, 1955.

Under clause (2) what is required is that the ship or aircraft must be registered in India. Registration of ships is governed by the Merchant Shipping Act, 1958.

Registration of aircraft is governed by the Indian Aircraft Act, 1934.

Illegal arrest: Even if a person is arrested outside India illegally for trial in India, the trial is not vitiated by the illegality of the arrest: Vinayak D. Saarkar,1920 ILR 35 Bom 225 (arrest alleged to be in violation of rules of Public International Law).

Basis of extra territorial jurisdiction: the most fundamental principle of extra- territorial jurisdiction is nationality. As early as the first authoritative commentator on jurisdiction, the Italian jurist Bartolus, himself a confirmed territoriality, it has been admitted that a state's laws may be applied extraterritorially to its citizens,

Individuals or corporations, wherever they may be found. See Bartolus on the conflict of Laws 51 (Beale trans. 1914).

A much more controversial form of extraterritorial jurisdiction is the so called effects principle. Extraterritorial though it may be in practice, in theory the effects principle is grounded on the principle of territorial jurisdiction. The premise is that a state has jurisdiction over extraterritorial conduct when the conduct has an effect within its territory.

The effects principle received its most notable enunciation in the Lotus case, where the permanent court of International Justice was asked to decide whether Turkey had violated "the principles of international law" by asserting criminal jurisdiction over a French officer who had been navigating a private French vessel, when it collided with, and sank, a Turkish ship on the high seas.

Lotus case: The issue was one of extra territoriality because the Frenchman had at all times during the collision been on French territory, i.e. aboard the French ship, although damage had been inflicted upon Turkish territory, i.e. on the Turkish ship. The Lotus court adopted a strictly positivist view of international law, seeing it as a law entirely generated by the positive acts of states and emanating "from their own free will as expressed in conventions or by usages generally accepted s expressing principles of law".

Lotus case at 18: The permanent court searched for "a rule of international law limiting the freedom of States to extend the criminal jurisdiction of their courts to a situation uniting the circumstances of the present case" and, finding move, ruled that Turkey had not acted improperly either in seizing the French Officer or in trying him for violation Turkey had not acted improperly either in seizing the French Officer or in trying him for violation Turkish law while outside Turkish territory.

Lotus case at 33: besides nationality and effects, there have been suggested and accepted from time to time a variety of other foundations for a state's exercise of extraterritorial jurisdiction. Three points should be mentioned here: the protective principle, the universality principle, and the passive personality principle. The protective principle provides that a state has jurisdiction to prescribe law with respect to "certain conduct outside its territory by persons not its nationals which is directed against the security of the state or a limited class of other state interests" Restatement (revised) supra note 8,402 (3).

5. Certain laws not to be affected by this Act: Nothing in this Act shall affect the provisions of any Act for punishing mutiny and desertion of officers, soldiers, sailors or airman in the service of the Government of India or the provisions of any special or local law.

Comments

Scope: Section 5 marks it clear that the Indian Penal Code is not exhaustive of the entire criminal law of the country: Motilal Shah, 1930 ILR 55 Bom 89.

But Section 26 of General Clauses Act, 1897 and article 20 of the Constitution prohibit double punishment for the same offence.

Section 5 saves the operation of two categories of laws, namely:-

(i) Enactments relating to armed forces, and

(ii) Special and local laws.

Armed forces: As to the category (i) mentioned above seen the Army Act, 1950, the Air Force Act, 1950 and the Navy Act, 1957.

Special and local laws: As to the category (ii) mentioned above see the expressions "Special law and Local law: as defined in sections 41-42 of the Indian Penal Code.

Double Jeopardy: Although the operation of certain other laws is saved by Section 5 of the Penal Code, it is to be remembered that a person cannot be punished twice for the same offence. See-

(i) Section 71, second Para, Indian Penal Code.

(ii) Section 26, General Clauses Act, 1897.

(iii) Article 20, Constitution of India.

Chapter-II

General Explanations

6. Definitions in the code to be understood subject to exceptions.-

Throughout this Code every definition of an offence, every penal provisions, and every illustration or every such definition or penal provision, shall be understood subject to the exceptions contained in the Chapter entitled "General Exceptions", though those exceptions are not respected in such definition, penal provision, or illustration.

Illustrations

(a) The sections in this Code, which contain defections of offences, do not express that a child under seven years of age cannot commit such offences, but the definitions are to be understood subject to the general exception which provides that nothing shall be an offence which is done by a child under seven years of age.

(b) A, a police officer, without warrant, apprehends Z, who has committed murder. Here A is not guilty of the offence of wrongful confinement for he was bound by law to apprehend Z and therefore the case falls within the general exception which provides that "nothing is an offence which is dine by a person who is bound by law to do it"

Comments

Scope: Section 6, in effect, provides that if the case of the accused falls within a general exception (Chapter 4) he is immune from criminal liability. It is not necessary to repeat in every section defining or punishing an offence that it is subject to Chapter 4.- About Latif v. State of Assam,1918 Cr LJ 1205 (Gau.); Khageswar Pujari v. State of Orissa, 1948 CR LJ 1984 Cr LJ 1108 (Orissa).

Effect : The effect of Section 6 (in broad terms) is that every penal provision of the Code is to be read as subject to the general exceptions continued in Chapter 4 (sections 76-106) of the Code.- Khageswar Pujari v. State of Orissa, 1984 Cr LJ 1108 (Orissa)

7. Sense of expression once explained: Every expression which is explained in any part of this Code in conformity with the explanation.

8. Gender: The pronoun " he" and its derivatives are used of any person, whether male or female.

9. Number: Unless the contrary appears from the context, words importing the singular number include the plural number, and words importing the plural number include the singular number.

Comments

Compare Section 13. General Clauses Act, 1897

10. Man, Woman: The word "man", denotes a male human being of any age; the word "woman" denotes a female human being of any age.

Comments

The principal's significance of Section 10 lies in the words "if any age." Thus "Woman" includes infant females as also mentioned in Section 354 of the Code. State v. Major Singh, AIR 1967 SC 63 : 1967 Cr LJ.

11. Person: The word "person includes any company or association or body of persons, whether incorporated or not.

Comments

Scope: Section 11 has the effect of including within the expression:

(a) Any company, whether incorporated or not;

(b) Any association of persons, whether incorporated or not; and

(c) Any body of persons, whether incorporated or not.

Criminal liability of corporations: Corporations are either:

(a) Corporations sole (one person or entity constituted by law as an artificial juridical person), or

(b) Corporations in aggregate (e.g. companies).

Corporations and their officers : The general proposition that corporations may be criminally liable gets some support from Section 11, which has also the effect of giving them the benefit of criminal law if they happen to become the victim of specific offences sentenced to imprisonment. Syndicate Transport Co., (1963) 66 Bom LR 197. Conversely, if the offence is punishable with fine only, the corporation (e.g. a local authority) can be punished: Girdharilal v. Lalchand, 1970 Cr LJ 987 (Raj).

More important is the question of liability of Directors and responsible officers of corporations. Where, technically, the offender is a corporation, the Directors, etc. may still is liable (in addition to the criminal liability of the corporation) if their own participation in the offence amounts to abetting the offence within the meaning of Sections 107 and 108 of the Indian Penal Code. Besides this , most special Acts enacted during the recent years contain provisions under which Directors and other Officers, who are in charge of the affairs of the corporation and responsible to the corporation for the conduct of the affairs of the corporation, are also declared criminally liable for an offence against that special Act, unless they can prove that the offence was committed without their knowledge, or that they exercised all due diligence to prevent the commission of that offence.

Criminal liability of partners: The Supreme Court, in Sham Sundar v. State of Haryana, (Judgment dated 21 August, 1989), JT 1989 (3) SC 523, has held that with reference to Section 10 of the Essential Commodities Act, 1955, the true position is that only a partner responsible for conduction the business of the firm could be convicted. The case related to breach of the Haryana Rice Procurement (Levy) Order, 1979. The offender was said to have failed to supply the necessary quantity of rice as per levy rules. Such short supply in contravention of Rice Procurement Order is punishable under Section 7 of the Essential Commodities Act. All the partners were convicted of the offence. It was urged by the appellants before the Supreme Court that there was no evidence that the appellants were in charge of the business of the firm, and for want of evidence, the conviction could not be sustained. The Supreme Court upheld the contention and allowed the appeal. It may be mentioned that Section 10 (1) of the Essential Commodities Act provides that if the person contravening an Order made under the Act is a company (which is defined to include a firm), every person who, at the time of contravention, was in charge of , and was responsible to , the company for the conduct of the business of the company (as well as the company), shall be deemed to be guilty of the contravention and shall be liable to be proceeded against and punished accordingly. However, this provision does not render any such person liable to any punishment if he proves that the contravention took place without his knowledge or that he exercised all due diligence to prevent such contravention.

The Supreme Court held that Section 10 of Essential Commodities Act was penal provision with a criminal liability, and must be construed strictly. Section 10 dies not provide for vicarious liability and dies not make all partners liable for an offence, whether they do business or not. The Court observed as under, in this context:-

"It is, therefore, necessary to add an emphatic note of caution in his regard. More often it is common that some of the partners of a firm may not even know of what is going on day to day in the firm. There may be partners, better known as sleeping partners, who are not required to take part in the business of the firm. There may be ladies and minors who were admitted for the benefit of partnership. They may not know anything about the bus anything about the business of the firm. It would be a travesty of justice to prosecute all partners and ask them to prove under the proviso to sub-section (1) that the offence was committed without their knowledge. It is significant to note that the obligation for the accused to probe under the proviso that the offence took place without his knowledge or that he exercised all due diligence to prevent such offence, arises only when the prosecution establishes that the requisite condition mentioned in sub section (1) is established. The requisite condition is that the partner we responsible for carrying on the business and was, during the relevant time, in charge of the business. In the absence of any such proof, no partner could be convicted. We, therefore, reject the contention urged by counsel for the State".

12. Public: The word public includes nay class of the public, or any community, any company, whether incorporated or not;
13. [Definition of Queen]: Repealed by the A.O.1950.
14. Servant Government: The words "servant of Government" denotes nay officer or servant continued, appointed or employed in India by or under the authority of Government.
15. [Definition of British India]: Repealed by the A.O.1937.
16. [Definition of Government of India]: Repealed.
17. Government: The word "Government" denotes the Central Government or the Government or the Government of a State.
18. India: "India" means the territory of India excluding the State of Jammu and Kashmir.

Comment

This definition dies not conflict with the Constitution: K.P.K. Vara Prasad v. Union of India, AIR 1980 AP 243.

It is only a verbal definition, confined to interpretation for the expression "India" as occurring in the code in various sections- such as Sections 108A, 121A, 359, 360, etc. The focus in Section 18 is not on India as a political entity, but on the geographical aspect of the territory intended to be connoted by the expression "India" as occurring in those sections of the Code where the territorial aspect is the crucial element. The definition would have been more expressive (and would have created less controversy) if it began something like this-"India" in relation to the territory...."

19. Judge: The word "judge" denotes not only every person who is officially designated as judge but also every person-who is empowered by law to give, in any legal proceeding, civil or criminal, definitive judgment by law to give, in any legal proceeding, civil or criminal, definitive judgment or a judgment which, if confirmed by some other authority, would be definitive or who is one of a body of persons if empowered by law to give such a judgement.

Illustrations

(a) A Collector exercising jurisdiction in a suit under Act 10 of 1859 is a Judge.

(b) A Magistrate exercising jurisdiction in respect of a charge on which he has power to sentence to fine or imprisonment, with or without appeal, is a judge.

(c) A member of a panchayats which has power, under Regulation VII, 1810, of the Madras Code to try and determine suits, is a judge.

(d) A Magistrate exercising jurisdiction in respect of a charge on which he has power only to commit for trial to another Court, is not a Judge.

20. Court of Justice: The words "Court of Justice" denote a Judge who is empowered by law to act judicially alone, or a body of judges who is empowered by law to act judicially as a body, when such judge or body of judges is acting judicially.

Illustrations

Panchayats acting under Regulation VII, 1816, of the Madras Code, having power to try and determine suits, is a Court of Justice.

21. Public servant: The words" public servant" denote a person falling under any of the descriptions hereinafter following, namely:-

2nd: Every Commissioned Officer in the Military, Naval or Air Forces of India;

3rd: Every Judge including any person empowered by law to discharge, whether by himself or as a member of any body of persons, any ad judicatory functions;

4th: Every; officer of a Overt of Justice (including a liquidator, receiver or commissioner) whose duty it is as such officer, to investigate or report on any matter of law or fact, or to make, authenticate, or keep any document, or to administer any oath, or to interpret, or to preserve order in the Court, and every person specially authorised by a Court of Justice to perform any of such duties;

5th: Every juryman, assessor, or member of a panchayats assisting a Court of Justice or public servant;

6th: Every arbitrator or other person to whom any cause or matter has been referred for decision or report by any Court of Justice, or by any other competent

1. Clause first omitted by the A.O. 1950.

7th: Every person who holds any office by virtue\e of which he is empowered to place or keep any person in confinement;

8th: Every officer of the Government whose duty it is. As such officer, to prevent offences, to give information of offences, to bring offenders to justice, or to protect the public health, safety or convenience;

9th: Every officer whose duty it is, as such officer, to take, receive, keep or expend any property on behalf of the Government, or to make any survey, assessment or contract on behalf of the Government, or to make any survey, assessment or contract on behalf of the Government, or to execute any revenue process, or to investigate, or to report, on any matter affection the pecuniary interests of the government, or to make m authenticate or keep any document relating to the pecuniary interests of the Government, or to prevent the infraction of any law for the protection of the pecuniary interests of the Government;

10th: Every person whose duty it is, as such officer, to take, receive, keep or expend any property, to made any survey or assessment or to levy any rate or tax for a y secular common purpose of any village, town or district, or to make, authenticate or keep any document for the ascertaining of the right of the people of any village, town or district;

11th: Every Person-

(a) in the service or pay of the Government or remunerated by fees or commission for the performance of any public duty by the government;

(b) in the service or pay of a local authority, a corporation establishment by or under a Central, Provincial or State Act or a Government company as defined in Section 617 of the Companies Act, 1956 (1 of 1956).

Appendix-VII

The Passport (Entry Into India) Amendment Act, 2000 Year: 1962

The Passport (Entry Into India) Amendment Act, 2000

Act No. 47 of 2000 [8th December, 2000]

An Act further to amend the Passport (Entry into India) Act, 1920. BE it enacted by Parliament in the Fifty-first Year of the Republic of India as follows:-

1. Short title.

1. Short title. This Act may be called the Passport (Entry into India) Amendment Act, 2000.

2. Amendment of section 3.2. Amendment of section 3. In section 3 of the Passport (Entry into India) Act, 1920 (34 of 1920) (hereinafter referred to as the principal Act), in sub-section (3), for the words "punishable with imprisonment for a term which may extend to three months, or with fine, or with both", the words "punishable with imprisonment for a term which may extend to five years, or with fine which may extend to fifty thousand rupees, or with both" shall be substituted.

3. Insertion of new section 3A.

3. Insertion of new section 3A. After section 3 of the principal Act, the following section shall be inserted, namely:-

"3A. Punishment for subsequent offences.-Whoever having been convicted of an offence under any rule or order made under this Act is again convicted of an offence under this Act shall be punishable with double the penalty provided for the later offence."

4. Amendment of section 4.4. Amendment of section 4.-In section 4 of the principal Act, in sub-section (2), for the words and figures "section 61 of the Code of Criminal Procedure, 1898 (5 of 1898)," the words and figures "section 57 of the Code of Criminal Procedure, 1973 (2 of 1974)," shall be substituted.

SUBHASH C. JAIN,

Secretary to the Government of India

Appendix-VIII

The Immigrants (Expulsion From Assam) Act, 1950

ACT NO. 10 OF 1950

[1st March, 1950]

An Act to provide for the expulsion of certain Immigrants from Assam, it enacted by Parliament as follows:--

1. Short Title and Extent

1. Short title and extent. (1) This Act may be called the Immigrants (Expulsion from Assam) Act, 1950.

   (2) It extends to the whole of India.

2. Power to order expulsion of certain immigrants.

2. Power to order expulsion of certain immigrants. If the Central Government is of opinion that any person or class of persons, having been ordinarily resident in any place outside India, has or have. whether before or after the commencement of this Act, come into Assam and that the stay of such person or class of persons in Assam is detrimental to the interests of the general public of India or of any section thereof or of any Scheduled Tribe in Assam, the Central Government may by order--

(a) direct such person or class of persons to remove himself or themselves from India or Assam within such time and by such route as may be specified in the order; and (b) give such further directions in regard to his or their removal from India or Assam as it may consider necessary or expedient; Provided that nothing in this section shall apply to any person who on account of civil disturbances or the fear of such disturbances in any area now forming part of Pakistan has been displaced from or has left his place of residence in such area and who has been subsequently residing in Assam.

3. Delegation Power

3. Delegation power. The Central Government may, by notification in the Official Gazette, direct that the powers and duties conferred or imposed on it by section 2 shall, subject to such conditions, if any, as may be specified in the notification, be exercised or discharged also by- (a) any officer subordinate to the Central Government; (b) the 2*[3*[Government of Assam, Meghalaya] or Nagaland] or any officer subordinate to that Government.

4. Power to give effect orders, etc. Any authority empowered by or in pursuance of the provisions of this Act to exercise any power may, in addition to any other action expressly provided for in this Act, take or cause to be taken such steps, and use or cause to be used such force, as may in its opinion be reasonably necessary for the effective exercise of such power.

5. Penalties

5. Penalties. Any person who (a) contravenes or attempts to contravene or abets the contravention of any order made under section 2, or (b) fails to comply with any direction given by any such order, or (c) harbours any person who has contravened any order made under section 2 or has failed to comply with any direction given by any such order, shall be punishable with imprisonment which may extend to three years and shall also be liable to fine.

6. Protection to Persons Acting Under this Act

6. Protection to persons acting under this Act. No suit, prosecution or other legal proceeding shall lie against any person for anything which in good faith done or intended to be done under this Act.

7. Construction of References to Assam

7. Construction of references to Assam. In this Act, except in section 3, references to Assam shall be construed as including also a reference to 2*[the States of Meghalaya and Nagaland and the Union territories of Arunachal Pradesh and Mizoram.

Appendix-IX

Registration of Foreigners Act 1939

ACT NO. 16 OR 1939*

[8th April, 1939]

An Act to provide for the registration of foreigners in British India. WHEREAS it is expedient to provide for the registration of foreigners entering, being present in, and departing from, British India;

Short Title and Extent

1. Short title and extent. (1) This Act may be called the Registration of Foreigners Act, 1939.

(2) It extends to 2 [the whole of India]

Definitions. 2. Definitions. In this Act- 3[(a) "foreigner" means a person who is not a citizen of India;] 4(b) "prescribed" means prescribed by rules made under this Act.

Power to make rules.

3. Power to make rules. [(1)]8 The Central Government may after previous publication, by power to notification in the Official Gazette, make rules 6 with respect to make rules. Foreigners for any or all of the following purposes, that is to say- (a) for requiring any foreigner entering, or being present in, 7 [India] to report his presence to a prescribed authority.

*This Act has been extended to Goa, Daman and Diu with modifications by Reg. 12 of 1962, s. 3 and Sch. Pondicherry with, modifications vide Notification No. G.S.R. 1557. dated 24-11-1962, Gazette of India, Part 11, Sec. 3 (i), p. 1886 ; brought into force in Dadra and Nagar Haveli by Reg. 6 of 1963, s. 2 and Sch. I. (w.e.f. 1-7-1965) ; Lakshadweep vide Reg. 8 of 1665, s. 3 and Sch. (w.e.f. 1-10-1967) Sch. (w.e.f. 1-10-1967). The State of Sikkim vides Notification No. G.S.R. 41 (E), dated 27-1- 1976 (w.e.f. 1-2-1976). 1 Subs. by Act 37 of 1949, s. 2, for "the Provinces of India". 2 Subs. by s. 3, ibid. for "all the Provinces of India". 3 The words "except the State of Hyderabad", ins. by the A.O. 1950, omitted by Act 3 of 1951, s. 3 and Sch. 4 Subs. by Act 11 of 1957, s. 8, for the former clause (w.e.f. 19-1- 1957). 5 Cl. (a), ins. by the A.O. 1950, omitted by Act 3 of 1951, s. 3 and Sch. 6 for Registration of Foreigners Rules. 1939 see Gazette of India, 1939, Pt. I, P. 1059. 7 Subs. by Act 37 of 1949, s. 4. For "the Provinces". 8 Renumbered by Act 4 of 1986, s. 2, such. (w.e.f. 15-5-1986) 4 within such time and in such manner and with such particulars as may be prescribed; (b) for requiring any foreigner moving from one place to another place in 1 [India] to report, on arrival at such other place, his presence to a prescribed authority within such time and in such manner and with such particulars as may be prescribed; (c) for requiring any foreigner who is about to leave 1[India] to report the date of his intended departure and such other particulars as may be prescribed to such authority. And within such period before departure as may. be prescribed; (d) for requiring any foreigner entering, being present in, or departing from, 1 [India] to produce, on demand by a prescribed authority, such proof of his identity as may be prescribed; (e) for requiring any person having the management of any hotel, boarding-house, sarai or any other premises of like nature to report the name of any foreigner residing therein for whatever duration, to a prescribed authority, within such time and in such manner and with such particulars as may be prescribed; (f) for requiring any person having the management or control of any vessel or aircraft to furnish to a prescribed authority such information as may be prescribed regarding any foreigner entering, or intending to depart from, 1 [India], in such vessel or aircraft, and to furnish to such authority such assistance as may be necessary or prescribed for giving effect to this Act.

2 (4) Every rule made under this section shall be laid as soon as may be after it is made, before each House of Parliament, while it is in session, for a total Period of thirty days which may be comprised in one session or in two or more successive sessions, and if, before the expiry of the session immediately following the session or the successive sessions aforesaid. Both Houses agree in making any

modification in the rule or both Houses agree that the rule should not be made. The rule shall there after have effect only, in such modified form or be of no effect, as the case may be; so, however, that any such modification or annulment shall be without prejudice to the validity of anything previously done tinder that rule.] (g) for providing for such other incidental or supplementary matters as may appear to the Central Government necessary or expedient for giving effect to this Act.

Burden of proof. 4. Burden of proof. If any question arises with reference to this Act or any rule made hereunder, whether any person is or is not a foreigner, or is or is not a foreigner of a particular class or description, the onus of proving that such person is not a foreigner or is not a foreigner of:

1. Subs. by Act 37 of 1949, s. 4, for "the Provinces" 2. Ins. by Act 4 of 1986, S. 2 & Sch (w.e.f. 15-5-1956) 4A such particular class or description, as the case may be, shall, not withstanding anything contained in the Indian Evidence Act, 1872 (1 of 1872) lie upon such person.

Penalties. 5. Penalties. Any person who contravenes, or attempts to contravene, or fails to comply with, any provision of any rule made under this Act shall be punished, if a foreigner, with imprisonment for a term which may extend to one year or with fine which may extend to one thousand rupees or with both, or if not a foreigner, with fine which may extend to five hundred rupees. Power to exempt from application of Act. 6. Power to exempt from application of Act. The Central Government may, by order 1, declare that any or all of the provisions of the rules made under this Act shall not apply

1 for Registration of Foreigners Exemption Order, 1949, see Gazette of India 1949, Pt. I, P. 1591. 5 or shall apply only with such modifications or subject to such conditions as may be specified in the said order, to or in relation to any individual foreigner or any class or description of foreigner: Provided that a copy of every such order shall be placed on the table of 1* * * Parliament as soon as may be after its promulgation.

Protection to persons acting under this Act. 7. Protection to persons acting under this Act. No suit, prosecution or other legal proceeding shall lie against any person for anything which is in good faith done or intended to be done under this Act.

Application of other laws not barred. 8. Application of other laws not barred. The provisions of this Act shall be in addition to, and not in derogation of, the provisions of the Foreigners Act, 2[1946] (31 of 1946.) and any other law for the time being in force.

Application of Act to Part B States. 9. Application of Act to Part B States. [Application of Act to Part B States.] Rep. by the Part B States (Laws) Act, 1951 (3 of 1951), s. 3 and Sch.

1 The words "both Houses of "rep. by the A.O. 1948. 2 Subs. by Act 37 of 1949, s. 5, for "1864". 3 Added, ibid, s. 6.

Appendix-X

Foreigners Order, 1948

In exercise of the powers conferred by Section 3 of the Foreigners Act, 1946, and in super session of the Foreigners Order, 1939, and of all notifications amending the same, the Central Government is pleased to make the following Order:-

1. Short title, Commencement and Extent

(1) This order may be called the Foreigners Order, 1948.

(2) It shall come into force at once.

(3) It extends to the whole of India.

2. Definitions

In this Order,-

(1) "Registration Officer" means a Registration Officer as defined in the Registration of Foreigners Rules, 1939 or any other officer as may be authorised by him to perform the functions of a Registration Officer under this Order;

(2) "Civil Authority" means such authority as may be appointed by the Central Government in this behalf for such an area as it thinks fit;

(3) "Port" includes an airport.

3. Power to Grant or Refuse Permission to Enter India

(1) No foreigner shall enter India-

(a) Otherwise than at such port or any other place of entry on the borders of India as a Registration Officer having jurisdiction at that port or place may appoint in this behalf; either for foreigners generally or for any specified class or descriptions of foreigners, or (b) Without the leave of the civil authorities having jurisdiction at such port or place.

(2) Leave to enter shall be refused if the civil authority satisfied that-

(a) The foreigner is not in possession of a valid passport or visa for India or has not been exempted from the possession of a passport or visa; (b) he is a person of unsound mind or a mentally defective person; (c) he is suffering from a loathsome or infectious disease in consequence of which, in the opinion of the Medical Officer of the port or the place of entry, as the case may be, the entry of the foreigner is likely to prejudice public health; (d) he has been sentenced in a foreign country for an extradition offence within the meaning of the Indian Extradition Act, 1903 (15 of 1903); (e) his entry is prohibited either under an order issued by a competent authority or under the specific orders of the Central Government.

(3) The civil authority may attach such conditions as it thinks fit to the grant of leave to enter and such conditions may be varied in such manner or cancelled as the Central Government deems fit.

(4) (a) Notwithstanding anything contained in sub-paragraphs (1) to (3) or in the Indian Passport Act, 1920 (34 of 1920) or in the rules made hereunder, a civil authority may, in the interests of public safety, prohibit the entry of any foreigner into India. (b) Whenever the civil authority issues an order under Clause (a), it shall report the matter forthwith to the Central Government which may cancel or modify the order in such manner as it thinks fit.

(5) Where leave to enter is refused to foreigner, he may be detained at some place approved by the civil authority and may, if he has come by sea, be placed temporarily on shore for that purpose, and whilst he is so detained, a foreigner shall be deemed to be in legal custody and not to have entered India.

4. Landing of Seamen

(1) No seamen or member of the crew of an aircraft, being a foreigner, shall land in India without a special permit from the

Superintendent of Police or any other Police Officer not below the rank of a Sub-Inspector or Sergeant.

(2) No such permit shall be granted unless the owners or agents of the vessel or aircraft have undertaken either generally in respect of all members of the crew of vessels or aircraft belonging to or managed by them or in an individual case, the responsibility for the maintenance of such seamen or member of the crew during his residence in India and for the expenses of his departure from India.

(3) For the purposes of this paragraph, "seamen" has the meaning assigned to it in the Registration of Foreigners Rules, 1939.

(4) The provisions of this paragraph are in addition to, and not in derogation of the provisions of paragraph 3.

5. Power to Grant Permission to Depart from India

(1) No foreigner shall leave India-

(a) otherwise than at such port or other recognised place of departure on the borders of India as a Registration Officer having jurisdiction at that port or place may appoint in this behalf, either for foreigners generally or for any specified class or description of foreigners; or (b) without the leave of civil authority having jurisdiction at such port or place.

(2) Leave shall be refused if the civil authority is satisfied that-

(a) the foreigner has failed to comply with the formalities of departure prescribed under the Registration of Foreigners Rules, 1939; (b) the foreigners' presence is required in India to answer a criminal charge; (c) the foreigner's departure will prejudice the relations of the Central Government with a foreign power; (d) the departure of the foreigner has been prohibited under an order issued by a competent authority.

(3) (a) Notwithstanding anything contained in the above sub-paragraphs, a civil authority may prohibit the departure of a foreigner where it is satisfied that such departure would not be conducive to the interest. (b) Whenever a civil authority issues an order under Clause (a), it shall report the matter forthwith to the Central Government which may cancel or modify the order in such manner as it thinks fit.

5. A. Power to examine persons.

The Civil Authority may examine any person who seeks leave to enter India or to depart there from or during his stay in India for the purposes of the Foreigners Act, 1946, or of any order made hereunder; and it shall be the duty of every such person to furnish to the Civil Authority such information, in such manner and at such times, as that authority may require.

6. Liability of Master of the Vessel, etc. to Remove a Foreigner

(1) A Civil Authority may require the master of the vessel or pilot of the aircraft in which a foreigner has arrived or the owners or agents of that vessel or aircraft, as may be appropriate in the opinion of such civil authority, to remove a foreigner who has been refused permission to enter or who has entered India without its permission or who has been landed in contravention of subparagraph (3) and the master, pilot, owner or agent, as the case may be, shall comply with such requisition, unless it is received for more than two months after the date of the arrival of the foreigner in India.

(2) The master of a vessel or the pilot of an aircraft, scheduled to call at any port outside India, shall, if so required by the Central Government, receive a foreigner in respect of whom an order directing that he shall not remain in India has been made, and his dependants, if any, on board the vessel or aircraft, as the case may be, and afford him and others a passage to the port and proper accommodation and maintenance during the passage.

(3) The master of any vessel or the pilot of any aircraft shall not, without the permission of the Civil Authority, land at any port in India any person, travelling by that vessel or aircraft against the wishes of such person, unless such person has been required by the Central Government to be brought to India.

(4) Nothing contained in the Foreigners (Exemption) Order, 1957, shall preclude the operations and applications of the provision of sub-paragraph (3).

7. Restriction of Sojourn in India

(1) Every foreigner who enters India on the authority of a visa issued in pursuance of the Indian Passport Act, 1920 (XXXIV of 1920), shall obtain from the Registration Officer having jurisdiction, "either at the place at which the said foreigner enters India or at the place at which he presents a registration report in accordance with Rule 6 of

the Registration of Foreigners Rules, 1939, a permit indicating the period during which he is authorised to remain in India and also indicating the place or places for stay in India, if any, specified in the visa. In granting such permit, the said Registration Officer may restrict the stay of the foreigner to any of the places specified in the visa.

(2) Every foreigner to whom the provisions of sub-paragraph (1) do not apply shall obtain a permit indicating the period during which he is authorised to remain in India from the Registration Officer to whom he presents a registration report in accordance with Rule 6 of the Registration of Foreigners Rules, 1939.

(3) Every foreigner to whom a permit is issued under sub-paragraph (1) or sub-paragraph (2):- (i)shall not, if the permit indicates the place unless the place or places for stay in India, visit any other place unless the permit is extended by the Central Government to such other place; (ii) shall, if the permit indicates the place or places for stay in India, report in person or in writing his arrival at, and departure from, any such place to the Registration Officer having jurisdiction at such place, within twenty-four hours after his arrival or, as the case may be. 1 [before his intended departure; provided that this clause shall not apply to the nationals of Pakistan who enter India on the authority of visa as valid for a period fourteen days or less.] (iii) shall, unless the period indicated in the permit is extended by the Central Government, depart from India before the expiry of the said period; and at the time of the foreigner's departure from India, the permit shall be surrendered by him to the Registration Officer having jurisdiction at the place from which he departs.

8. Prohibited Places

(1) No foreigner shall, without the permission of the civil authority having jurisdiction at such place, visit, or reside in any prohibited place as defined in the Indian Official Secrets Act, 1923 (19 of 1923).

(2) Where any foreigner is, on the commencement of this Order, residing in any prohibited place and is not permitted to continue to reside there, he shall within such time as may be specified by the Civil Authority, remove himself from such place.

(3) The civil authority may impose on any householder or other person in such prohibited place the obligation to report to the police or to any Naval, Military, or Air Force authority the presence of any

foreigner in his household or in any premises occupied by him or under his control and the departure of any such foreigner and such other particulars with respect to such foreigner as may be prescribed by such authority.

9. Protected Areas

(1) The Central Government or, with its prior sanction, a civil authority may by order declare any area to be a protected area for the purposes of this Order.

(2) On such declaration, the civil authority may, as to any protected area, by order,-

(a) prohibit any foreigner or any class of foreigners from entering or remaining in the area;

(b) impose on any foreigner or class of foreigners entering or being entered in the area, such conditions or restrictions as it may think fit as to,- (i) reporting to the Police or any Naval, Military, or Air Force Authority; (ii) surveying or making sketches or photographs; (iii) the use or possession of any machine, apparatus or other article of any description; (iv) the acquisition of land or any interest in land within the area; (v) any other matter or thing as to which it may deem it necessary in the interests of public safety to impose conditions or restrictions;

(c) impose on any householder or other person the obligation to report to the Police or any Naval, Military, or Air Force Authority the presence of any foreigner in his household or in any premises occupied by him or under his control, and the departure of any such foreigner and such other particulars with respect to any such foreigner as may be prescribed by the order:

Provided that the civil authority may, subject to any general or specific direction of the Central Government, grant to an individual foreigner a special permit exempting him from any or all of the conditions or restrictions imposed under this sub-paragraph.

10. Restrictions on Employment

(1) No foreigner shall, without the permission in writing of the Civil Authority, either enter any premises relating to or accept employment in, or in connection with:

(i) any undertaking for the supply of light, petroleum, power or water to Government or to the public; or (ii) any other undertaking which may be specified by the Central Government in this behalf.

(1-A) No foreigner employed without the permission in writing of the civil authority before the commencement of the Foreigners (Amendment) Order, 1964, in any undertaking referred to in Clause (i) of sub-paragraph (1) shall remain employed in such undertaking, without the permission in writing of the civil authority, after the expiry of a period of three months from the commencement of the Foreigners (Second Amendment) Order, 1964.

(1-B) No foreigner employed in any undertaking specified in Clause (ii) of sub-paragraph (1) before the undertaking was so specified shall remain employed in such undertaking, without the permission in writing of the civil authority, after the expiry of a period of one month from the date of commencement of the Foreigners (Second Amendment) Order, 1964, or the date on which the undertaking was so specified, whichever is latter:

Provided that no Pakistani national, shall remain employed in any such undertaking as is referred to in clause (ii) of sub-paragraph (1), which has been, or may be specified after the 1st September, 1965, unless he has obtained permission in writing from the civil authority within twenty-four hours from the date of commencement of the Foreigners (Second Amendment) Order, 1964 or from the date on which the undertaking is so specified, whichever is latter.

(2) The management of any undertaking referred to in subparagraph (1) shall furnish to the civil authority such information regarding foreigners employed in that undertaking and make available for inspection such records and registers as may be called for by the authority.

11. Powers to Impose Restrictions on Movements, etc.

The civil authority may, by order in writing, direct, that any foreigner shall comply with such conditions as may be specified in the order in respect of:-

(1) his place of residence;

(2) his movements;

(3) his association with any person or class of persons specified in the order; and

(4) his possession of such articles as may be specified in the order.

11-A. Restrictions on Certain Activities

Notwithstanding anything contained in the Foreigners (Exemption) Order, 1957, no foreigner shall produce, or attempt to produce, or cause to be produced, any picture or film, including a documentary or feature films for television or the screen, intended for public exhibition, except with the permission in writing of, and subject to such conditions as may be specified in this behalf, by the Central Government.

11-B. Restrictions on Mountaineering Expeditions.

Notwithstanding anything contained in the Foreigners (Exemption) Order, 1957, no foreigner or group of foreigners shall climb, or attempt to climb, any mountain peak in India without obtaining the prior permission in writing, of the Central Government on an application made in that behalf through the Indian Mountaineering Foundation, a registered society having its registered office in the Union Territory of Delhi and without complying with such condition including specification of route to be followed, accompaniment by Liaison Officer, use of photographic and wireless communication equipment, as may be laid down in this behalf by the Central Government.

12. Powers to Remove Foreigners from Cantonments

The Military Officer for the time being in command of the forces in a Cantonment may, by order in writing; direct any foreigner to remove himself from the Cantonment within such time at may be specified in the order.

13. Powers to Close Clubs and Restaurants

(1)A civil authority may direct, that any premises in its jurisdiction which in its opinion are used for the sale of refreshments to be consumed on the premises, or as a place of public resort or entertainment or as a club, and which are or have recently been frequented by foreigners, shall be either closed altogether or kept closed during such hours or for such purposes as may be required by it, if in its opinion either-

(a) the foreigners so frequenting the premises are of criminal or disloyal associations or otherwise undesirable; or

(b) the premises are conducted in a disorderly or improper manner; or in a manner prejudicial to the public good; and if any premises are kept open in contravention of any such direction the occupier or person having control of the premises shall be deemed to have acted in contravention of this Order.

(2) where any premises have been closed under this paragraph the occupier or person having control of the premises shall not occupy or control any other premises which are used for the sale of refreshment or as a place of public resort or entertainment, or as a club without the consent of the civil authority of the area in which the premises are situated.

(3) Any police officer, if authorised by a civil authority may, for the purpose of enforcing the provisions of this paragraph, enter, if necessary, by force, and search or occupy any premises in respect of which an order under this paragraph has been made by the civil authority.

(4) Any action taken by the civil authority under sub-paragraphs (1) to (3) above shall be reported forthwith to the Central Government which may cancel or modify such order in such manner as it deems fit.

14. Expenses of deportation

Where an order is made in the case of any foreigner directing that he shall not remain in India or where a foreigner is refused permission to enter India or has entered India without permission, the Central Government may, if it thinks fit, deport any money or property of the foreigner in payment of the whole or any part of the expenses of, or incidental to the voyage from India and the maintenance until departure of the foreigner and his dependants, if any.

Appendix-XI

Illegal Migrants (Determination by Tribunals) Act 1983

ACT NO. 39 OF 1983

[25th December, 1983]

An Act to provide for the establishment of Tribunals for the determination, in a fair manner, of the question whether a person is an illegal migrant to enable the Central Government to expel illegal migrants from India and for matters connected therewith or incidental thereto. WHEREAS a good number of the foreigners who migrated into India across the borders of the eastern and north-eastern regions of the country on and after the 25th day of March, 1971, have, by taking advantage of the circumstances of such migration and their ethnic similarities and other connections with the people of India and without having in their possession any lawful authority so to do, illegally remained in India; AND WHEREAS the continuance of such foreigners in India is detrimental to the interests of the public of India; AND WHEREAS on account of the number of such foreigners and the manner in which such foreigners have clandestinely been trying to pass off as citizens of India and all other relevant circumstances, it is necessary for the protection of the citizens of India to make special provisions for the detection of such foreigners in Assam and also in any other part of India in which such foreigners may be found to have remained illegally; BE it enacted by Parliament in the Thirty-fourth Year of the Republic of India as follows:- CHAP PRELIMINARY CHAPTER I PRELIMINARY.

1. Short Title, Extent and Commencement

(1) This Act may be called the Illegal Migrants (Determination by Tribunals) Act, 1983.

(2) It extends to the whole of India.

(3) It shall be deemed to have come into force in the State of Assam on the 15th day of October, 1983 and in any other State on such date as the Central Government may, by notification in the Official Gazette, appoint and different dates may be appointed for different States and references in this Act to the commencement of this Act shall be 322 construed in relation to any State as references to the date of commencement of this Act in such State.

2. Application

Nothing in this Act shall apply to or in relation to-

(a) any person who was in any State and who had been expelled from that State or India before the commencement of this Act in that State or in relation to whose expulsion from such State or India any order made before such commencement under any other law is in force; (b) any person detected as a foreigner at the time of his entry across any border of India; (c) any foreigner who, having entered into India under a valid passport or travel document, continued to remain therein after the expiry of the period for which he was authorised to remain in India under such passport or travel document.

3. Definitions and Construction of References

(1) In this Act, unless the context otherwise requires, - (a) "Appellate Tribunal" means an Appellate Tribunal established by the Central Government under sub-section (1) of section 15; (b) "foreigner" has the same meaning as in the Foreigners Act, 1946; (31 of 1946.) (c) "illegal migrant" means a person in respect of whom each of the following conditions is satisfied, namely:- (i) he has entered into India on or after the 25th day of March, 1971, (ii) he is a foreigner, (iii) he has entered into India without being in possession of a valid passport or other travel document or any other lawful authority in that behalf; (d) "notification" means a notification published in the Official Gazette; (e) "prescribed" means prescribed by rules made under this Act; (f) "Tribunal" means a Tribunal established by the Central Government under sub-section (1) of section 5. (2) Any reference in this Act to any law which is not in force in any area shall, in relation to that area, be construed as a reference to the corresponding law, if any, in force in that area.

4. Overriding Effect of the Act

(1) The provisions of this Act or of any rule or order made hereunder shall have effect notwithstanding anything contained in the Passport (Entry into India) Act, 1920 (34 of 1920) or the Foreigners Act, 1946 (31 of 1946) or the Immigrants (Expulsion from Assam) Act, 1950 (10 of 1950) or the Passports Act, 1967 (15 of 1967) or any rule or order made under any of the said Acts and in force for the time being. (2) In particular and without prejudice to the generality of the provisions of sub-section (1), nothing in the proviso to section 2 of the Immigrants (Expulsion from Assam) Act, 1950 (10 of 1950) shall apply to or in relation to an illegal migrant as defined in clause (c) of sub-section (1) of section 3.

5. Establishment of Illegal Migrants (Determination) Tribunals

(1) The Central Government may, by notification, establish, for the purposes of this Act, as many Illegal Migrants (Determination) Tribunals as it may deem necessary and specify the principal place of sitting of, and the territorial limits within which, each such Tribunal shall exercise its jurisdiction. (2) No person shall be appointed as a member of any such Tribunal unless he is or has been a District Judge or an Additional District Judge in any State. (3) Each Tribunal shall consist of two members. (4) On the establishment of a Tribunal, the Central Government shall appoint one of the members thereof as the Chairman of such Tribunal. (5) Each Tribunal shall sit in its principal place of sitting and in such other place or places as its Chairman may, from time to time, appoint.

6. Filling of vacancies

If, for any reason, any vacancy occurs in the office of the Chairman or the member of a Tribunal, the Central Government may fill the vacancy by appointing any person who fulfils the qualifications specified in sub-section (2) of section 5, as the Chairman, or, as the case may be, member of such Tribunal.

7. Staff of the Tribunals

The Central Government shall make available to every Tribunal such staff as may be necessary for the discharge of its functions under this Act.

8. References or Applications to Tribunals

(1) If any question arises as to whether any person is or is not an illegal migrant, the Central Government may, whether such question has arisen on a representation made by such person against any order under the Foreigners Act, 1946 (31 of 1946) requiring him not to remain in India or to any other effect or has arisen in any other manner whatsoever, refer such question to a Tribunal for decision. (2) Any person may make an application to the Tribunal, for its decision, as to whether the person whose name and other particulars are given in the application, is or is not an illegal migrant: (3) "Provided that no such application shall be entertained by the Tribunal unless the person in relation to whom the application is made is found, or resides, within the jurisdiction of the same police station wherein the applicant has his place of residence."; 1 Subs. by Act 24 of 1988, s. 2. 2 Subs. by s. 3, ibid. 3 Omitted and rules. by s. 4, ibid. (3) Every application made under sub-section (2) shall be made in such form and in such manner as may be prescribed and shall be accompanied by affidavits sworn by not less than two persons residing within the jurisdiction of the same police station in which the person referred to in the application is found, or residing, corroborating the averments made in the application, and shall also be accompanied by such fee, being not less than ten and not more than one hundred, rupees, as may be prescribed.

1*["(4) Every reference under sub-section (1) shall be made to the Tribunal within the territorial limits of whose jurisdiction the place of residence of the person named in such reference is, at the time of making such reference, situated: Provided that where such person has no place of residence, the reference shall be made to the Tribunal within the territorial limit of whose jurisdiction such person is, at the time of making such reference, found.

(5) Every application under sub-section (2) shall be made to the Tribunal within the territorial limits off whose jurisdiction the person named in such application is found or, as the case may be, has his place of residence, at the time of making such application."]

2*["8A. Application to the Central Government for reference. (1) Any person may make an application to the Central Government, for decision by a Tribunal, as to whether the person whose name and other particulars are given in the application, is or is not an illegal migrant, and where any such application is received by the Central Government, it may, on the basis of any information in its possession or after making such inquiry as it deems fit, reject the application on the ground that the application is frivolous or vexatious or it does not comply with the requirements of this section or refer such application to a Tribunal for decision.

(2) Every application made under sub-section (1) shall be made in such form and in such manner as may be prescribed and shall be accompanied by a declaration by another person residing within the jurisdiction of the same revenue sub-division in which the applicant resides in such form as may be prescribed to the effect that the particulars mentioned in the application are true to his knowledge, information and belief: Provided that no person shall make more than ten such apply- captions or more than ten such declarations.

(3) Every reference under sub-section (1) shall be made to the Tribunal within the territorial limits of whose jurisdiction the place of residence of the person named in such reference is, at the time of making such reference, situated: Provided that where such person has no place of residence, the reference shall be made to the Tribunal within the territorial limits of whose jurisdiction such person is, at the time of making such reference, found."]

9. Powers of the Tribunal

Every Tribunal shall have the same powers as are vested in a civil court under the Code of Civil Procedure, 1908, (5 of 1908.) while trying a suit, in respect of the following matters, namely:- (a) summoning and enforcing the attendance of witnesses and examining them on oath; (b) discovery and production of any document; (c) reception of evidence on affidavits; (d) requisitioning of public records from any court or office; (e) issuing of any commission for the examination of witnesses.

10. Procedure with Respect to References under Sub-section (1) of Section 8

On receipt of a reference under sub-section (1) of section 8 or sub-section (1) of section 8A the Tribunal shall serve on the person named in such reference, a notice, accompanied by a copy of such reference, calling upon him to make, within a period of thirty days from the date of receipt of such notice, such representation with regard to the averments made in the reference, and to produce such evidence as he may think fit in support of his defence: Provided that if the Tribunal is satisfied that the person aforesaid was prevented by sufficient cause from making his representation and from producing evidence in support of his defence within the said period of thirty days, it may permit him to make his representation and to produce evidence in support of his defence, within such further period, not exceeding thirty days, as it may, by order, specify.

11. Procedure with Respect to Applications under Sub-section (2) of section 8

(1) On receipt of an application under sub-section (2) of section 8, the Tribunal shall issue a notice, accompanied by a copy of the application, to the prescribed authority calling upon it to furnish, after making such inquiry as that authority may deem fit, a report to the Tribunal with regard to the averments made in the application. 1 Subs. by Act 24 of 1988, s. 4. 2 Ins. by s. 5, *ibid.* 3 Subs. b s. 6, *ibid*. 325 (2) If, on a consideration of the report made by the prescribed authority, the Tribunal is satisfied that- (a) the person named in the application is not an illegal migrant or that the application is frivolous or vexatious, or has not been made in good faith, the Tribunal shall, after giving the applicant an opportunity to be heard, reject the application; (b) there are reasonable grounds to believe that the person named in the application is an illegal migrant, the Tribunal shall issue a notice accompanied by a copy of the application, to the person named in the application, calling upon him to make, within thirty days from the date of receipt of the notice, such representation with regard to the averments made in the application and to produce such evidence as he may think fit in support of his defence: Provided that if the Tribunal is satisfied that the person aforesaid was prevented by sufficient cause from making his representation and from producing evidence in support of his defence within the said period of thirty days, it may permit him to make his representation and to produce evidence in support of his defence, within such further period, not exceeding thirty days, as it may, by order, specify.

12. Determination of the Question as to whether a Person is an Illegal Migrant

(1) The Tribunal to which a reference has been made under ["section 8, or section 8A, or to which an application has been made under section 8"] shall after taking such evidence as may be adduced before it may think fit and after hearing such persons as it may deem

appropriate, by order, decide the question as to whether the person named in such reference or application, as the case may be, is or is not an illegal migrant: Provided that where for the determination of such question in any case the decision on any issue renders any decision on any other issue or issues unnecessary, the Tribunal may not decide such other issue or issues.

1*["(2) Where the members of the Tribunal differ in their opinion on any point, the Chairman of the Tribunal shall state the point or points on which they differ and make a reference to the President of the Appellate Tribunal which exercises jurisdiction in relation to the Tribunal who shall refer the case for hearing on such point or points by a member of another Tribunal under its jurisdiction and such point or points shall be decided according to the opinion of that member and such decision shall be deemed to be the decision of the Tribunal.."]

(3) The Tribunal shall send a copy of every order passed by it to the prescribed authority or authorities and to the parties to the reference, or the application, as the case may be.

(4) Every order passed under sub-section (1) shall, subject to the decision of the Appellate Tribunal, be final and shall not be called in question in any court.

13. Reference and Application to be Disposed of within Six Months

Every reference made to a Tribunal under ["section 8A or Application made to Tribunal under section 8"] shall be inquired into as expeditiously as possible and every endeavour shall be made to conclude such inquiry within a period of six months from the date of the service, on the person concerned, of a copy of such reference or application. 1 Subs. and ins. by Act 24 of 1988, s. 7. 2 Subs. by s. 8, *ibid.* 326

14. Appeal

The Central Government, or any person, named in a reference or an application under section 8, or any applicant under sub-section (2) of that section ["or any person named in a reference under section 8 "] may, if or he is not satisfied with any order made by a Tribunal under section 12, prefer an appeal to the Appellate Tribunal against such order.

15. Appellate Tribunal

(1) The Central Government may, by notification, establish for each State in which this Act is in force an appellate tribunal to be known as the Illegal Migrants (Determination) Appellate Tribunal for deciding appeals preferred under section 14 against orders made by tribunals in the state and specify the principal place of sitting of such Appellate Tribunal. (2) No person shall be appointed as a member of an Appellate Tribunal unless he is or has been a Judge of a High Court. (3) An Appellate Tribunal shall consist of as many members, not being less than two and more than six, as the central government may think fit. (4) The Central Government shall appoint one of the members of an Appellate Tribunal to be the President thereof. (5) An Appellate Tribunal shall sit in its principal place of sitting or any such other place or places as the President thereof may, from time to time, appoint.

(6) The powers and functions of an Appellate Tribunal may be exercised and discharged by benches constituted by the President thereof from amongst the members thereof ["which may either be single member benches or benches consisting of not less than tow members"]. (7) The Central Government shall make available to every Appellate Tribunal such staff as may be necessary for the discharge of its functions under this Act. (8) Every memorandum of appeal to an Appellate Tribunal shall be made in such form and in such manner as may be prescribed, and, in the case of an appeal preferred by an applicant under sub-section (2) of section 8, shall also be accompanied by such fee, not being less than 25 and more than 100 rupees, as may be prescribed. (9) Every appeal shall be preferred within thirty days from the date on which the order sought to be appealed against was communicated to the appellant: Provided that the Appellate Tribunal may, if it is satisfied that the appellant was prevented by sufficient cause from preferring the appeal within the said period, admit an appeal after the expiry of the aforesaid period of thirty days. 2*["(10) Every appellate tribunal shall have the same powers as are vested in an appellate court under the Code of Civil Procedure, 1908, while hearing an appeal."]. 1 Ins. by Act 24 of 1988, s. 9. 2 Subs. by s. 10, *ibid.* 327

16. Order of the Appellate Tribunal

(1) The Appellate Tribunal may, after giving the parties to the appeal a reasonable opportunity of being heard, pass such orders thereon as it may think fit, confirming, modifying or annulling the

appeal to the Appellate Tribunal may be preferred and the fee which shall accompany such appeal, as required by sub-section (8) of section 15; 1*["(ca) the manner of arrest and detention under the proviso to section 21A;"] (d) any other matter which is required to be, or may be, prescribed.

(3) Every rule made by the central government under this Act shall be laid, as soon as may be after it is made, before each House of Parliament, while it is in session, for a total period of thirty days which may be comprised in one session or in two or more successive sessions, and if, before the expiry of the session immediately following the session or the successive sessions aforesaid, both Houses agree in making any modification in the rule or both Houses agree that the rule should not be made, the rule shall thereafter have effect only in such modified form or be of no effect, as the case may be; so, however, that any such modification or annulment shall be without prejudice to the validity of anything previously done under that rule.

29. Repeal and Saving

(1) The Illegal Migrants (Determination by Tribunals) Ordinance, 1983, (8 of 1983.) is hereby repealed.

(2) Notwithstanding such repeal, anything done or any action taken under the said ordinance shall be deemed to have been done or taken under the corresponding provisions of this Act. 1 Ins. & Subs. by Act 24 of 1988, s. 16.

Appendix- XII

UNHCR Projected Global Resettlement Needs 2009

By Country of Asylum

Sub-Regiou	*Country of Asylum*	*Individuals iu ueed of Resettlement*	*Capacity to Process Individual Needs (^including group submissions)*	*UNHCR Resettlement Capacity Shortfall*
	AFRICA			
Great Lukes	Burundi	525	175	350
	Cameroon	650	375	275
	Central African Republic (CAR)	150	150	0
	Democratic Republic of Congo (COD)	580	330	250
	Gabon	300	300	0
	Republic of Congo (COB)	540	240	300
	Rwanda	4.010	1.750	2.260
	Tanzania	8.925	2.500	6.425
East and Horn of Africa	Djibouti	1.000	650	350
	Eritrea	3.930	350	3.580
	Ethiopia	25.730	2.350	23,380
	Kenya	44.335	8.475	35.860
	Somalia	4,280	800	3.480
	Uganda	11,300	1.500	9.800
West and Central Africa	Benin, Burkina Faso. Niger and Togo	280	280	0
	Cote dTvoire	125	125	0
	Ghana	300	300	0
	Guinea	50	50	0
	Liberia	40	40	0
	Nigeria	100	10	90
	Senegal (incl. Gambia. Guinea Bissau and Mali)	230	170	60
	Sierra Leone	50	50	0
Southern ifiica	Angola	95	30	65
	Botswana	39	11	28
	Malawi	260	260	0
	Mozambique	200	200	0
	Namibia	70	20	50
	South Africa	1.025	375	650
	Zambia	1.295	1.270	25
	Zimbabwe	500	300	200
Chad and Sudau Operation	Chad	4.300	1.800	2500
	Sudan	1.250	1.000	250
Africa TOTAL:		**116,464**	**'26,236**	**90.228**

	THE AMERICAS			
	Caribbean	25	25	0
	Costa Rica	175	175	0
	Cuba	50	50	0
	Ecuador	865	680	185
	Peru	25	S	17
	Venezuela	112	62	50
The Americas TOTAL:		**1.252**	**1,000**	**252**
			ASIA	
South Asia	Bangladesh	500	500	0
	India	1.420	1,160	260
	Sepal	30.031	28,531 (*25,931)	1.500
	Sri Lanka	110	110	0
East Asia	Cambodia	130	130	0
	[3]RC (including Hong Kong SAR) and Mongolia)	350	350	0
	Indonesia	487	487	**0**
	Malaysia	13.500	8,500 (*7,000)	5.000
	Thailand	23.425	22.815	610
Central Asia	Kazakhstan	370	310	60
	Kyrgyzstan	236	136	100
	Tajikistan	36	36	0
	Turkmenistan	47	1	46
	Uzbekistan	407	51	356
South West 4sia	Iran	88,200	1,400	86.800
	Pakistan	171,700	1.600	170.**100**
Asia TOTAL:		**330,949**	**66,117**	**264.832**

EUROPE				
Eastern Europe	Armenia	5	5	0
	Azerbaijan	330	70	260
	Belarus	25	25	0
	Georgia	15	15	0
	Moldova	20	10	10
	Russian Federation	350	350	0
	Jkraine	400	400	0
5outh-EasterD **Europe**	3osnia and Herzegovina	207	177	30
	Former Yugoslav Republic of Macedonia (fyROM)	20	20	0
	Malta	1600	500	1.100
	Serbia	5	5	0
	Turkey	4.500	4.500	0
Europe TOTAL:		**7,477**	**6,077**	**1.400**

MENA				
VIÉNA	Algeria	80	0	80
	Egypt	600	600	0
	Iraq	13.590	2.400	11.190
	Tordan	10,500	10.500	0
	Lebanon	8.443	1,600	6.843
	Libva	500	500	0
	Morocco	50	50	0
	Saudi Arabia. Bahrain. Qatar. Kuwait, **UAE** and Oman	650	650	0
	Svria	65.500	10.500	55.000
	Tunisia	26	26	0
	Yemen	5.056	750	4.306
MEN A TOTAL:		**104,995**	**27.576**	77,419
GrLOBAL TOTAL:		**561,137**	**127,006**	434,131

Global Resettlement Needs 2009 By Country of Origin

Country of Origin	*Country of Asylum*	*Individuals in need of Resettlement*	*Capacity to Process Individual Needs ("including group submissions)*	*INHCR Resettlement Capacity Shortfall*
	A F R I C A			
Angola	Botswana	4	2	2
	Namibia	20	5	15
	Zambia	170	170	0
	Total	194	**177**	**17**
Burundi	Democratic Republic of Congo (COD)	500	250	250
	Malawi	75	75	0
	Mozambique	20	20	0
	Rwanda	644	348	296
	South Africa	90	45	45
	Tanzania	1.985	1.400	585
	Uganda	200	50	150
	Zambia	60	50	10
	Zimbabwe	55	35	20
	Total	**3.629**	**2.273**	**1.356**
Chad	Cameroon	250	150	100
	Central African Republic	45	45	0
	Total	**295**	**195**	**100**
Central African Republic (CAR)	Cameroon	200	100	100
	Chad	1.500	700	800
	Total	**1.700**	**800**	**900**
Congo (COD)	Angola	60	15	45
	Benin. Burkina Faso, Niger & To so	100	100	0
	Burundi	500	160	340
	Cameroon	150	100	50
	Central African Republic (CAR)	75	75	0
	Malawi	150	150	0
	Morocco	28	28	0
	Mozambique	150	150	0
	Nigeria	60	5	55
	Republic of Congo (COB)	500	200	300
	Rwanda	3.356	1.392	1.964
	South Africa	200	90	110

Country of Origin	*Country of Asylum*	*Individuals in need of Resettlement*	*Capacity to Process Individual Needs (^including group submissions)*	*INHCR Resettlement Capacity Shortfall*
	Tanzania	6.840	1.000	5.840
	Uganda	10.000	600	9.400
	Zambia	980	975	5
	Zimbabwe	350	200	150
	Total	**23.499**	**5.240**	**18.259**
Congo (COB)	Benin	45	45	0
	Gabon	250	250	0
	Total	**2.95**	**295**	**0**
Cote tlTvoiie	Guinea	25	25	0
	Liberia	10	10	0
	Morocco	7	7	0
	Senegal. Gambia. Guinea-Bissau & **Mali**	70	50	20
	Tunisia	10	10	0
	Total	**122**	**102**	**20**
Eritrea	Djibouti	150	150	0
	Libya	300	300	0
	Malta	500	150	350
	Saudi Arabia	20	20	0
	Sudan	1.000	900	100
	Uganda	100	100	0
	Total	**2.070**	**1.620**	**450**
Ethiopia	Djibouti	350	250	100
	Eritrea	50	50	0
	Somalia	4.180	750	3.430
	South Africa	90	35	55
	Uganda	100	100	0
	Yemen	150	150	0
	Total	**4.920**	**1.335**	**3,585**
Liberia	Cote d'Ivoire	100	100	0
	Ghana	20	20	0
	Guinea	20	20	0
	Sierra Leone	50	50	0
	Total	**190**	**190**	**0**
Mauritania	Senegal. Gambia. Guinea-Bissau & Mali	90	50	40
	Total	**90**	**50**	**40**
Namibia	Botswana	16	4	12
	Total	**16**	**4**	**12**

Country of Origin	*Country of Asylum*	*Individuals in need of Resettlement*	*Capacity to Process Individual Needs (including group submissions)*	*UNHCR Resettlement Capacity Shortfall*
Rwanda	Angola	25	10	15
	Burundi	25	15	10
	COD	30	30	0
	Malawi	30	30	0
	Mozambique	30	30	0
	Republic of Congo (COB)	20	20	0
	South Africa	85	40	45
	Uganda	100	50	50
	Zimbabwe	45	30	15
	Total	**390**	**255**	**135**
Sierra Leone	Liberia	15	15	0
	Total	**15**	**15**	**0**
Somalia	Botswana	14	3	11
	China (PRC)	65	65	0
	Djibouti	500	250	250
	Egypt	100	100	0
	Eritrea	3.880	300	3.580
	India	250	140	110
	Indonesia	34	34	0
	Kenya	38,500	7.500	31.000
	Lebanon	12	10	2
	Malta	1,000	300	700
	Pakistan	40	40	0
	South Africa	260	85	175
	Uganda	500	500	0
	Ukraine	50	50	0
	Yemen	3.910	400	3,510
	Total	**49.115**	**9.777**	**39.338**
Sudan	Chad	2.500	1,000	1,500
	Central African Republic (CAR)	30	30	0
	Egypt	100	100	0
	Ghana	100	100	0
	Lebanon	60	30	30
	Saudi Arabia	30	30	0
	Uganda	300	100	200
	Total	**3.120**	**1.390**	**1,730**
Togo	Benin	75	75	0
	Ghana	50	50	0
	Total	**125**	**125**	**0**
Zimbabwe	South Africa	300	80	220

Country of Origin	*Country of Asylum*	*Individuals in need of Resettlement*	*Capacity to Process Individual Needs ("including group submissions)*	*UNHCR Resettlement Capacity Shortfall*
	Total	**300**	**80**	**220**
AFRICA TOTAL		*96,085*	*23,923*	*66,162*
THE AMERICAS				
Columbia	Costa Rica	165	165	0
	Pent	18	5	13
	Venezuela	97	54	43
	Total	**280**	**224**	**56**
AMERICAS TOTAL		*280*	*224*	*56*
ASIA				
Afghanistan	Belarus	20	20	0
	India	50	50	0
	Indonesia	40	40	0
	Iran	88.000	1.200	86,800
	Kazakhstan	100	50	50
	Kyrsyzstan	20	20	0
	Pakistan	171.600	1.500	170,100
	Russian Federation	300	300	0
	Tajikistan	35	35	0
	Turkey	50	50	0
	Turkmenistan	47	1	46
	Uzbekistan	400	50	350
	Total	**260.662**	**3.316**	**257,346**
Bhutan	Nepal	30.031	28.531 (*25.931)	1,500
	Total	**30.031**	**28,531 ("25.931)**	**1,500**
Cambodia	Thailand	100	30	70
	Total	**100**	**30**	**70**
China (PRC)	Kazakhstan	50	50	0
	Kyrsyzstan	6	6	0
	Thailand	150	75	75
	Total	**206**	**131**	**75**
Iran	India	50	40	10
	Indonesia	6	6	0
	Iraq	900	900	0
	Lebanon	15	5	10
	Pakistan	30	30	0
	Turkey	1.300	1.300	0
	Total	**2.301**	**2.281**	**20**
Laos	Thailand	425	425	0

Country of Origin	*Country of Asylum*	*Individuals in need of Resettlement*	*Capacity to Process Individual Needs {*iuchiding group submissions)*	*INHCR Resettlement Capacity Shortfall*
	Total	**425**	**425**	**0**
Myanmar	Bangladesh	500	500	0
	India	800	750	50
	Malaysia	13.000	8.200	4.800
	Thailand	22.000	22.000	0
	Total	**36.300**	**31.450**	**4,850**
Pakistan	China (PRC)	85	85	0
	Sn Lanka	95	95	0
	Total	**ISO**	**180**	**0**
Sri Lanka	China (PRC)	70	70	0
	Indonesia	90	90	0
	Thailand	300	100	200
	Total	**460**	**260**	**200**
Uzbekistan	Kazakhstan	150	150	0
	Kyrgyzstan	195	95	100
	Russian Federation	20	20	0
	Total	**365**	**265**	**100**
Vietnam	Cambodia	100	100	0
	Total	**100**	**100**	**0**
ASIA TOTAL		***331,130***	***66,969***	***264,161***
		E U R O P E		
Kosovo	Bosnia and Herzegovina	200	170	30
	Macedonia	20	20	0
	Total	**220**	**190**	**30**
Russian Fed. (Chechnya)	Azerbaijan	200	30	170
	Georgia	15	15	0
	Kazakhstan	70	60	10
	Kyrgyzstan	5	5	0
	Ukraine	100	100	0
	Total	**390**	**210**	**180**
Turkev	Iraq	100	0	100
	Total	**100**	**0**	**100**
EUROPE TOTAL		***710***	***400***	***310***
		M E N A		
Algeria	Tunisia	10	10	0

Bibliography

Primary Sources

UN Documents, Petitions, Reports, Judgements and other Primary Documents

AAPSU (1994), An Appeal, Issued on the Occasion of its Historic Delhi March Programme, All Arunachal Pradesh Student Union, 8-20 May, New Delhi.

---------------- (1994), Memorandum Submitted to the Prime Minister of India, All Arunachal Pradesh Student Union, New Delhi, May.

---------------- (1994), Why Arunachalees are Opposed to Permanent Settlement of Chakma and Hajong Refugees in Arunachal Pradesh, All Arunachal Pradesh Student Union, Itanagar, Arunachal Pradesh.

Aga Khan, Sadruddin (1981) Study on Human Rights and Massive Exoduses. United Nations, Economic and Social Council, Commission on Human Rights, E/CN.4/ 1503.

Amnesty International (1997), Refugees: Human Rights Have no Borders, Amnesty International Publications, New York.

Asian Centre for Human Rights (2006), India Human Rights Report, New Delhi.

—————————— (2007), India Human Rights Report, Arunachal Pradesh, New Delhi.

Capotorti, F. (1978), Study on the Rights of Persons belonging to Ethnic, Religious and Linguistic Minorities, UN document E/CN/4/ Sub.2/384/Rev. I.

Census of India (1991), Arunachal Pradesh, District Census Handbook, Changlang, Series-3, Part-A and B, Directorate of Census Operations, Arunachal Pradesh.

——————————— (1991), Arunachal Pradesh, District Census Handbook, Lohit, Series-3, Part-A and B, Directorate of Census Operations, Arunachal Pradesh.

————————————— (1991), Arunachal Pradesh, District Census Handbook, Lower Subansiri, Series-3, Part-A and B, Directorate of Census Operations, Arunachal Pradesh.

Christensen, Hanne (1982), Survival Strategies for and by Camp Refugees, UN Research Institute for Social Development, Geneva.

CHT Commission (1997), Life is not Ours Land and Human Rights in Chittagong Hill Tract, Bangladesh, Copenhagen and Amsterdam.

Committee for Citizenship Rights of the Arunachal Pradesh (CCRAP), A Report Submitted by Subimal Bikash Chakma (President, CCRCP) to the NHRC on 12th December, 1997.

Constitution of India, The Citizenship Act of 1955 and all Citizenship Amendments.

Deng, F. (1993), Comprehensive Study on the Human Rights Issues relating to Internally Displaced Persons, UN document, E/CN.4/ 1993/35.

——————— (1994), Internally Displaced Persons, Report of the Representative of the Secretary-General, UN document, E/ CN.4/1994/44.

Direction was given by the National Human Right Commission, Letter (No. 2/12/96 LD), to protect the refugees in the state of Arunachal Pradesh.

ECI (2004), Election Commission of India, Nirvachan Sadan, Ashoka Road, New Delhi Order No. 23/ARUN, 2003, March.

Elles, Baroness (1980), International Provisions protecting the Human Rights of Non-Citizens, UN document, E/ CN.4/Sub.2/392/Rev. 1.

Human Rights Committee, General Comments, No. 15, UN document, CCPR/C/21/ Rev. 1 (19 May 1989).

Ingles, J. (1964), Study of Discrimination in Respect of the Right of Everyone to leave any Country, including his own, and return to his Country, UN document, E/CN.4/ Sub.2/229/Rev. 1.

Internally Displaced Persons, Analytical Report of the Secretary-General, UN document, E/CN.4/1992/23, 14 Feb. 1992.

International Law Commission, Draft Statute of the International Criminal Court (1994), Text in Report of the International Law Commission, (1994), UN GAOR, 49th Sess., Suppl. No. 10 (A/49/10).

Jaeger, G. (1985), Study on Irregular Movements of Asylum Seekers and Refugees Working Group on Irregular Movements of Asylum Seekers and Refugees, Geneva.

Justice A. S. Anand, Chairman NHRC, Complaint for full implementation of the Supreme Court judgment in the Case of NHRC vs. State of Arunachal Pradesh (CPW 720 of 1995) of 9 January 1996, New Delhi, p. 3.

Lewis, Herbert S. and Wisner, Benjamin (1981), Refugee Rehabilitation in Somalia, Report of a Mission, March, Report prepared under USAID Contract No; ALD/DSAN-C-0060, June.

Malvika Karlekar versus Union of India (Criminal Writ Petition No. 583 of 1992), (Right of asylum seekers to approach UNHCR).

Martinez Cobo, J.R (1979), Study of the Problem of Discrimination against Indigenous Populations, UN document, E/CN.4/Sub.2/L.707.

Moon, Anson and Tashima, Nathaniel (1982), Help Seeking Behaviour and Attitudes of Southeast Asian Refugees, San Francisco: Pacific Asian Mental Health Project.

Murphy, H.B.M. (1955), The Extent of the Problem, in Murphy, H.B.M., (ed.) Flight and Resettlement. Paris: UNESCO.

National Human Rights Commission 2002-2003, The Eight Annual Reports.

National Human Rights Commission versus State of Arunachal Pradesh and another 1996, SCC (1) 742 (Right to Life and Liberty) Article 21 of the Constitution of India.

Randhawa (1954), Out of Ashes: An Account of the Rehabilitation of Refugees from West Pakistan in Rural Areas of East Punjab, Punjab Public Relations Department, Chandigarh, p. 25.

Rao, U B (1967), The Story of Rehabilitation, Ministry of Relief and Rehabilitation, Government of India.

Rees, E. (1960), Common Psychological Factors in Refugee Problems throughout the World in Uprooting and Resettlement, World Federation for Mental Health, London.

Refugees and Persons in Refugee-Like Situations in Kazakhstan, Central Asia and CIS 403 Report of the Secretary-General on the Meeting on Refugees and Displaced Persons in South East Asia, Geneva, 20–21 July 1979, and subsequent developments, UN document, A/34/637 (1979).

Reiterer, M. (1984), The Protection of Refugees by their State of Asylum, Wilhelm Braumhller, Vienna.

Report of the Group of Governmental Experts on International Co-operation to Avert New Flows of Refugees, UN document, A/41/324 (May 1986).

Report of the Secretary-General (1995), Strengthening of the Coordination of Humanitarian and Disaster Relief Activities, etc., UN document, A/50/203; E/1995/79 (14 June 1995), also Add. 1, 27 June.

Ruhashyankiko, N. (1978), Study of the Question of the Prevention and Punishment of the Crime of Genocide, UN document, E/CN.4/Sub.2/416.

Stein, Barry N. (1981), Refugees and Economic Activities in Africa, Research report to Washington, D.C., United States Agency for International Development, August.

The Sarbananda Sonowal versus Union of India (2005), Supreme Court Cases 665 (Aliens, Aggression, Illegal Migrants, Powers of State).

The State of Arunachal Pradesh versus Khudiram Chakmas 1994 Supp, (1) SCC 615, (Citizenship of Chakma Refugees).

UNHCR (1993), The State of the World's Refugees: The Challenge of Protection. Oxford: Oxford University Press.

UNHCR (1995), The State of the World's Refugees: In Search of Solutions. Oxford: Oxford University Press.

UNHCR (1997), World Refugee Survey, Washington, D.C. : Immigration and Refugee Services of America.

UNHCR (1998), The State of the World's Refugees : A Humanitarian Agenda. Oxford: Oxford University Press.

UNHCR (2000), Human Rights and Human Development, Human Development Program, United Nations, New York.

UNHCR (2000), The State of the World's Refugees: Fifty Years of Humanitarian Action, Oxford University Press, Oxford.

United Nations (1951), Convention Relating to the Status of Refugees, UN Doc.A/Res/429.

Secondary Sources

Books

Abbi, B. L. (ed.) (1984), Northeast Region: Problems and Prospects of Development Centre for Research in Rural and Industrial Development, Chandigarh.

Adhikari, O. S. (1988), Four Immigrants Tribes of Tripura, Tripura Directorate of Research, Government of Tripura.

Agrawal, M.M. (1996), Ethnicity, Culture and Nationalism in N.E. India, Indus Publishing Company, New Delhi.

Aiyar, S (1994), Violence and the State in the Partition of Punjab, University of Cambridge, Cambridge.

Aleinikoff, T.A. and Martin, D.A. (1981), Immigration: Process and Policy, West Publishing Co., St. Paul, Minn.

Alston, P. (1992), The United Nations and Human Rights: 3 Critical Appraisal, Clarendon Press, Oxford.

Ambedkar, B.R. (1945), Pakistan or the Partition of India, Thacker and Co., Bombay.

Aziz, Qutubuddin (1974), Blood and Tears, United Press of Pakistan, Karachi.

Baehr, Peter R. (1999), Human Rights: Universality in Practice, Macmillan Press Ltd., New Delhi.

Balwally, Darshan (2003), Growth of Totalitarianism in Arunachal Pradesh, Mizoram and Nagaland, Spectrum Publications, Delhi.

Barber, B. (1984), Strong Democracy, University of California Press, Berkeley.

Barua, Sanjib (1999), India against Itself: Assam and the Politics of Nationality, Oxford University Press, New Delhi.

------------------ (2005), Durable Disorder: Understanding the Politics of North East India, Oxford University Press, New Delhi.

Basu, D.D (1992), Introduction to the Constitution of India, Prince-Hall of India, Pvt. Ltd., New Delhi.

Bates, T. (1997), Race, Self-Employment, and Upward Mobility: An Illusive American Dream, Woodrow Wilson Center Press, Washington D.C.

Bauer, Jaanner R. and Beel, Daniell A (ed.) (1999), The East Asian Challenge for Human Rights, Cambridge University Press, Cambridge.

Bayefsky, Anne F. And Joan Fitzpatrick, (ed.) (2000), Human Rights and Forced Displacement, Martinus Nijhoff Publishers, London.

Benhabib, S. (2004), The Rights of Others, Aliens, Residents and Citizens, Cambridge University Press, Cambridge.

Bhabha, J. and Coll, G. (eds.) (1992), Asylum Law and Practice in Europe and North America, Federal Publications, Washington, D.C.

Bhan, Susheela (1999), Impact of Ethnic Violence on Youth: A Study of Tribal-Nontribal Violence in Kokrajhar, Shipra Publications, New Delhi.

Bhargava, Rajiv and Reifeld, Helmut (2005), Civil Society, Public Sphere and Citizenship, Dialogues and Perceptions, Sage Publication, New Delhi.

Bhargava, Rajiv (2008), Politics and Ethics of the Indian Constitution, Oxford University Press, New Delhi.

Bhattacharjee, Chandana (1996), Ethnicity and Autonomy Movement, Vikas Publishing House, New Delhi.

Bhattacharjee, J.B. (1995), North East Indian Perspectives in History, Vikas Publishing House, New Delhi.

Bhattacharyya, Hiranya Kumar (2001), The Silent Invasion: Assam Versus Infiltration, Spectrum Publications, Delhi.

Bhattacharyya, N.N. (1995), Religious Culture of North-Eastern India, Manohar Publishers & Distributors, New Delhi.

Bhaumik, Subir (1996), Insurgent Cross Fire: North-East India, Lancer Publishers, New Delhi.

Bhuyan, B.C. (1989), Political Development of the North East, Omsons Publications, New Delhi.

Bindra, S.S (1982), Indo-Bangladesh Relation, Deep and Deep Publication, New Delhi.

Borgohain, Bani (1999), Human Rights, Social Justice and Political Change, Kanishka Publisher, New Delhi.

Borjas, George (1990), Friends or Strangers: The Impact of Immigrants on the U.S. Economy, Basic Books, New York.

Bose, Manilal (1977), History of Arunachal Pradesh, Concept Publication, New Delhi.

———————— (ed.) (1979), Historical and Constitutional Documents of Northeast India, 1824-1973, Concept Publishing House, Delhi.

Bose, Pradip Kumar (ed.) (2000), Refugees in West Bengal: Institutional Practices and Contested Identities, Calcutta Research Group, Calcutta.

Bose, Tapan K and Manchanda, Rita (ed.) (1997), States, Citizens and Outsiders: The Uprooted People of South Asia, South Asian Rights for Human Rights, Katmandu.

Brass, Paul R. (1991), Ethnicity and Nationalism: Theory and Comparison, Sage Publications, New Delhi.

——————————— (1994), Language, Religion and Politics in North India, Vikas Publication, Delhi.

——————————— (ed.) (1985), Ethnic Groups and the State, Barnes and Noble Books, Totowa.

Brighouse, H. (2000), School Choice and Social Justice, Oxford University Press, Oxford.

Brownlie, I. (ed.) (1995), Basic Documents in International Law, Clarendon Press, Oxford.

Brubaker, R. (1992), Citizenship and Nationhood in France and Germany, Harvard University Press, London.

C. Mouffe (ed.) (1992), Dimensions of Radical Democracy, Pluralism, Citizenship, Community, Verso, London.

C.R. Abrar and Shahdeen Malik (2000), Towards National Refugee Laws in South Asia, Refugee and Migratory Movement's Research Unit, University of Dhaka, Bangladesh.

Callan, E. (1997), Creating Citizens, Oxford University Press, Oxford.

Carasco, Aiken, Galloway, and Macklin (2006), Immigration and Refugee Law: Cases, Materials, and Commentary, Emond Montgomery Publications, Canada.

Carens, J.H. (2000), Culture, Citizenship, and Community: A Contextual Exploration of Justice as Evenhandedness, Oxford University Press, Oxford.

Castles, Stephen, and Kosack, G. (1984), Immigrant Workers and Class Structure in Western Europe, Oxford University Press, Oxford and New York.

Chakarvarty, Manik (1998), Human Rights and Refugees Problems, Law and Practices, Deep and Deep Pvt. Ltd., New Delhi.

Chaube, S.K. (1973), Hill Politics in Northeast India, Orient Longman Limited, Patna.

———————— (1985), Electoral Politics in Northeast India, University Press, India Pvt. Ltd, Madras.

Chaudhuri, Dipak Kumar (1993), Autonomy Movements in Assam, Omsons Publications, New Delhi.

Chimni, B.S. (2000), International Refugee Law: A Reader, Sage Publications, New Delhi.

———————— (1999), From Resettlement to Repatriation: Towards a Critical History of Durable Solutions to Refugee Problems, UNHCR.

Chiranjivi J. Nirmal (ed.) (2000), Human Rights in India: Historical, Social and Political Perspectives, Oxford University Press, New York.

Chowdhury, J.N. (1990), The Tribal Culture and History of Arunachal Pradesh, Daya Publishing House, Delhi.

Das, Samir Kumar (ed.) (2008), Blisters on Their Feet; Tales of Internally Displaced Persons in India's North East, Sage Publication, New Delhi.

Das, Gurudas and Purkayastha, R.K. (ed.) (2000), Border Trade: North-East India and Neighbouring Countries, Akansha Publishing House, New Delhi.

Dasgupta, R.K. (1971), The Revolt of East Bengal, Calcutta, A Dasgupta Publication, Calcutta.

Datta, P.S. (ed.) (1995), North East and the Indian State: Paradoxes of a Periphery, Vikas Publishing House, New Delhi.

Debbarma, P.K. and George Sudhir Jacob (1993), The Chakma Refugees in Tripura, South Asian Publishers, New Delhi.

Deka, Kanak Sen (1991), Youths in Turmoil: Assam, Gurupada Chaudhury Publication, Calcutta.

———————— (1993), Assam's Crisis Myth and Reality, Mittal Publications, New Delhi.

Diwan, Paras and Diwan, Peeyushi (1996), Human rights and the law, Deep and Deep Publication, New Delhi.

Drez, Jean and Sen, Amartya (1995), India: Economic Development and Social Opportunity, Oxford University Press, New Delhi.

Dunne, Tim and Wheeler, Nicholas J. (ed.) (1999), Human Rights in Global Politics, Cambridge University Press, Cambridge.

Dutta, N.C. (ed.) (1997), Politics of Identity and Nation Building in North-East India, South Asian Press, New Delhi.

Dutta, P and Ahmad, S.I. (1995), The People of Arunachal Pradesh: People of India, Vol. XIV, General editor K.S. Singh, Seagull Books, Calcutta.

Dutta, P. (1976), The Story of Origin and Migration of the Noctes, Resarun Publication, Itanagar.

Dutta, S (1998), Student Movements in Arunachal Pradesh, Himalayan Publishers, Delhi.

———————— (ed.) (2000), Studies in the History, Economy and Culture of Arunachal Pradesh, Revised ed., Himalayan Publishers, Itanagar.

Dutta, Sreeradha (2004), Bangladesh: A Fragile Democracy, Institute for Defense Studies and Analyses, Shipra Publication, New Delhi.

Eisenstadt, S.N. (1954), The Absorption of Immigrants, Routledge and Kegan, London.

Elwin, Verrier (1959), India's North-East Frontier in the Nineteenth Century, Oxford University Press, Bombay.

———————— (1970), A New Book of Tribal Fiction, Directorate of Research, Government of Arunachal Pradesh, Itanagar.

———————— (1957), A Philosophy for NEFA, Directorate of Research, Government of Arunachal Pradesh, Itanagar.

Fürer-Haimendorf, C. Von. (1950), Ethnographic Notes on the Tribes in the Subansiri Region, Assam Government Press, Shillong.

———————— (1962), The Apatanis and Their Neighbours: A primitive Civilization of the Eastern Himalayas, Routledge and Kegan Paul, London.

———————— (1983), Himalayan Adventure: Early Travels in Northeast India, Sterling Publication, New Delhi.

G. Loescher (1993), The Origins of the International Refugee Regime, in Beyond Charity: International Co-operation and the Global Refugee Crisis, Oxford University Press, Oxford.

Gait, Edward (1925), A History of Assam, Lawyers Book Stall, Guwahati.

Gangopadahyay, Niladri Sekhar (2002), Insurgency and Media: A Study on Tripura, Nabankur, Agartala.

Gangualy, Rajat and Macduff Ian (ed.) (2003), Ethnic Conflict and Secessionism in South and Southeast Asia: Causes, Dynamics Solution, Sage Publication, New Delhi.

Gangualy, Rajat and Phadnis, Urmila (2001), Ethnicity and nation-building in South Asia, Sage Publication, New Delhi.

Garcia-Mora, M.R. (1956), International Law and Asylum as a Human Right, Public Affairs Press, Washington D.C.

Gassah, L.S. (1999), Survey of Research in Political Science on North-East India 1970-1990, Regency Publication, New Delhi.

Gassah, L.S. (ed.) (1992), Regional Political Parties in North East India, Omsons Publications, Guwahati.

Ghai, U.R. (1998), Foreign Policy of India, New Academic Publishing Co., Jalandhar.

Giles, W. and H. Moussa (eds.) (1996), Development and Diaspora: Gender and the Refugee Experience, Dudas, Ontario, Artemis Publishers, Canada.

Gohain, Hiren (1985), Assam: A Burning Question, Spectrum Publications, Guwahati.

Gold, Steven (1992), Refugee Communities, Newbury Park, Sage Publications, California.

Goodwin-Gill, G.S. (1978), International Law and the Movement of Persons between States, Clarendon Press, Oxford.

Gopalkrishnan, R. (1995), Insurgent North-Eastern Region of India, Vikas Publishing House, New Delhi.

Gordenker, L. (1987), Refugees in International Politics, Croom Helm, London.

Goswami, M.C. & Das, P.B. (1990), The people of Arunachal Pradesh: A physical Survey, Directorate of Research, Government of Arunachal Pradesh, Itanagar.

Gowlland, Vera (1995), The Problem of Refugees in the Light of Contemporary International Law Issues, Dordrecht, Martinus, Nijhoff.

Grahl-Madsen, A. (1972), The Status of Refugees in International Law, vols. 1 and 2, Sijthhoff, Leyden.

Grewal, D.S. (1997), The Tribes of Arunachal Pradesh, Vol. 2, South Asia Publications, Delhi.

Gupta, D.N and Singh, Chandrachur (2003), Human Rights: Acts Statues and Constitutional Provisions, Vol. I, Kalpaz Publication, Delhi.

Guy S. Goodwin, Gill (ed.) (1996), The Refugee in International Law, 2 ed., Clarendon Press, Oxford.

Hampton, Janie, (ed.) (1997), Internally Displaced People: A Global Survey, Earth-Scan Publications Ltd., London.

Hansen, Art and Oliver-Smith, Anthony (eds.) (1982), Involuntary Migration and Resettlement: The Problems and Responses of Dislocated People, West view Press, Boulder.

Hathaway, J. (1991), The Law of Refugee Status, Butterworths, Toronto.

Hazarika, Sanjoy (1995), Strangers of the Mist: Tales of War and Peace from India's Northeast, Penguin Books, New Delhi.

---------- (2000), Rites of Passage: Border Crossings, Imagined Homelands, India's East and Bangladesh, Penguin Books India, New Delhi.

Holborn, L.W. (1956), The International Refugee Organisation: The Specialised Agency of the United Nations, Its History and Work 1946-1952, Oxford University Press, London.

Holmes, S. (1984), Benjamin Constant and the Making of Modern Liberalism, Yale University Press, New Haven.

Horowitz, Donal L. (1985), Ethnic Groups in Conflict, University of California Press Ltd., London.

Hughey, Michal.W (1998), New Tribalism: The Resurgence of Race and Ethnicity, Macmillan Press Ltd., London.

Hussain, M. (1993), The Assam Movement: Class, Ideology and Identity, Har-Anand Publications, New Delhi.

Hutchison, R.H.S. (1978), Chittagong Hill Tracts, Vivek Publishing House, New Delhi.

Hutnic, Nimmi (1991), Ethnic Minority Identity, Clarendon Press, Oxford.

Hyndman, Jennifer (2000), Managing Displacement: Refugees and the Politics of Humanitarianism. Minneapolis: University of Minnesota Press.

Joshep, K.V. (1988), Migration and Economic Development of Kerala, Mittal Publications, Delhi.

Joshi, P.M. (1972), Student Revolt in India: Story of Pre-Independence Youth Movement, Joshi Publications, New Delhi.

Kamei, Gangmumei (2002), Ethnicity and Social Change: An Anthology of Essays, Pouganglu Gangmei Publication Imphal.

Karn, Anil (1986), Politics of Population Influx and Labour Problem, UDH Publication, Delhi.

Kazi, Jigme N (1993), Inside Sikkim against the Tide, Hill Media Publications, Gangtok.

Keely, Charles (1981), Global Refugee Policy: The Case for a Development-Oriented Strategy, Population Council, New York.

Keller, S.L. (1975), Uprooting and Social Change: The Role of Refugees in Development, Manohar publishers, Delhi.

Kent, D.P. (1953) The Refugee Intellectual: The Americanization of the Immigrants of 1933-1941, Columbia University Press, New York.

Khan, Adeel (2005), Politics of Identity: Ethnic Nationalism and the State in Pakistan, Sage Publication, New Delhi.

Khanna, D.P (2001), Reforming Human Rights, Manas Publication, New Delhi.

Kharat, Rajesh S. (2003), Tibetan Refugees in India, Kaveri Books, New Delhi.

Kloosterman, Robert, and Jan Rath (2003), Immigrant

Entrepreneurs: Venturing Abroad in the Age of Globalisation, Berg, Oxford and New York.

Koehn, Peter H. (1991), Refugees from Revolution: U.S. Policy and Third-World Migration, West View Press, Colorado.

Kumar, B.B. (1995), Tensions and Conflict in Northeast India, Cosmo Publications, New Delhi.

Kuper, A. (2004), Democracy Beyond Border; Justice and Representation in Global Institutions, Oxford University Press, Oxford.

Kymlicka, W. (1995), Multicultural Citizenship, Oxford University Press, Oxford.

Lauterpacht, H. (1950), International Law and Human Rights, Stevens, London.

———————— (1958), The Development of International Law by the International Court, Stevens, London.

Lauterpacht, H. and Monahan, L. (eds.) (1989), Refugees and International Relations, Oxford University Press, Oxford.

Loescher, Gil (1993), Beyond Charity: International Cooperation and the Global Refugee Crisis. Oxford: Oxford University Press.

Loizos, Peter (1981), The Heart Grown Bitter: A Chronicle of Cypriot War Refugees, Cambridge University Press, Cambridge.

Luthra, P.N. (1993), Constitutional and Administrative Growth of the Arunachal Pradesh, Directorate of Research, Government of Arunachal Pradesh, Itanagar.

M. Marrus (1985), The Unwanted European Refugees in the Twentieth Century, Oxford University Press, Oxford.

Macedo, S. (1990), Liberal Virtues: Citizenship, Virtues, and Community in Liberal Constitutionalism, Clarendon Press, Oxford.

Mackenzie, Alexander (2001), The North East Frontier of India, Mittal Publications, New Delhi.

Mamdani, M. (1973), From Citizen to Refugee: Uganda Asians Come to Britain, Frances Pinter Limited, London.

Mamta, Rajwat (ed.) (2001), Burning Issue of Human Rights, Kalpaz Publications, Delhi.

Manin, B. (1997), Principles of Representative Government, Cambridge University Press, Cambridge.

Manoj Kumar Sinha (2000), Basic Documents on International Human Rights and Refugee Laws, Manak Publications, New Delhi.

Mansukhani, G.S (ed.) (1975), Student Power in India, Oxford Publication, New Delhi.

Marrus, M. (1985), The Unwanted: European Refugees in the Twentieth Century, Oxford University Press, New York.

Marshall, T.H. (1950), Citizenship and Social Class and other Essays, Cambridge University Press, Cambridge.

Massey, D.S., Arango, J., Hugo, G., Kouaouci, A., Pellegrino, A. and Taylor, J. E. (1998), Worlds in Motion: Understanding International Migration at the End of the Millennium, Oxford University Press, Oxford.

McClure, Vimala Schneider (1989), Bangladesh: Rivers in a Crowded Land, Dillon Press, Minneapolis, the U.S.

McGoldrick, D. (1991), The Human Rights Committee: Its Role in the Development of the International Covenant on Civil and Political Rights, Clarendon Press, Oxford.

Meron, T. (1989), Human Rights and Humanitarian Norms as Customary Law, Clarendon Press, Oxford.

Mirza, Loraine (1998), Internment Camps of Bangladesh, Crescent International, Markham, Canada.

Miller, D. (1995), On Nationality, Clarendon Press, New York.

——————— (2000), Citizenship and National Identity, Polity Press, Cambridge.

Mishra, Omprakash and Majumdar, Anindyo J. (ed.) (2003), The Elsewhere People, Lancer Book Publisher, New Delhi.

Misra, Udayon (1988), North East India: Quest for Identity, Omsons Publications, Guwahati.

—————————— (2000), The Periphery Strikes Back: Challenges to the Nation-State in Assam and Nagaland, Indian Institute of Advanced Study, Shimla.

Modood, T., Triandafyllidou, A., Zapata-Barrero, R. (eds.) (2006), in Multiculturalism, Muslims and Citizenship, A European Approach, Routledge, London.

Muni, S.D. and Baral, Lok Raj (ed.) (1996), Refugees and Regional Security in South Asia, Konark Publishers Pvt. Ltd., Delhi.

Muntarbhorn, V. (1992), The Status of Refugees in Asia, Clarendon Press, Oxford.

Nag, Sajal (1990), Roots of Ethnic Conflict: Nationality Question in Northeast India, Manohar Publications, New Delhi.

---------- (1998), India and North-East India: Mind, Politics and the Process of Integration 1946-1950, Regency Publications, New Delhi.

---------- (2002), Contesting Marginality: Ethnicity, Insurgency and Subnationalism in North-East India Manohar, New Delhi.

Narasimham, R.K. (1999), Human Rights and Social Justice, Commonwealth Publishers, Delhi.

Nautiyal, Annpurna (ed.) (2002), Fifty Years of Human Rights: Expectations and Challenges, Sarita Book House, Delhi.

Nepram, Binalakshmi (2002), South Asia's Fractured Frontier: Armed Conflict, Narcotics and Small Arms Proliferation in India's North East, Mittal Publications, New Delhi.

Nibedon, Nirmal (1981), North-East India: The Ethnic Explosion, Lancers Publishers, New Delhi.

----------- (2002), Northeast India: A Bibliography, Nehru Memorial Museum and Library, New Delhi.

Nuh, V.K. (2001), Struggle for Identity in North-east India: A Theological response, Spectrum Publications, New Delhi.

Osik, N.N. (1999), Modern History of Arunachal Pradesh (1825-1997), Himalayan Publication, Delhi.

P.R. Chari, Mallika Joseph and Suba Chandran (ed.) (2003), Missing Boundaries: Refugees, Migrants, Stateless and Internally Displaced Persons in South Asia, Manohar Publishers, New Delhi.

Pakem, B. (1997), Insurgency in North-East India, Om Sons Publications, New Delhi.

Patil, V.T. & Trivedi, P.R. (2000), Migration Refugee and Security in the 21st Century, Authors Press, Delhi.

Perry, Michael J. (1998), The Idea of Human Rights, Oxford University Press, New York.

Phanjoubam, Tarapot (1983), Insurgency Movement in North East India, Vikas, Delhi.

Phillips, A. (1999), Which Equalities Matter?, Polity Press, Cambridge.

Phukon, Girin (1996), Politics of Regionalism in Northeast India, Spectrum Publications, New Delhi.

Oberoi, Pio (2006), Exile and Belonging: Refugees and State Policy in South Asia, Oxford University Press, New Delhi.

Pipher, Mary (2002), The Middle of Everywhere: The World's Refugees Come to Our Town Harcourt Inc, London.

Pitkin, H.F. (1967), The Concept of Representation, University of California Press, Berkeley.

Plaut, W.G. (1985), Refugee Determination in Canada, Minister of Supply and Services, Ottawa.

Pogge, T.W (2002), World Poverty and Human Rights, Polity Press, Cambridge.

R. Beiner (ed.) (1995), Theorizing Citizenship, State University of New York Press, Albany.

R. Cohen (ed.) (1999), The Cambridge Survey of World Migration, Cambridge University Press, Cambridge.

R. E. Goodin (eds.) (1992), The Transnational Migration of People, The Pennsylvania State University Press, Pennsylvania.

R. Kharat (2003), Tibetan Refugees in India, Kaveri Books, New Delhi.

Rao, V.Venkata (1976), A Century of Tribal Politics in North- East India 1874-1974, S. Chand and Company, New Delhi.

Rawls, J. (1972), A Theory of Justice, Oxford University Press, Oxford.

——————- (1999), The Law of People's, Harvard University Press, London.

Robinson, N. (1953), Convention Relating to the Status of Refugee: A Commentary, Institute of Jewish Affairs, New York.

Robinson, W. (1841), A Descriptive Account of Assam, Rock Publication, London.

Roy, Sanjay K. (ed.) (2001), Refugees and Human Rights: Social and Political Dynamics of Refugee Problem in Eastern and North-Eastern India, Rawat Publications, Jaipur.

Rustomji, Nari (1971), Enchanted Frontiers, Oxford University Press, Delhi.

---------- (1983), Imperiled Frontiers: India's North-east Borderlands, Oxford University Press, Delhi.

Rystad, G. (ed.) (1990), The Uprooted: Forced Migration as an International Problem in the Post-War Era, Lund University Press, Lund.

Sachar, Rajinder (2004), Human Rights: Perspectives and Challenges, Gyan Publishing House, New Delhi.

Sachdeva, Gulshan (2000), Economy of the North-East: Policy, Present Conditions and Future Possibilities, Konark Publishers, Delhi.

Saikia, Anil, Goswami, Homeswar, Goswami, Atul (2003), Population Growth in Assam 1951-1991: With Focus on Migration, Akansha Publishing House, New Delhi.

Saikia, Mrinal Kr. (1995), Assam towards Islamisation, Omsons Publications, Guwahati.

Saksena, K.P. (ed.) (2003), Human Rights and the Constitution: Vision and Reality, Gyan Publishing House, New Delhi.

Saksena, R.N. (1961), Refugees: A Study in Changing Attitudes, Asia Publishing House, Bombay.

Salomon, K. (1991), Refugees in the Cold War: Toward a New International Refugee Regime in the Early Postwar Era, Lund University Press, Lund.

Samaddar, Ranabir (1999), The Marginal Nation Trans Border Migration from Bangladesh to West Bengal, Sage Publication, New Delhi.

----------- (ed.) (2003), Refugees and the State; Practices of Asylum and Care in India, 1947-2000, Sage Publication, New Delhi.

Sarin, V.I.K. (1982), India's North-East in Flames, Vikash Publishing House, Uttar Pradesh.

Savic, Obrad (ed.) (1999), The Politics of Human Rights, Verso, London.

Sen, Amartya (1999), Development as Freedom, Oxford University Press, New York.

———————————- (2004), Social Exclusion; Concept Application Scrutiny, Critical Quest, New Delhi.

Sen, Sankar (1998), Human Rights in a Developing Society, APH Publishing Corporation, New Delhi.

Sharma, N.R. (1999), Human Rights in the World, Pointer Publisher, Jaipur.

Shinde, A.B. (1972), Political Consciousness among College Students, Thacker and Co. Ltd., Bombay.

Shklar, J.N. (1991), American Citizenship: The Quest for Inclusion, Harvard University Press, Cambridge.

Simpson, J.H. (1939), The Refugee Problem, Royal Institute of International Affairs, Oxford University Press, London.

Singh, B.P. (1987), The Problem of Change: A Study of North-East India, Oxford University Press, Delhi.

Singh, Deepak K. (2010), Stateless in South Asia; The Chakma Between Bangladesh and India, Sage Publication, New Delhi.

Singh, K.S. (ed.) (1995), People of India: Arunachal Pradesh Vol. XIV, Seagull Books, Calcutta.

------------------ (ed.) (1995), People of India: Mizoram Vol. XXXIII, Seagull Books, Calcutta.

------------------ (ed.) (1996), People of Tripura Vol. XLI, Seagull Books, Calcutta.

------------------ (ed.) (2003), People of India: Assam Volume XV Part Two, Seagull Books, Calcutta.

Saksena, K.P. (ed.) (1994), Human Rights Perspective and Challenges, Institute for World Congress on Human Rights (IWCHR), New Delhi.

----------------- (ed.) (1999), Human Rights: Fifty Years of India's Independence, Gyan Publishing House, New Delhi.

Singh, Mahavir (ed.) (2005), Home Away from Home: Inland

Movement of People in India, Anamika Publishers & Distributers Pvt. Ltd., Kolkatta.

Singhal, Sushila (1977), Academic Leadership and Student Unrest, New Man Group of Publication, New Delhi.

Sinha, A.C. (ed.) (1994), Youth Movements in North-East India: Structural Imperatives and Aspects of Change, Indus Publishing Company, New Delhi.

Sinha, Manoj Kumar (1999), Implementation of Basic Human Rights, Manak Publications Pvt. Ltd. Delhi.

--------------------- (2000), Basic Documents on International Human Rights and Refugee Laws, Manak Publications, New Delhi.

Sinha, P.C (2003), India's Human Rights Regime: A Comprehensive Presentation, Kaniska Publishers and Distributors, New Delhi.

Skran, C. (1995), Refugees in Inter-War Europe: The Emergence of a Regime, Oxford University Press, Oxford.

Smith, James P. and Edmonston, Barry (1997), The New Americans: Economic, Demographic and Fiscal Effects of Immigration, National Academy Press, Washington, D.C.

Snellgrove, D. (1987), Indo-Tibetan Buddhism: Indian Buddhists and their Tibetan Successors, Serindia Publications, London.

Soysal, Y.N. (1994), Limits of Citizenship; Migrants and Post-national Membership in Europe, University of Chicago Press, Chicago.

Spinner, J. (1994), The Boundaries of Citizenship; Race, Ethnicity, and Nationality in the Liberal State, Baltimore, John Hopkins University Press, London.

Sanajaoba, Naorem (ed.) (1994), Human Rights Principles: Practice and Abuses, Omson Publication, New Delhi.

Sukhdeo, Thorat and Kumar, Narender (2008), B.R. Ambedkar: Perspective on Social Exclusion and Inclusive Policy, Oxford University Press, New Delhi.

Syiemlieh, R. David (2000), Survey of Research in History on North-East India 1970-1990, Regency Publication, New Delhi.

T. Aleiniko? and V. Chetail (eds.) (2003), Migration and International Legal Norms, Asser Press, The Hague.

Talukdar, S.P. (1988), The Chakmas: Life and Struggle, Gyan Publishing House, New Delhi.

------------------ (1994), Chakmas: An-Embattled Tribes, Uppal Publishing House, New Delhi.

Tan, K.C. (2004), Justice without Borders; Cosmopolitanism, Nationalism and Patriotism, Cambridge University Press, Cambridge.

Ted, Robert. Gurr & Harff, Barbara (1994), Ethnic Conflict in World Politics, West View Press, Oxford.

Thomas, C. Joshua (2002), Dimensions of Displaced People in North-East India, Regency Publications, New Delhi.

Trakroo, A. Bhat, and S. Nandi (eds.) (2006), Refugees and the Law, Human Rights Law Network, Delhi.

Tyson, Geoffrey (1992), Forgotten Frontier, Spectrum Publications, New Delhi.

V. Bader (ed.) (1997), Citizenship and Exclusion, St. Martin's Press, New York.

V. Suryanarayan and V. Sudersen (2000), Between Fear and Hope: Sri Lankan Refugees in Tamil Nadu, T.R. Publications Pvt. Ltd., Chennai.

Vansina, J. (1985), Oral Tradition as History, James Currey Publication, London.

Varman, S. B. K. Dev (1999), A Study Over the Jhum and Jhumia Rehabilitation in the Union Territory of Tripura, Directorate of Research, Agartala.

Verghese, B. George (1996), India's Northeast Resurgent: Ethnicity, Insurgency, Governance, Development, Konark Publishers, Delhi.

Vernant, J. (1953), The Refugee in the Post-War World, Yale Press, New Haven.

Vierdag, E.W. (1973), The Concept of Discrimination in International Law, The Hague, Nijhoff.

Vijapur, Abdulrahim P and Kumar, Suresh (ed.) (1999), Perspectives on Human Rights, Manak Publication, Pvt. Ltd, New Delhi.

W. F. Schwartz (ed.) (1995), Justice in Immigration, Cambridge University Press, Cambridge.

W.R. Brubaker (ed.) (1984), Immigration and the Politics of Citizenship in Europe and America, University Press of America, Lanham.

Wain, B. (1982), The Refused: The Agony of the Indo-china Refugee, Simon and Schuster, New York.

Walzer, M. (1983), Spheres of Justice, A Defense of Pluralism and Equality, Basic Books, New York.

------------------ (1989), Citizenship, in Political Innovation and Conceptual Change, T. Ball, J. Farr, R. L. Hanson, Cambridge University Press, Cambridge.

Weiner Myron (1978), Sons of the Soil: Migration and Ethnic Conflict in India, Oxford University Press, Delhi.

----------------- (1995), The Global Migration Crisis: Challenge to States and to Human Rights. New York: Addison-Wesley Longman Publishers.

Williams, M.S. (1998), Voice, Trust, and Memory; Marginalized Groups and the Failings of Liberal Representation, Princeton University Press, Princeton.

Woodbridge, G. (1950), UNRRA: The History of the United Nations Relief and Rehabilitation Administration, 3 Vols. Columbia University Press, New York.

Young, I. M. (2000), Inclusion and Democracy, Oxford University Press, Oxford.

Zolberg, A.R., Suhrke, A., and Aguayo, S. (1989), Escape from Violence: Conflict and the Refugee Crisis in the Developing World, Oxford University Press, New York.

Journals and Magazines

A. Pecoud and P. Guchteneire (2005), "Migration without Borders: An Investigation into the Free Movement of People", Global Migration Perspectives, No. 27, April.

A. Portes and J. DeWind (2004), "A Cross-Atlantic Dialogue: The Progress of Research and Theory in the Study of Migration", International Migration Review, Vol. 38, No. 3, Fall, pp. 828-851.

Adams, Jr., Richard H., and Alderman, H. (1992), "Sources of Inequality in Rural Pakistan: A decomposition analysis", Oxford Bulletin of Economics and Statistics, Vol. 54, No. 4, London.

Ahsan, Syed Aziz-Al and Chakma Bhumitra (1989), "Problem of

National Integration in Bangladesh: The Chittagong Hill Tracts", Asian Survey, Vol. xxix, No. 10, October, Berkeley, pp. 959-970.

Allen, R. and Hiller, H.H. (1985), "Social Organization of Migration: An Analysis of the Uprooting and Flight of Vietnamese Refugees", no. 23, International Migration, p. 439.

Ansari, Sarah (1985), "Partition, Migration and Refugee: Response to the Arrival of Muhajirs in Sind During 1947-48", South Asia special issue on North India: Partition and Independence, Vol.18, pp. 95-108.

Avery, C. (1983), "Refugee Status Decision-making: The Systems of Ten Countries", 19 Stan. JIL, p. 235.

Bader, V. (1995), "Citizenship and Exclusion; Radical Democracy, Community, and Justice, What is Wrong with Communitarianism?", Political Theory, 23 (2), pp. 211-246.

Bagambiire D. (1993), "Terrorism and Convention Refugee Status in Canadian Immigration Law: The Social Group Category according to Ward v. Canada", 5 IJRL, p. 183.

Banks, D.L. (1986), "The Analysis of Human Rights Data over Time", 8 HRQ, p. 654.

Barbora, Sanjay, Thieme, Susan, Astrid Siegmann, Karin, Menon, Veneetha and Gurung, Ganesh (2008), "Migration matters in South Asia: Commonalities and Critiques", *Economic and Political Weekly*, June 14, pp. 57-65.

Barham, Bradford and Boucher, Stephen (1998), "Migration, Remittances, and Inequality: Estimating the Net Effects of Migration on Income Distribution", Journal of Development Economics, Vol. 55, Issue No. 2, April.

Barpujari, H.K. (1981), "Problem of the Hill Tribes of North-East Frontier, 1873-1962", Vol. 3, Spectrum, Gauhati.

Barrett, G. A., Jones, T.P. and McEvoy, D. (1996), "Ethnic Minority Business: Theoretical Discourse in Britain and North America", Urban Studies, Vol. 33, pp. 4-5.

Baruah, Sanjib (2001), "Generals as Governors: The Parallel Political Systems of Northeast India", Himal, Vol.14, No.6, Pp. 10-20.

------------------- (2002), "Gulliver's Troubles: State and Militants in North-East India", Economic and Political Weekly, Vol.37, No.41, 12-18 October, Pp. 4178-82.

------------------- (2003), "Citizens and Denizens: Ethnicity, Homelands and the Crisis of Displacement in Northeast India", Journal of Refugee Studies, vol.16, no.1, Pp. 44-67.

------------------- (2003), "Nationalizing Space: Cosmetic Federalism and the Politics of Development in Northeast India", Development & Change, Vol.34, No.5, pp. 915-40.

------------------- (2005), "A new Politics of Race: India and its North-East", IIC Quarterly, Vol. 32, No. 2 & 3, Monsoon-Winter, pp. 165-76.

Bettati, M. (1992), "The Right of Humanitarian Intervention or the Right of Free Access to Victims?" ICJ Review, No. 49, 1, December.

Beyer, G.A. (1990), "Monitoring Root Causes of Refugee Flows and Early Warning: The Need for Substance", 2 IJRL, Special Issue, September, p. 71.

Bhagwati, Jagdish (1991), "International Migration and Income Taxation", Political Economy and International Economics, Vol. 18, August.

Bhattacharjee, T.K. (1975), "The Adis, their Origin and Migration", Resarun, Pp. 40-43.

Blay, S.K.N. & Tsamenyi, B.M. (1990), "Reservations and Declarations under the 1951 Convention and the 1967 Protocol relating to the Status of Refugees", 2, IJRL, p. 527.

Bradley, Don E. (2004), "A Second Look at Self-Employment and Earnings of Immigrants", International Migration Review, Vol. 38, No. 2, Summer.

Calabia, Dawn T. (1992), "Refugee admissions for fiscal year 1993", Migration World Magazine, V. 20, n. 5, Nov-Dec, p. 32.

Dalton, E.J.T. (1845), "On the Meris and the Abors of Assam", Journal of the Royal Asiatic Society of Bengal, Vol.14, No.1, pp. 426-30.

Carens, J. H. (1987), "Aliens and Citizens: The Case for Open Borders", The Review of Politics, 49 (2), pp. 252-273.

Cernea, Michael M. (1995), "Understanding and Preventing Impoverishment from Displacement: Reflections from the State of Knowledge", Journal of Refugee Studies, 8 (3), pp. 245-264.

Cernea, Michael M. (1997), "The Risks and Reconstruction Model for Resettling Displaced Populations", World Development, 25(10), Pp. 1569-1587.

Cervenak, C.M. (1994), "Promoting Inequality: Gender-Based Discrimination in UNRWA's Approach to Palestine Refugee Status", 16 HRQ, p. 300.

Chakma, Sugata (1982), "Chakma Culture, Folklore", The Journal of the Folklore Research Institute, Bangladesh, 7 January, pp. 58-75.

Chakma, Suhas (1989), "Four Rays of Hope, Eastern" Economic Review, 23 March.

Chandrahasan, N. (1993), "Use of Force to ensure Humanitarian Relief: A South Asian Precedent examined', 42 ICLQ, p. 664.

Chimni, B. S. (1994), "The Legal Condition of Refugees in India", Journal of Refugee Studies, Vol. 7, No. 4, pp. 394-398.

------------------ (1991), "Perspectives on Voluntary Repatriation: A Critical Note", 3 IJRL, p. 541.

------------------ (1993), "The Meaning of Words and the Role of UNHCR in Voluntary Repatriation", 5 IJRL, p. 442.

Clark, T. (1992), "Human Rights and Expulsion: Giving Content to the Concept of Asylum", 4 IJRL, p. 189.

Cohen, C.P. (1991), "The Rights of the Child: Implications for Change in the Care and Protection of Refugee Children", 3 IJRL, p. 675.

Cohen, J. (1999), "Changing Paradigms of Citizenship and the Exclusiveness of the Demos", International Sociology, 14 (3), pp. 245-268.

Cohon, J. Donald (1981) "Psychological Adaptation and Dysfunction among Refugees", International Migration Review, XV.

Crawford, J. (1990), "Australian Immigration Law and Refugees: The 1989 Amendments", 2 *IJRL*, p. 626.

D. Massey, J., Arango, G. Hugo, A. Kouaci, A. Pellegrino, and E. Taylor (1993), "Theories of International Migration: A Review and Appraisal", *Population and Development Review*, Vol. 19, no. 3, September, pp. 431–466.

David, H.P. (1969), "Involuntary International Migration: Adaptation of Refugees", *International Migration*, 7(3/4), pp. 67-81.

De, Prabir and Ghosh, Buddhadeb (2008), "Reassessing Transaction Coats of Trade at the India-Bangladesh Boarder", *Economic and Political Weekly*, July 19, pp. 69-79.

De Zayas, A. (1975), "International Law and Mass Population Transfers", 16 *Harv, ILJ*, p. 207.

Deng, F.M. (1995), "The International Protection of the Internally Displaced", 7 *IJRL*, Special Issue, Summer, p. 74.

Deng, Francis M. (1995), "Dealing with the Displaced: A Challenge to the International Community", *Global Governance*, 1, winter, pp. 45-57.

DeVoe, Drosh Marie (1981), "Framing Refugees As Clients", *International Migration Review*, XV.

DeWind, Josh (1990), "Alien justice: the exclusion of Haitian refugees", *Journal of Social Issues*, V.46, N.1, Spring, p. 121.

Dhavan, Rajeev (1996), "Treaties and People: Indian Reflections", 44 JILI pp. 362-376.

Dieng, A. (1995), "Addressing the Root Causes of Forced Population Displacements in Africa: A Theoretical Model", 7 *IJRL* Special Issue, Summer p. 119.

Doheny, Kevin (1981), "The Plight of the Refugee: A Case in Point – Africa", *Migration News*, 1 January.

Donnelly, J. & Howard, R.E. (1988), "Assessing Nations Human Rights Performance: A Theoretical Framework", 10 *HRQ*, p. 214.

Dowty, Alan and Loescher, Gil (1996), "Refugee flows as grounds for international action", *International Security*, Vol.21, N.1, Summer, p. 43.

Dutta, S (1996), "Chakma-Hajong Refugee Problem in Arunachal Pradesh: Historical Background", *IASSI Quarterly*, Vol.15, No.1, July-September, pp. 111-26.

Fehervary, A. (1993), "Citizenship, Statelessness and Human Rights: Recent Developments in the Baltic States", 5, *IJRL*, p. 392.

Fitzpatrick, J. (1996), "Revitalizing the 1951 Refugee Convention", *Harvard Human Rights Journal*, Vol. 9, pp. 229-53.

Fonteyne, J. P. (1994), "Overview of Refugee Determination Procedures in Australia", 6, *IJRL*, p. 253.

Fox, Gregory H. (1989), "Aliens refugee status asylum well-founded fear of persecution advisory opinion by Bureau of Human Rights and Humanitarian Affairs, *American Journal of International Law*, v.83, n.3, July, pp. 569-573.

Frelick, B. (1992), "Preventive Protection and the Right to Seek Asylum: A Preliminary Look at Bosnia and Croatia", 4, *IJRL*, p. 439.

Fullerton, M. (1993), "A Comparative Look at Refugee Status based on Persecution due to Membership in a Particular Group", 26, *Cornell Int'l L.J*, p. 505.

Gallagher, Dennis (1989), "The Evolution of the International Refugee System, *International Migration Review*, Vol.23, n.3, Fall, p. 579.

Gasarasi, C.P. (1990), "The Mass Naturalization and further Integration of Rwandese Refugees in Tanzania: Process, Problems and Prospects", 3, *JRS*, p. 88.

Gerhart, Gail M. (1996), "African Exodus: Refugee Crisis, Human Rights and the 1969 OAU Convention", *Foreign Affairs*, Vol.75, n.5, Sept-Oct, p. 161.

Ghatak, Subrata, Levine, Paul & Price, Stephen Whealey (1996), "Migration Theories and Evidence: An Assessment", *Journal of Economic Surveys*, Vol.10, No.2, pp. 159-198.

Gibney, Mark (1988), "A well-founded fear of persecution", *Human Rights Quarterly*, Vol.10, n.1, Feb, pp. 109-121.

Goodwin Gill, Guy S. (1989), "International law and human rights: trends concerning international migrants and refugees", *International Migration Review*, Vol.23, n.3, Fall, p. 526.

———————— (1986), "International Law and the etention of refugees and Asylum-Seekers", 20, *International Migration Review*, p. 193.

———————— (1986), "*Non-refoulement and the New Asylum Seekers*", 26 *Virg. JIL*, p. 897.

———————— (1993), "UNHCR and International Protection: Old Problems, New Directions", 5, *IJRL* 1.

Gohain, Hiren (2010), "Positions on Assam History", *Economic and Political Weekly*, February 20, pp. 37-42.

Gordenker, L. (1986), "Early Warning of Disastrous Population movements", 20, *International Migration Review*, p. 170.

Gorlick, B. (1995), "Refugee Protection and the Committee against Torture", 7, IJRL, p. 504.

Grahl-Madsen, A. (1986), "Protection of Refugees by their Country of Origin", 11, Yale JIL, p. 362.

Gray, Andrew (1993), "The Protection of Minorities and Human Rights", Journal of Refugee Studies, 6, 3, pp. 305-307.

Greene, I. & Schaffer, P. (1992), "Leave to Appeal and Leave to commence Judicial Review in Canada's Refugee Determination System: Is the Process Fair?", 4, IJRL, p. 71.

Gulati, Chandrika (1986), "Foreign Infiltration: Tension in Indo-Bangladesh Relations", Asian Thought and Society, Vol. XI, No.32-33, July-November.

Gupta, Rakesh (1991), "Extend Democracy to Chittagong People", Link, October, p. 27.

Gupta, Sekhar (1984), "Mizoram: Chakma Crisis", India Today, 15 June.

Hailbronner, K. (1986), "Non-refoulement and "Humanitarian" Refugees: Customary International Law or Wishful Legal Thinking?", 26 Virg. JIL, p. 857.

Hansen, Art (1981), "Refugee Dynamics: Angolans in Zambia 1966 to 1972", International Migration Review, XV.

Hazarika, Sanjoy (2000), "Title India's North-East and the Problem of Migration: What is to be Done?", Dialogue, Vol.1, No. 3, January-March, pp.11-20.

Helton, Arthur C. (1994), "Displacement and human rights: current dilemmas in refugee protection", Journal of International Affairs, v.47, n.2, winter, Pp. 379-398.

Horowitz, Michael M. (1989), "Victims of Development", Development Anthropology Network, 7(2), pp. 1-8.

-------------------- (1991), "Victims Upstream and Down", Journal of Refugee Studies, 4(2), pp. 164-181.

Jacobson, Gaynor I. (1977), "The Refugee Movement: An Overview", International Migration Review, 11, 4, winter, pp. 514-523.

Jafa, Jyoti (1987), "Victims of Colonialism and Ethno-Centric Nationalism", Mainstream, Annual, pp. 107-108.

Jenkins, J. Craig; Schmeidl, Susanne (1995), "Flight from Violence: The Origins and Implications of the World Refugee Crisis", Sociological Focus, 28, 1, Feb, pp. 63-82.

Jennings, R.Y. (1939), "Some International Law Aspects of the Refugee Question", 20, BYIL, p. 98.

Johnsson, A.B. (1989), "The International Protection of Women Refugees", 1, IJRL, p. 221.

Joly, D. (1994), "The Porous Dam: European Harmonization on Asylum in the Nineties", 6, IJRL, p. 159.

Jonassohn, Kurt (1993), "Famine, Genocide, and Refugees", Society, 30, 6(206), Sept-Oct, pp. 72-76.

Jordan, June (1994), "We are all Refugees; Just Inside the Door", Progressive, Vol. 58, n. 7, July, 16.

Knox Thames (1999), "India's Failure to Adequately Protect Refugees", 7 Human Rights Brochure, p. 20.

Konow, S. (1902), "Notes on the Languages Spoken between the Assam Valley and Tibet", Journal of the Royal Asiatic Society, Dec, pp. 127-37.

Kunz, E.F. (1981), "Exile and Resettlement: Refugee Theory", International Migration Review, XV.

Kymlicka, W., and W., Norman, (1994), "Return of the Citizen: A Survey of Recent Work on Citizenship Theory", Ethics, 104 (2), pp. 352-381.

Lama, Mahendra P. (2000), "Managing Refugees in South Asia: Protection Aid, State Behaviour and Regional Approach", Occasional Paper, no.4, Refugee and Migratory Movement, Research Unit, University of Dhaka, Bangladesh.

L. Holborn (1938), "The Legal Status of Political Refugees, 1920-1938", American Journal of International Law, Vol. 32, No. 4, October, pp. 680-703.

Lister, M. (2005), "Marshalling Social and Political Citizenship: Towards a Unified Conception of Citizenship", Government and Opposition, 40 (4), pp. 471-492.

Loescher, Gil (1994), "The international refugee regime: stretched to the limit?", Journal of International Affairs, Vol.47, N.2, Winter, pp. 351-377.

Ludlow, F. (1937), "Expeditions: The Sources of the Subansiri and Siyom", Himalayan Journal, Vol. 9, pp. 142-47.

Lumby, Catherine (1992), "A poor record on human rights", United Nations policy on refugees, World Press Review, Vol.39, n. 4, April, p. 35.

M. Malik, Sadia (2009), "Horizontal Inequalities and Violent Conflict in Pakistan: Is There a Link", *Economic and Political Weekly*, August 22, pp. 21-24.

Macklin, Audrey (1995), "Refugee Women and the Imperative of Categories", Human Rights Quarterly, 17(2), pp. 213-277.

Maluwa, T. (1991), "The Domestic Implementation of International Refugee Law: A Brief Note on Malawi's Refugee Act of 1989", International Journal of Refugee Law, 503.

Massey, D.S. and others (1993), "Theories of International Migration: A Review and Appraisal", Population and Development Review, Vol. 19, No. 3.

Mayotte, Judy (1994), "Civil war in Sudan: the paradox of human rights and national sovereignty", Journal of International Affairs, Vol.47, n.2, winter, pp. 497-524.

Menon, Ramesh (1987), "Chakmas: Shattered Lives, India Today", 15 March.

Mitra, Subrata (2010), "Citizenship in India: Some Preliminary Results of a National Survey", Economic and Political Weekly, February 27, pp. 46-53.

Nagy, B. (1992), "Asylum Seekers and Refugees: Hungarian Dilemmas", 34 Acta Juridica Hungarica, No. 1-2, p. 27.

Nath, Manoj Kumar (2004), "Mapping Northeast on India's Foreign Policy: Looking Past, Present and Beyond", The Indian Journal of Political Science, Vol. LXV, Nos.4, October-December, pp. 637-652.

Nepram, Binalakshmi (2003), "Accord into Discord: Conflict and the 1997 Peace Accord of Chittagong Hill Tract", Himalayan and Central Asian Studies, Vol.7, Nos. 3-4, July-December, pp. 147-175.

Newland, Kathlean (1993), "Ethnic Conflict and Refugees", Survival, 35(1), Spring.

Newland, Kathleen (1994), "Refugees; the rising flood", World Watch Vol.7, N.3, May-June 10.

Okin, S. M. (1992), "Women, Equality, and Citizenship", Queen's Quarterly 99 (1), pp. 57-72.

Opondo, Enoch O. (1992), "Refugee Repatriation during Conflict: Grounds for Skepticism", Disasters, 16, 4, December, pp. 359-362.

Osborne, M. (1980), "The Indo-Chinese Refugees: Causes and Effects", International Affairs, p. 37.

P. Saxena (2007), "Creating Legal Space for Refugees in India: the Milestones Crossed and the Roadmap for the Future", International Journal of Refugee Law, Vol. 19, pp. 246-272.

Page, Melvin E. (1991), "Malawi and Mozambique: the human frontier", Africa Today, Vol.38, N.4, p. 59.

Panda, Architesh (2010), "Climate Refugees: Implications for India", Economic and Political Weekly, May 14, Vol. XLV, No. 20, pp. 76-79.

Patra, Saral (1991), "Bangladesh Factor", World Focus, 13, 1 January.

Pedersen, S. (1949), "Psychopathological Reactions to Extreme Social Displacements", Psychoanalytic Review, 36, Pp. 344-354.

Perluss, D. and Hartman, J. (1986), "Temporary Refugee: Emergence of a Customary International Norm", 26, Virg, JIL, p. 551.

Portes, A. (1969), "Dilemmas of a Golden Exile: Integration of Cuban Refugee Families in Milwaukee", American Sociological Review, 34(4), August, pp. 505-518.

Prasad, Chunnu (2010), Looking for Whose Identity; A Critical Overview of the Concept Dalit and Social Justice, Third World Impact, January-March, pp. 29-32.

----------------- (2009), Understanding the Political Economy of Arunachal Pradesh, Political Economy Journal of India, Vol. 18, Issue 3 and 4, July-December, pp. 86-93.

----------------- (2008), Political Economy and Social Exclusion: A Case of Scheduled Castes in Arunachal Pradesh, South India Journal of Social Sciences, Vol. vi, No. 2, December, pp. 47-58.

----------------- (2008), Natural Resource Management and Sustainable Development: A Study in Arunachal Pradesh, Social Action, Vol. 58, April-June, pp. 200-207.

----------------- (2008), India Pakistan: Man who Divided", Third World Impact", April-June, Vol. XIX, No. 178, pp. 23-29.

--------------- (2008), Chakma Refugees in Arunachal Pradesh: Question of Identity and Citizenship, Eastern Anthropologist, Vol. 61, No.1, January-March, pp. 95-104.

--------------- (2007), Student Movement In Arunachal Pradesh: A Case of Chakma-Hajong Refugee Problem, Economic and Political Weekly, Vol. XLII, No.15, April 14-20, pp.1373-1379.

--------------- (2007), Arunachal Pradesh and the Inner-Outer Line Regulation of 1873-1874 of North East Frontier Agency, Third World Impact, Vol. XVIII, No.173, January-March, pp.15-19.

--------------- (2006), Migration and the Question of Citizenship: People of Chittagong Hill Tract in Arunachal Pradesh, Indian Journal of Political Science, Vol. LXVII, No. 3, July-September, pp. 471-490.

--------------- (2006), Victims of Partition: A Case of Chakma and Hajong Refugees of Arunachal Pradesh, Think India, Vol. 9, No.4, October-December, pp. 59-71.

--------------- (2006), Citizenship Rights in North East: The Case of Chakmas and Hajongs in Arunachal Pradesh, Journal of Peace Studies, Vol. 13, Issue 4, October-December, pp. 49-55.

--------------- (2006), Arunachal Pradesh Denies the Rights to Scheduled Caste in the State, Radical Humanist, Vol. 433, April, pp. 33-34.

--------------- (2006), Chakma-Hajong Refugee Problem and Politics of their Settlement in Arunachal Pradesh (1947 to 2004), South Asia Politics, Vol.5, No.1, May, pp. 46-50.

--------------- (2006), Arunachal Pradesh as the Factor in Indo-China Relation, Third Concept, April, Vol. 331, pp. 51-55.

--------------- (2010), Refugees and Human Rights: Comparative Studies Between Chakmas in India and Biharis in Bangladesh, in an edited book by M. R. Biju in Development Issues in Contemporary India, Concept Publishing Company Pvt. Ltd., New Delhi, pp. 238-262.

--------------- (2010), Democracy, Dalits and Exclusive Policies: A Case of Scheduled Castes in Arunachal Pradesh, in an edited book by Yagati Chinna Rao and Karakoti Sudhakara in Exclusion and Discrimination; Concepts, Perspectives and Challenges, Kanishka Publishes and Distributors, New Delhi, pp. 120-144.

--------------- (2010), Naxalism Fighting for what: Question of

Exclusion, Dignity and Livelihood, in an edited book by Pradeep Basu in Discourse on Naxalite Movement (1967-2009); Insights into Redical Left Politics, Setu Prakasan, Kolkatta, pp. 238-251.

R. Skeldon (2008), "International Migration as a Tool in Development Policy: A Passing Phase?", Population and Development Review, Vol.34, no.3, March pp. 1-18.

Scudder, Thayer (1993), "Development-Induced Relocation and Refugee Studies: 37 Years of Change and Continuity among Zambia's Gwembe Tonga", Journal of Refugee Studies, 6(2), pp. 123-152.

Singh, Deepak K. (1996), "The Arunachal Tangle: Migration and Ethnicity, Journal of Peace Studies", Vol.3, Issue, 18-19, September-December, p. 54.

-------------------- (2001), "Refugee question in Arunachal Pradesh: Some Conflicting Currents", Journal of Anthropological Survey of India, 50(4), December, pp. 95-102.

-------------------- (2001), Stateless Chakmas in Arunachal Pradesh: From Rejected Peoples to Unwanted Migrants, Social Science Research Journal, 9(1), pp. 47-82.

Soskis, P. (1967), "The Adjustment of Hungarian Refugees in New York", International Migration Review, 2(1), p. 40.

Stein, Barry N. (1979), "Occupational Adjustment of Refugees: The Vietnamese in the United States", International Migration Review, 13(1), spring.

-------------------- (1981), "The Refugee Experience: Defining the Parameters of a Field of Study", International Migration Review, 15, pp. 1-2.

Tran, Peter (1994), "Refugees and Displaced People: An Approach by the Church of Africa on Preventive Actions", Migration World Magazine, 22, 1, pp. 15-19.

Weiner, Myron (1983), "The Political Demography of Assam's Anti-Migrant Movement", Population and Development Review, June, pp. 279-92.

-------------------- (1993), "Rejected People and Unwanted Migrants in South-Asia", *Economic and Political Weekly*, August 21, pp. 1737-1746.

Young, I. M. (1989), "Polity and Group Difference: A Critique of the Ideal of Universal Citizenship", Ethics, 99, pp. 250-274.

Young, Lincoln (1985), "A General Assessment of the Environmental Impact of Refugees in Somalia with Attention to the Refugee Agricultural Program", Disasters, 9(2), pp. 122-133.

News Papers

The Arunachal Times, 7 October, 1991.

Highland Observer, 15 September, 1994.

Highland Observer, 30 September, 1994.

The Arunachal Times, 26 February, 1995.

The Arunachal Times, 2 April, 1995.

The Assam Tribune, 2 April, 1995.

The Arunachal Times, 4 April, 1995.

The Assam Tribune, 22 April, 1995.

The Assam Tribune, 7 August, 1995.

The Arunachal Times, 10 August, 1995.

The Arunachal Times, 15 August, 1995.

Eco of Arunachal, 15 August, 1995.

Eco of Arunachal, 25 August, 1995.

The Arunachal Times, 29 August, 1995.

The Arunachal Times, 14 September, 1995.

Highland Observer, 7 October, 1995.

The Arunachal Times, 26 October, 1995.

The Hindu, 31 August, 2001.

The Hindu, 24 June, 2004.

The Assam Tribune, 5 September, 2004.

The Asian Age, 3 August 2006.

The Telegraph, 13 December, 2006.

The Hindu, 24 February, 2007.

The Hindu, 4 March, 2007.

The Indian Express, 18 July, 2007.

The Hindu, 16 July, 2009.

Websites

http://www.ceoarunachal.nic.in.

http://www.achrweb.org.

http://www.aitpn.org.

http://www.bangla.org.

http://www.banglarights.net.

http://www.chakmafriends.com.

http://www.cldem.umd.edu.

http://www.forcedmigration.org

http://www.hrea.org.

http://www.hri.ca.

http://www.hvk.org.

http://www.ipcs.org.

http://www.legalserviceindia.com.

http://www.nhpcindia.com.

http://www.refugeesinternational.org.

http://www.rsc.ox.ac.uk.

http://www.sacw.net.

http://www.safhr.org.

http://www.sneha.org.in.

http://www.south-asia.org.

http://www.state.gov.

http://www.statelesspeopleinbangladesh.net.

http://www.virtualbangladesh.com.

http://www.worldlii.org.

http://www.yespakistan.com.

https://www.msu.edu.

Index